BATHS

Warren Dickerson. *New York City-East Side*. Los Angeles County Museum of Natural History.

Portraits of the American Jew

An Anthology of Short Stories by American Jewish Writers

Edited by
Max Nadel

Barron's Educational Series, Inc.
Woodbury, New York

Library of Congress Catalog Card No. 75-34066
Paper Edition
International Standard Book No. 0-8120-0578-3

Library of Congress Cataloging in Publication Data
Main entry under title:
Portraits of the American Jew.
  Bibliography: p.
  CONTENTS: Fast, H. Where are your guns?—Brinig,
M. Day of atonement.—Litwak, L. The oath. [etc.]
    1. Short stories, American—Jewish authors.
2. American fiction—20th century. I. Nadel, Max.
II. National Curriculum Research Institute. Com-
mission on Jewish Studies in Public Schools.
PZ1.P8364 [PS647.J4] 813'.01 75-34066
ISBN 0-8120-0578-3

Acknowledgements

This anthology as prepared as a project of the Commission on Jewish Studies for Public Schools of the American Association for Jewish Education.
Dr. Theodore H. Lang, Chairman
Dr. Hyman Chanover, Director of the National Curriculum Research Institute of the AAJE
Max Nadel, Editor

Arbor House Publishing Co., Inc., for "The Only One in Town" from *Summer* by Jack Ansell. Copyright 1973 by Arbor House. Reprinted by permission of Arbor House Publishing Co., Inc.

Myron Brinig for "Day of Atonement" from *Singermann* by Myron Brinig. Copyright by Myron Brinig. First published (1929) by Rinehart and Company. Reprinted by permission of the author.

Curtis Brown, Ltd. for "The Crime of Ezechiele Coen" by Stanley Ellin from *Ellery Queen's Mystery Magazine*, November, 1963. Reprinted by permission of Curtis Brown, Ltd. Copyright 1963 by Stanley Ellin.

James Brown Associates, Inc., for "The Oath" by Leo Litwak from *Commentary*, August 1969. Copyright 1969 by Leo Litwak. Reprinted by permission of the author and his agent, James Brown Associates, Inc.

Farrar, Straus & Giroux, Inc., for "The Throne of Good" by Hugh Nissenson from *In the Reign of Peace*; copyright 1968, 1969, 1970, 1972 by Hugh Nissenson. For "Man in the Drawer" by Bernard Malamud from *Rembrandt's Hat*; copyright 1968, 1972, 1973 by Bernard Malamud. Reprinted with the permission of Farrar, Straus & Giroux, Inc.

Yaacov Luria for "My Medical Career." Copyright 1953 by Jack Luria. First appeared in *The New Yorker*. Reprinted by permission of the author.

Contents

Preface

A major department of the American Association for Jewish Education (the central Jewish educational agency in the United States for community service, research, and coordination) is its National Curriculum Research Institute. In 1971 the NCRI, in response to requests from school systems in various parts of the country for materials dealing with the Jewish experience, organized a Commission on Jewish Studies in Public Schools whose major function was to assist school supervisors and teachers in adding a Jewish component to programs of ethnic studies that were being introduced into the schools.

The educational and cultural work of the Commission—including the preparation of the present anthology—in part has been supported by a grant from the Memorial Foundation for Jewish Culture.

This collection of short stories with study guides was prepared to fill a need in the public schools for a work that illumines the character of the American Jew. The study guides emphasize the substance of the Jewish experience and seek also to achieve the goals that motivate the teaching of English and creative writing in secondary schools. Study materials have been included to enable the teacher and the student to deal creatively with each story and to draw from each a view of the historical and sociological experience of the American Jew that would lead to a deeper understanding.

There are a plethora of analytic questions that follow each story. It is the editor's belief, as a veteran teacher of English, that only a searching study of a work of art can reveal the talent and artistry that produced it and bring to the reader the added pleasure of inquiry and discovery. The editor of this anthology was formerly chairman of the English department of the Bronx High School of Science in New York City and is at present consultant to the Commission on Jewish Studies in Public Schools.

He wishes to thank Dr. Hyman Chanover, Director of the National Curriculum Research Institute, for initiating the work and for providing him with information, direction, and guidance while the anthology was in progress; Dr. Mark F. Goldberg, Assistant Administrator at the Shoreham-Wading River Middle and High School in Long Island, New York, for reading the manuscript and making many valuable suggestions; Mrs. Berte Gellis for patiently typing and re-typing the manuscript and, in the process, offering many suggestions from her wealth of background; and his wife, Elizabeth, who assisted him in this work and helped to shape it.

Introduction

Partly in response to new social and political currents in society and partly as an extension of the desires of the visible minority groups in schools all over the country for a study of their past and for recognition of the part they played in American history and culture, there has gradually evolved in all ethnic groups in America a wish to be identified and to have their contributions to American history and American life recognized.

Americans are not single-faceted personalities. They are the product of at least two, and generally more, rich social and cultural influences. First, there is the American heritage. Whatever its sources in Europe, the American life-style has, since its inception, acquired a unique character, the product of a turbulent history of political and social growth, wars for survival and for the integrity of democratic institutions, movement into new territories, industrial and technological expansion, and cultural and esthetic maturation. Second, since America was a land of refuge for many diverse peoples, no ethnic group could live in total physical isolation from other groups and remain unaffected by their values, beliefs, and mores. A way of life evolved wherein each group's basic religious, cultural, and social usages were tempered by a myriad of indigenous and ethnic thrusts.

Ethnic Americans have taken a second look at themselves. They have recognized that 1) a study of the ethnic elements that colored the American character not only points the way to the fulfillment of the American ideal but also can contribute to lessening the possibility of tension among the varied groups; 2) knowledge of the customs and traditions of one's neighbors encourages mutual understanding and helps allay the fears and suspicions that generate group conflicts; and 3) ethnic cultures provide emotional and intellectual experiences and lead one to go beyond purely parochial American values and concerns.

History and heritage play tricks on people. When groups seem ready to slough off what they conceive to be the trammels of their past, events keep reminding them who they are. This has happened to the many ethnic groups that make up American society; it has happened frequently and intensely to the Jews. Anti-Semitism, whose ugliest and most brutal manifestation occurred more than a generation ago under

Nazi rule and whose contemporary expression is the resistence of the government of the Soviet Union to permit its Jewish citizens either to maintain their culture or to emigrate to a country where they may practice their faith, has reminded Jews all over the world that they have roots and that they are descended from a noble and ill-treated people to whom they owe a deep loyalty. This concern for Jewish identity has been intensified by the birthpangs of the State of Israel and its struggle to survive.

The growing awareness of identity among the Jews of America has led to a movement to introduce programs of Jewish studies in schools and communities, designed to develop an understanding in the population of the nature, historic experience, and faith of the Jewish people and of the creative part they played in the story of Western civilization and in the growth of the United States. Christian as well as Jewish educators are fast coming to believe that American students ought to have more than a superficial familiarity with the main elements of the history and culture of the Jewish people, in order to root out the misconceptions and the misinformation about the Jew that abound in so many homes, schools, and communities. Such knowledge is also needed to fill in the gaps where no information exists. Presenting a true image of the Jew should help neutralize the falsehoods and distortions that are often heard.

To the Teacher

When a teacher is dealing with literature of an ethnic nature, a backdrop of the group's characteristics—social values, distinctive views of life, even salient historical experiences—must be furnished against which the work acquires genuine meaning. The editor's introductions to the stories used in this volume were designed to serve part of this purpose. Students should be directed to other sources for the additional ethnic understandings that will give them a deeper comprehension of the material.

To the Student

This anthology attempts to do two things: first, it seeks to demonstrate how the past and present culture and history of a people—in this case the Jewish people—influence its writers and provide the substance for some of their work; second, it tries to show how a writer takes the raw details of the experiences of life and gives them artistic shape and design.

For each of the stories in this anthology, there is an introduction which will give you its historical background—the events that impelled the author to write it. After you read the story, you should seek to determine how the author used the events.

In addition, each story is followed by questions for analysis and discussion, as well as by suggested activities. Writing fiction is a craft and an art. When you read a work of fiction, you should find pleasure not only in vicarious participation in the story but also in the skill and talent that went into its creation. A major purpose of the questions for analysis and discussion is to help read critically and to exchange your perceptions and interpretations with those of your classmates. You will enjoy determining the author's point of view, his relationship to the narrator and the characters of the story, the decisions he made at strategic points, his skill in writing descriptions and dialogue, and his power to move into the minds of his characters. If you follow the analysis and find in the story, as well as in your knowledge and experience, the evidence to support your answers and judgment, the story will become more than a piece of entertainment for you. You will see it as a unique expression of the author's creative energies.

Furthermore, as you begin to disassemble a work of fiction and become aware of its parts—in a way similar to disassembling a machine—you learn the craft, and you become ready to try your own hand at writing fiction. Try writing a description of a scene in nature, an accident you witnessed, an angry dialogue between a cab driver and a passenger, the thoughts that run through a student's mind as he prepares to take a state-wide examination.

The suggested activities after each story should encourage many such experiments in fiction writing. In addition, they direct you to further reading and investigation into history and literature dealing with themes similar to those in the selection you have read, studied, and analyzed.

The Julius Meyer store in Omaha, Nebraska. Courtesy of American Jewish Archives, Hebrew Union College, Jewish Institute of Religion.

By HOWARD FAST

Where Are Your Guns?

Introduction: **The Colonial Period and the Revolution**

Jewish people first came to America in 1654. Twenty-three Jews, who had lived in peace in the Jewish community in Recife, Brazil, under a benign Dutch rule, left the city when it was re-taken by Portuguese forces. Instead of returning to Europe as many of their compatriots did, they sailed to New Amsterdam, then a Dutch colony. Peter Stuyvesant, its governor, at first refused to accept them, but he was ordered by the directors of the Dutch West India Company to let them land. In time, the Jews became part of the New Amsterdam community.

More Jews, though not many, came to the New World in the years that followed. In 1700 there were at most between 200 and 300 Jews in the colonies. They settled in five seaboard communities which at that time were becoming centers of trade and which practiced a tolerance that made it possible for Jews to live there. The five communities were New York (the new name given to New Amsterdam when the town was captured by the British); Newport, Philadelphia, Charleston, and Savannah.

These colonies offered economic, social, and religious opportunities to the Jews that were denied them in the lands from which they came. Although there were some restrictions, they were permitted to engage in almost all activities open to other members of these communities. Many of them were merchants, shopkeepers, and importers; some became wealthy members of their growing towns. A few, in the South, were farmers and planters. Others were artisans, tailors, bakers, and silversmiths. And a rare few went into the wilderness to trade for furs among the Indians. Fur was much in demand in colonial commerce with the West Indies and with Europe.

In the colonies, the Jews remained loyal to their faith. They had suffered much to remain Jews, and they were not ready to give up Judaism easily. They struggled to attain two goals: to practice their way of life, which meant in part to get permission to build a house of worship, and to participate in the economic and political activities in the communities in which they settled. They were able gradually to win both rights.

Like all subjects of Britain in America, they found themselves involved in the struggles of the English against the French and their Indian allies for territory and power in the New World. With rare exceptions, they fought on the side of Britain. Later, when the American colonists fought for freedom from England, Jews were on both sides, caught up by loyalties fashioned by their economic situations. Most of the Jews, however, realizing the importance in their lives of a truly free society, joined the Revolution and contributed what they could to the cause of liberty.

In any struggle, the innocent will sometimes suffer, especially if they do not know why the opposing sides are at war. Howard Fast conceived a tale of an apolitical Jewish fur trader in pre-Revolutionary America when the conflict between the British and French was intense. His protagonist spent many years with his son away from civilization, living in the forests and trading with the Indians, coming into town on rare occasions to join the Jewish community on the High Holy Days. What values would he cherish? What relationships and loyalties would govern his life? What would be his fate in a turbulent, changing world? What influences would shape the attitudes of his son toward this world? These are the concerns of Where Are Your Guns?

I N THE land of the Goyim, my father traded with the Indians. We traded for beaver, and my father's word was as good as his bond, and we never carried a weapon except for our knives. From the lakes in the north to the canebrake in the south and as far west as the great river—there we traded and we never carried a weapon, never a musket or a rifle or a pistol, for these are weapons of death; and if you deal with

death, what else can you expect in return? Is it not said in the Book, "Thou shalt not hate thy brother in thy heart"? And is it not also said, "I will also give thee for a light to the Gentiles"?

Among the Mingoes, we dwelt and traded, and among the Delawares, too, and among the Wyandottes and the Shawnees and the Eries and the Miamis and the Kickapoos, and even among the Menomini, where only the French have been, and never did we carry a weapon. "Men do not kill for the sake of killing," my father answered once to a hunter who could not understand why we didn't walk in fear of the red savage. "My people walked in fear for too long," my father said. "I don't fear what is different."

The hunter was one who slew his meat and ate it, even as the red men do, but our law is different. We kept the Law. Would you understand if I told you how we suffered to keep the Law? The Law says that when a beast is slain, it must be with the hand of a holy man, so that the lifeblood will run out as an offering to God rather than as a wanton slaughter of one of His creatures—with God's will and God's blessing.

Long, long ago, when I was only nine, my father said, "The high holy days are coming, and we have not sat down with our own people since your mother's death three years ago," speaking in the old tongue, which he taught me so carefully, being a man of learning. "I would have you pray for your mother's soul, and I would be with my own people for a little while, there is such a hunger in me." So we saddled our horses and made the long journey eastward to Philadelphia, where were a handful of our people. Not that they welcomed us so well, we were two such wild buckskin folk, my father's great black beard falling to his waist;

but we prayed with them and we ate meat with them.

You would have thought that we were unclean, they were such fine people there in Philadelphia, and when they talked about certain things, politics and who ruled over whom, indeed we sat as silent as the red men in their own woods. What does a man who trades with the Indians know of politics, my father thought? And what is it to a Jew who rules over a land? A Jew is a Jew, whether it be the old world or this new world, where the forest rolls like the sea. But when they talked of the Law and of holy things, then it was different, for my father was a man of learning, and when he lifted the meat to this mouth, he pointed out that this was the first meat he or I had eaten in years— and even after that day in Philadelphia, no unclean meat passed our lips.

I speak of this because I must make you understand my father, the man who traded with the Indians, so you will not judge me too harshly. I am not my father. My father fared forth to a wild land from far-off Poland, and of Poland I know no more than a dream and a legend, nor do I care. With his own hands he buried his wife in the wilderness, and he was mother and father to me, even though he left me with the Indians when I was small, and I lived in their lodges and learned their tongue. I am not like my father. He had a dream, which was to trade with the Indians until there was enough money to buy freedom, peace, security—all those things which, so it goes, only money can buy for a Jew; and because he had that dream, he never knew any comfort and the taste of meat was a strange thing to him. A stream of beaver skins went back to the Company on the donkeys and the flatboats that were owned by the Company, and all of it went to a place called London, and in this place there was a thing called an *account*.

Those were names and words and without meaning to me. I cared nothing of the beaver skins and nothing of the account, but my father said that these things were of such importance, then indeed, they were, even as the Law was. I knew other things; I knew the talk of the Shawnees and Algonquin talk, and I could make palaver with the men of the Six Nations too, if need be. I knew Yankee talk, the talk of those long-boned hunters of the East, and I knew the French talk and the high-pitched nasal talk of the British, who claimed to own the land, but knew nothing of it and stayed huddled in their outposts and stockades. I spoke the old language of the Book and I knew the Law, and I could catch trout with my bare hands and steal the eggs from under the nesting bird never disturbing it. I knew the step and

the stride of nineteen moccasins, and where the wild parsnip grows and the wild turnip too, and with only a knife I could live the year round in the dark woods, where never the sky is seen. By heart in the old Hebrew, I knew the Song of Songs, which is Solomon's, and I knew forty psalms. And from the time I was thirteen, I prayed twice a day.

I also knew what it is to be a Jew.

But not like my father, whom you would have remembered, had you seen him come into Fort Pitt on that day. My father was six feet and two inches tall; fifteen stone he scaled; and never an ounce of fat, but hard as rock, with a black beard that fell to his waist. All though the woods, in those times, which are the old times now, the half-forgotten times, were Jews who traded with the Indians and went where no other white man had ever trod, but there was no one like my father, you may believe me. No one so tall or so wide or so heavy—or so sweet of speech and gentle of mien, yet I remember so well a cart and horse mired belly-deep, and my father heaved the horse out and the cart too. Or the time a year before at the company post of Elizabeth, where two Delawares were crazed with drink; they would have been slain, for what is better sport for a redcoat than to slay a drunken Indian? But my father lifted them from the ground like puppies and shook them until the drink went out of them, and instead of going to their deaths they went home to their lodges and were grateful.

I am not like my father, believe me. No man touches my forehead, unless he kill me first; but when a hunter met my father and saw that he was a Jew and begged to feel for the two horns nestling in his hair, my father would smile and agree, and then kindly commiserate with the man when he discovered that the old wives' tale was no more than that. Nor did my father sign for surety—ever, be it old MacTavish, who fended for the company in the north, or Ben Zion, who provided trade goods in Philadelphia, or Pontiac, whom my father told me to look at and heed, so I would know what was best in my own people in the ancient time when they followed the way of war and not of peace.

That was my father, who bound the phylacteries on his head faithfully every morning, and kept the Law, and did justice to all who knew him. That was my father, who came into Fort Pitt with me on this day. We drove seven donkeys and they carried eleven hundred skins, and for a month I had listened to my father plan how now we would go to New York and demand an accounting from the Company, and there we would live with our own people and roam the woods no more. He

was filled with it. A mile from the fort, we had stopped to drink water at the outhouse and mill of MacIntyre, and my father told him.

"No more this way, Angus," my father said, "but eastward and the boy will wear woven cloth on his back."

"Ye been a woodsy man these twenty year," MacIntyre said somberly.

"I'll be woodsy no more. And young Reuben here will make a company of his own, the good Lord willing."

"Heed the new commandment. He has no love for Jews, or for Scots either. I am glad to see you safe, because there is war with the Mingoes."

My father laughed because we had bought two hundred skins from the Mingoes, and there was no war talk in their cities. But when we came to the fort, there was a new guard at the gate. The doors were closed, and the men on the walls wore yellow facings and shakos I had not seen before. It was a new regiment for the woods.

"Who goes there?" a sergeant called.

"Two traders with skins."

"And where are your guns?"

"We bear no guns," my father said. "We are Jews who trade with the Indians."

Then the doors opened, and we entered with our donkeys, but there was never a smile or a nod.

I looked at my father and he looked at me, but there was nothing to make out of his face; and when we looked around us, we saw that these were new men. Their cloth clothes were still fresh with the East, and they stared at us as if we were creatures; were we not Jews, they would have stared at us too, but there was that in their eyes that was singular for Jews.

Where, I wondered, were the Yankee folk, Benson, the smith, Bryan, the cooper, Wheelbury, the harness maker? Where were the Indians, who were always a crowd in the fort? Where were the woodsy folk, the hunters, the French, in their green buckskin and red hats? Where were Stuart and Stevenson, the storekeepers? That too was in my father's mind, as I could see, but his broad face was calm, and he smiled at me as we prodded our donkeys into the low town. As if this were the first time we had come to old Duquesne, soldiers barred our way and a British subaltern demanded of us:

"Who are you and what are your names?"

"We are Jews who trade with the Indians," my father said. "My name is David, and this is my son, Reuben. Twelve years I have been in and out of this place, even when it was Duquesne, and I am known in the forest country."

"I don't know you," the young man said, as if we were dirt and less than dirt.

"Then I be sorry," my father said. "Stevenson knows me, for I have always traded with him and paid my loanings. Benson knows me, for he shod my beasts, and Bryan knows me, for he boxed my goods. I am not a stranger here."

"You are a Jew and damned insolent," the young man replied. "As for the scum of this place, they know the dregs of the woods. Where are your arms?"

"We bear no arms but our knives."

"And how did you come through the Mingoes? There is war with the Mingoes."

A mass of soldiers were around us now, and now I could see Benson and some of the others, but keeping off. I am not like my father. I would have made a story then, but it was not in him to speak anything but the truth. He was going to New York, but I knew of a sudden that he would be lonely and forsaken in such a place. The green woods was his home, and it was not in him to speak anything but the truth.

"There is no war with the Mingoes," he said slowly. I traded two hundred skins with the Mingoes, and I lay in their lodges this fortnight past. There is no war with the Mingoes."

The young officer said, "You're a damned liar, a filthy Jew, and a spy as well."

My father's face was sad and hard and woeful. I moved, but he moved quicker, and he struck the officer a blow that would have felled an ox. Then we fought a little, but there were too many of them.

They put us in a cell and they gave us no food and no water. We were bleeding and bruised, but it was not hard to go without food. It was hard for my father to go without his phylacteries, but after the second day I didn't care. They came every few hours and asked us to tell what we knew of the Mingoes, but what we knew was of no interest to them.

The colonel came finally. It is so different now that you cannot know what a colonel was in those days in a place like Fort Pitt. He was an English gentleman and he was God too, and he prodded us with his stick.

"How old are you?" he asked me.

"I am fifteen," I croaked.

"You are large for fifteen," he lisped, holding a lace handkerchief over his nose. "The Yankees come large, but I should not think it would be so with a Jew. I shall hang your father tomorrow, but if you will tell me what you know of the Mingoes, you may go free and take your seven beasts with the skins."

"I know nothing of the Mingoes."

"And how do you travel in the woods without guns? I am very curious."

"That you could never know," my father said, almost sadly.

Even these days, you will hear things said of Jews; it is that way; but once my father found a robin with a broken wing, and made splints for the wing and a sling, so that we could carry the bird with us, and he nursed it until it flew away. So I will remember until I die how the British drums rolled as they hanged my father, who traded with the Indians in the land of the goyim, and whose word was as good as his bond. And then they gave me thirty lashes until I bled like a pig, and drove me from the fort to die in the forest.

A Jew dies hard, they say. I crawled a mile to Angus MacIntyre's mill, and he washed my back and cared for me until I returned to my senses and could walk again.

"Weep for your father," he said, "for you are only a laddie, and he was much of a man."

"I weep no more and pray no more. My father is dead, and I am not like him."

"You will be like him, lad."

"I will never be like him, Angus, but I will make my word like my bond. I give you my word I will bring you forty beaver skins if you give me a musket and powder and shot."

A long time the old Scot looked at me, measuring me and weighing me. "Go to the land of the

Yankees, lad," he said, "and wear woolen clothes on your back."

"The Yankees stood by while my father was hanged. When that redcoat filth drove the Mingoes from the fort, the Yankees stood by. When two Mingoes came back for the little they left behind and were slain at the gate, the Yankees said nothing."

"How many of them were there?" the Scot said quietly. "They are a strange folk, dirty, and bragging and mean and sometimes, in a most curious way, a little noble. Will they be silent forever?"

"Will you give me the gun?"

"You are one of them," the Scot said.

"When they are no longer silent —I will be one of them. When they strike, I will strike with them."

"And your father traded in the woods with never more than a knife. For the Company. Are you for the Company?"

"I am against any man in a uniform."

"I will give you the gun, lad," the Scot said sadly, "and you will slay your meat and eat it."

"And other things."

"Then put no price on it, for what you seek has no price but a man's blood. You are one of them."

He gave me the gun, and I left him and walked eastward.

Questions for Analysis and Discussion

This is a story of a father and son, of the love between them, and of the change in the son's attitude toward the world because of a tragic event. It is a story also of what makes a fighter and a rebel.

1. Who is the narrator? What is the relationship between him and his father? How does the father make his living? What kind of life do the father and son have together? Where did the father come from? What did he seek in the new world?

2. At what period in the history of the United States does this story occur? How do we know? How does the father care for his son? What knowledge and what skills had the narrator acquired as a result of his father's tutelage and the kind of life they led?

3. What religious observances did the father and son follow? Why

were these observances important to the father? What was the father's attitude toward the Indians? Why did the father never carry weapons? Why didn't he fear the Indians? Why did he have no interest in politics? What was the political situation at the time?

4. The son says, "I am not like my father, believe me. No man touches my forehead unless he kills me first." What is the son referring to? In what ways is the son different from the father? How did father and son appear to the Jews of Philadelphia when they attended High Holy Day services there? How does the son characterize the people among whom they lived: the Indians, the Yankees, the French, the British? Why do father and son find welcome in the home of Angus MacTavish?

5. After twenty years in the woods, the father decides to settle down in a town and live a quiet life. What had happened politically to make this impossible? How are father and son greeted when they arrive at Fort Pitt? Of what are father and son accused? What is the nature of the evidence against them? Why do they not receive a trial? Why do not the Yankees at the fort, who know them, come to their defense? How are father and son punished? How does Angus help the son? What has the son learned from the shock of this cruel experience? Who are the enemies? Who are the friends? When will he join the friends? What will be his revenge?

6. Howard Fast is a writer of historical fiction. The setting of this story is the untamed country of America before the Revolution. But Howard Fast's fiction has relevance to our day. Can you see the connection? The father is a good man, and despite his physical strength, a peaceful man. He also refuses to acquaint himself with the political issues of the time. How are his ignorance of the political situation and his dedication to peace responsible for the disaster that befalls him and his son? How could he have avoided the tragedy? What does the son learn from his father's death? What will the son now do? What is the message of this story? State your views on when peace is desirable and when militancy becomes necessary.

7. Does a story lose quality when it is written to convey a message or prove the truth of a doctrine? In such a story is there likely to be a distortion of truth, a manipulation of incident? In this tale by Howard Fast do you find any characters or any incidents that are not convinc-

ing? Are the characters portrayed as either all good or all bad? Why does the author omit the actual scene in which the father was hanged? Would you have included it?

Suggested Activities

1. One of the leaders of the small group of twenty-three Jews that sought permission to land in New Amsterdam was a man called Asser Levy, who later won civil rights for Jews living in the settlement. Create a scene in which Asser Levy confronts Peter Stuyvesant and demands rights for his compatriots. Write the dialogue for the scene. You will find the background information for such a dramatic bit in Lee J. Levinger's *A History of the Jews in the United States* and in Lee M. Friedman's *Early American Jews*.

2. It would be interesting to discover what life was like in a typical early colonial community which had a variety of settlers. A good society to study is that in colonial Philadelphia. How was the colony founded? What forces were responsible for the religious freedom that prevailed there? What different peoples settled in the colony? What were their occupations? What were their forms of recreation and entertainment? What made possible the growth of the Jewish community in this settlement? Prepare a report on your findings and present it to the class.

3. The Indians played an important role in colonial life in America. Prepare a report describing the relationships between the settlers and the Indians. Be sure to include the trade that occurred between the two groups and the extent to which the Indians were used in the conflicts between the English and the French. Comment on the authenticity or lack of it in Howard Fast's story. Comment also on the extent to which the Indians were either exploited or mistreated.

4. Write a short story in which the son in Howard Fast's *Where Are Your Guns?* takes revenge for the hanging of his father and the lashing which he received at the hands of the British authorities.

5. Howard Fast apparently intended his story as a parable for our day. Write an essay in which you demonstrate how the themes and events of the story are applicable to what has happened to the Jewish people during and since World War II.

6. Write a short "stream of consciousness" essay in which you record the musings that go on in MacTavish's mind as he thinks about the life and fate of the Jewish fur trader who was his friend. Or play the role of MacTavish and recite his musings as a performance in class.

7. Most of the Jews who lived in America during the colonial period contributed to the cause of the Revolution. Outstanding among these were Haym Salomon, Francis Salvador, Mordecai Sheftall, Isaac Franks, and Solomon Bush. Write poems in the manner of Edgar L. Masters' *Spoon River Anthology* in which these men tell about themselves; their aspirations, achievements, and disappointments; and the part they played in the American Revolution. You can find biographical information about these men in Lee Friedman's *Pilgrims in a New Land* and Anita Libman Lebeson's *Jewish Pioneers in America*. A pamphlet (for 25¢), *The Jew and the American Revolution* by Jacob R. Marcus, is available from the American Jewish Archives, Hebrew Union College, Cincinnati, Ohio 45220, which will give you helpful information.

8. The Hebrew Scriptures play a great role in the culture of the Puritans who established the Plymouth colony in Massachusetts. They would not permit people whose faith was different from theirs to join them. There were therefore no Jews in the colony. Nevertheless, the Hebrew Bible served as a guide for many of their customs. Write an essay in which you demonstrate the extent to which the Hebrew Bible influenced the structure of Puritan society and many of its practices.

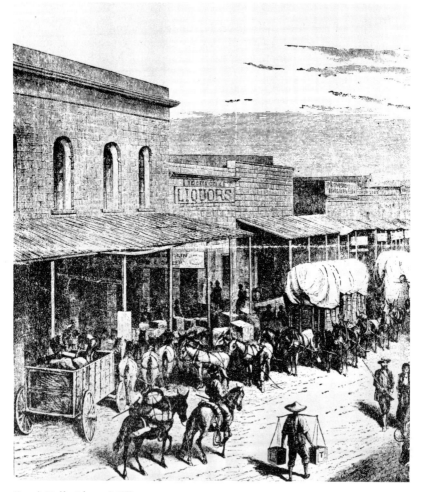

Harper's Weekly, February 2, 1878

BY MYRON BRINIG

Day of Atonement

Introduction: **The Northwest**

Between the years 1820 and 1861, there was a second immigration of Jews to America. They came primarily from Central Europe, from countries where religious freedom, economic opportunities, and political equality were denied them. The victories of Napoleon had brought them a taste of liberty. Under the leadership of men like Moses Mendelssohn, they had begun to break down the ghetto walls. They wanted a taste of Western culture and the opportunity for professional education. However, with the defeat of Napoleon and the restoration of reactionary governments, their hopes were dashed. They found themselves once again cast into the inferior role of ghetto dwellers. Many could not accept the status of a repressed and persecuted minority, and so they left for America.

America at this time was a big, sprawling country. The Jews were only one of the many peoples from abroad who came seeking opportunities in the New World. Many of the German-Jewish immigrants joined their brethren in the cities, found work, learned trades, and settled down. Others, without trades and uneducated, turned to peddling. They purchased, usually on credit, clothing, medicines, household utensils, trinkets and other merchandise that they believed pioneering families would need, placed them in a pack, and peddled their wares in outlying communities. As their business improved, they bought a wagon and horses. This made it possible for them to carry a larger and more varied store of goods and to travel farther. Eventually, a number of them settled down in small communities, opened stores, sent for their families, and joined the social and political life of their town.

As peddlers, they journeyed to the farthest places of the growing land, places like California, Oregon, Texas, Oklahoma. They became part of the pioneering movement that helped build the country. They *were the "newspapers" of their day, bringing stories of events from place to place as they traveled with their wares. They brought elements of romance and color into the hard lives of the early pioneers. They were often treated as guests, and their appearance was anticipated with pleasure. Their lives were arduous, and they looked forward to the time when they, too, could settle down.*

The German-Jewish peddlers and storekeepers maintained the traditions and observances of their fathers as best as they could. Frequently, however, circumstances forced them to modify their way of life. Coming from countries where there were movements to liberalize religious observances, many of them began to do the same in the new land. An immigrant rabbi from Bavaria, Isaac Mayer Wise, became the founder of the Reform movement in Judaism in this country. Many of the congregations established by Jews in growing communities during this period were Reform Jewish congregations, where the services were conducted largely in English, where men and women were permitted to sit together in the sanctuary, where the men could pray without head covering, where some of the traditional vestments of prayer, like the prayershawl and phylacteries, were discarded, and where the major two-day holidays were observed only one day. The fundamental tenets of the Jewish faith—the belief in one God and the ethical structure enunciated in the Bible and Talmud—remained at the heart of the reformed religion.

The holiest day of the year for the Jew is Yom Kippur, the Day of Atonement. It is a time of fasting, confession, and repentance. The Jewish peddlers made every effort to reach a town in time to join their fellow Jews for the Jewish New Year and the Day of Atonement. The Jewish storekeepers closed their shops on these High Holy Days and attended services in their synagogues. This is the background of Myron Brinig's "Day of Atonement," an excerpt from his novel Singermann.

R OSH HASHANAH, the Jewish New Year, commenced on a Thursday, and would be followed the week from Saturday by Yom Kippur, the Day of Atonement. These particular Saturdays happened to be pay days for the miners, and the coincidence made it particularly hard for the Jewish merchants of Silver Bow. Those who were sincere in their beliefs did not worry unduly about this coincidence. They were willing, even eager, to sacrifice profits for the sake of their religion. Moses was such a one. Much as he loved his store and greatly as he looked forward to these golden pay days, he did not for a moment tolerate the thought of keeping his store open for business.

On the holy days it was Moses' custom to rise at six so that he might be in the synagogue an hour later. Rebecca, too, was up at that early hour and roused the children. Since the holidays occurred in the latter part of September, it was already cold in Montana. In Rumania, it had been pleasant to wake in the autumnal morning and walk through the rich red and gold countryside to the shul. Moses and Rebecca remembered the voices of the Rumanian congregation, a steady humming sound pierced by the rising supplications of the rabbi, a golden overtone in a full-bodied symphony. The contrast of Silver Bow was overwhelming and depressing, particularly on Rosh Hashanah. It did not matter so much on Yom Kippur, for that was the day of mourning, of deep grief for the sins committed during the past twelve months. The dark skies of Silver Bow and the penetrating winds that swept through the town were in keeping with the doleful nature of the day.

Cold as it was, no fire was started in any of the stoves; and whatever servant there happened to be in the house at the time was given the day off. It was not proper that servants should work on the holy days, no matter what their beliefs might be. Rebecca and Moses dressed in their cold bedchamber, and the children shivered in their own icy rooms. There was no hot coffee for breakfast, but Rebecca served cake and wine. Since Yom Kippur was a day of fasting, there was nothing to warm up congealed bodies, and the Singermanns formed a frozen, despondent group when they left their house to attend the services in the synagogue. They left a gloomy, cold house to emerge into a dim street harsh with smoke and sulphur. But it was comforting to reach the modest shul, dark and musty, warmed by the presence of many worshipers. The men with their hats worn low over their eyes, their shoulders draped by the inevitable prayer shawl, stood in many attitudes; some were bent low over the benches peering with a desperate concentration into the Hebrew prayer books; others stood with their eyes to the wall as though ashamed to show their faces agonized by grief and supplication.

On this Yom Kippur, Moses occupied a bench near the altar, and it was to this corner of the shul that he shepherded his flock, his wife and five children. Michael was still too young to appear in the synagogue, and Mary O'Brien had taken him to her home in Walkerville for the day. Last year Joseph had been here, praying by the side of his father; but now he was married and his wife was a Christian Scientist. There was a yawning gap where he should have stood, his slim shoulders draped by the prayer-shawl. There had been for Moses a kind of security in the knowledge of Joseph's presence in a shul, a warmth of kinship that cannot be far from God. But now he was gone—sold to the devil! "O Lord, have mercy upon my son and show him the right way!" Moses prayed, and his voice transformed the ugly wooden shack into an immortal place. He sang and all else seemed fugitive and dying; but his songs were one with the million nights that have passed over the earth since Abraham and David and Solomon. "This was my son, Joseph. Now I am bereft of him. Forgive Thou his many sins, O Lord! *Adenoi Elohenu, Adenoi Echod!* Hear, O Israel! The Lord our God, The Lord is One!"

At noon time, Moses went outside for a breath of air. He walked up and down the sidewalk in front of the synagogue, refreshing his body and lungs and feeling the wind in his eyes. Members of the congregation stood about in small groups holding earnest conversation with one another, seeking diversion and rest in gossip—aye, even on the Day of Atonement! When the afternoon prayers began, they would be able to renew their supplications to Jehovah with a more devout and strengthened ardor. After a minute, Moses became aware that they were casting furtive, uneasy glances in his direction. They

would look at him and then resume talking with great heat and animation. He caught detached words . . . "His son, Joseph . . . Such a shame . . . the son keeps open his store on Yom Kippur . . . With my own eyes . . . disgrace . . . Only of money he thinks . . . Should I have such a son, I would hang my head . . . And we keep our stores closed that such a one . . ."

Moses knew that they were talking of his oldest son. He dared not meet their reproachful eyes, yet every word they spoke was a wound in his body. Usually the most courageous of men, he was moved now by a desire to flee from these critical eyes and hide away. He looked towards the door of the synagogue and saw David emerge, David so tall and strong, with grace in his walk and assurance in his manner. Moses felt suddenly free, and as he moved forward to meet his third son, he thought that Jehovah would not hold Joseph so much against him since there was David, so alive, so vivid in his young beauty.

But as David caught sight of his father, a frown appeared on his forehead, and his eyes blinked with troubled anger. For a moment, Moses was hurt by his son's expression; but it turned out that it was not with his father that David was angry. On the contrary, this was one of those rare occasions when David was thoroughly sympathetic with his father's attitude.

"Did you know that Joseph was keeping his store open today?" David whispered, drawing Moses to the edge of the walk. "Everybody's talking about it and cursing at us behind our backs. It's a shame!" David kicked at the rocks in the street.

"It was not like this before he married that woman," said Moses, throwing the blame on Daisy rather than on his favorite son. "She's to blame." And he added in Yiddish, "She should roll in the dust!"

"It ain't so much because I'm religious that I care," said David truthfully, and Moses looked moody at these words. "But how does it look for other people? Every Jewish store in the block closed for the holidays, and his open with the Gentiles."

"It is the woman," persisted Moses stubbornly, but he only half believed his own words. "She is to blame. She with her Christian Science! Do you think I don't know? I have seen her go into the church with the Christians. But why do I talk? He is no more a son of mine. Let her give him flesh of the swine to eat."

The worshipers returned into the synagogue. The rabbi's voice that had been droning on and on during the interlude, in a kind of passive monotone, was once more raised to its high pitch of intense supplication. Its sharpness, its vehemence of expression stabbed the quietness of the street and recalled the men and women to their various places within. "It is beneath me to talk from such a son," said Moses and returned within the shul, leaving David to stand alone on the sidewalk.

David stood there in front of the synagogue staring at the cheap colored glass windows parallel with his eyes. A weak, timid-appearing sun shot its gleams through the dark, smoky clouds for a short space, and the answering reflections of the glass were imprisoned in David's eyes. He became, thus, for the slightest interval, a very striking young man, a crusader striding out of the muddled cheapness of his background. For that moment he was all beauty, all young manhood attempting to free itself from the grasping tendons of a materialistic octopus. But David's thoughts were less concerned with beauty than with ideas of right and wrong; and even his ideas of right and wrong were by no means straightened out in his mind. He only knew that it was a sin to transact commerce on Yom Kippur. Joseph was therefore sinning. David did not bother to argue the question to himself. For all he cared, religion might be useless and out of date. Indeed, he had entertained a suspicion of this sort for some time. But futile or worthy as his religion might be, it was his religion, and no member of his family had ever scorned it as Joseph was doing today.

Since Joseph had opened his own store, he had dug a chasm between himself and his younger brothers, a chasm filled with bitterness. David acknowledged that his oldest brother had worked hard; he acknowledged, too, a certain initiative and hustle in Joseph that the younger members of the family did not possess. But these worthier qualities of Joseph's were overshadowed by the indubitable fact that he had seized, by stealth, what he had no right to have. He had built up a new business on the money that he and Daisy had taken from the original Singermann store. Joseph was a hard worker and Daisy a clever manager, but that did not alter the truth of the situation.

"It makes me sore!" said David to himself, and without quite realizing it, started to walk away from the synagogue towards the business part of town. He was not clear in his mind about what he wanted to do, but he was filled with that soreness, that blind anger against Joseph and Daisy. As he neared East Park Street, his thoughts became less amenable to discipline. "It's a shame!" he kept repeating to himself. "That guy thinks he can get away with anything!"

So intensely was David wrapped up with his angered thoughts that he started with some surprise when he found himself in front of his brother's store.

Doubts began to enter his mind and he hesitated. Like his younger brothers, David had always held Joseph in a certain awe. The oldest son had always been a dictator to his brothers; he had always sneered in a superior way at any idea Louis or David had set in motion, as though no one his junior could possibly say or do anything that would bear the scrutiny of an intelligent human being. Since his marriage to Daisy, he had exhibited even less patience where the rest of the family was concerned. David was fully aware of this attitude on Joseph's part, and it tended to create within him a certain despondent feeling of inferiority. So now, as he stood in front of Joseph's store, he wondered what he had better do. All his hatred and jealousy had ceased to be effective weapons. He must be sure of himself before he entered within to do battle with Joseph. And now, he felt sure of nothing. He even wondered whether he had the right to interfere in his oldest brother's business. The fact that they were brothers meant very little as they grew older. Each man for himself . . . that was it. If Joseph chose to look out for himself, who could blame him?

David turned his eyes to the opposite side of the street and regarded his father's store with the sign, *Closed acc't Holidays,* hanging behind the door. How deserted the place looked, how cold!

And here, on the other side of the street, everything was light and business. Joseph's was the only store open on the block, and he was profiting at the expense of his father and younger brothers. All these customers thronging the aisles of Joseph's store, their pockets jingling with money, their fingers eagerly caressing the merchandise! And on the Day of Atonement, the day that Singermanns for generations past had set aside for the worship of the one God, the true God!

It was this thought, concerned with the mysterious Deity, that set David's fears at rest. He cast off his inferiority with one stride and passed into the crowded aisles of Joseph's store. There, in the center of the floor, seated on a chair that was like a throne, was Daisy, pressing the keys of the cash register and calling out instructions to the clerks who scurried like ants beneath her. Like a queen she commanded all; with one hand she reached for money and counted change; with the other she delved absently into a bag of peanuts, cracking each shell between her strong, pointed teeth. A sudden realization of her power overcame David as he halted in the aisle looking up at her. He knew, without stopping to formulate any logical train of thought in his mind, that it was this handsome, formidable woman who had ordered Joseph to keep his store open on a Jewish holiday.

And with that thought came a succeeding one, painfully obvious to him, that it would be worse than useless to argue with Joseph who was dominated by this stubborn, crafty woman.

As David continued to look up at her, almost drugged by her power, she caught sight of him. For a moment she was taken aback by his abrupt materialization out of a crowd of milling shoppers; but she was quick to regain her composure, perceiving, almost instantly, David's motive for coming into the store. She waved at her brother-in-law gaily. "Hello, Dave! How's tricks?" At the same time there was an interrogative glint in her hard blue eyes, as if she were saying: Out with it! You might as well tell me why you've come.

"Where's Joe?" asked David in a voice that was this side of rudeness. And as he asked the question, he began edging away from the chair upon which Daisy was enthroned, his eyes darting in many directions.

"He's in the rear waiting on a customer," was Daisy's almost mechanical response. "Is it something important you wanted to see him about, dear?" She had a habit of calling her brothers-in-law "dear" thus instantly placing them on the defensive. The term caused them to feel ridiculously young, mere children, and served to fortify Daisy's self-esteem.

David did not answer his sister-in-law's last question. He had caught a momentary glimpse of Joseph in the rear of the store; for an instant their eyes met, and the older brother's face had turned a trifle pale. Joseph quickly lowered his gaze and pretended an almost fierce interest in the customer he was waiting upon. Like his wife, he knew why David had come, and the realization threw him into one of his peculiar, spasmodic fits of action. He talked rapidly to his customer, shifting about nervously on his feet. He was in the midst of selling a suit of clothes, and his agile hands were in bewildering movement, patting the back of the coat, running along the man's collar, pulling at the sleeves. "It fits you perfect—just perfect," Joseph said with a deliberate, intense concentration. "You don't have to take my word for it. Just take a look for yourself, here in the glass." And as the customer turned to the mirror, Joseph followed him, petting, cajoling, assuming the slightly cringing attitude of a clever salesman who wants to flatter his prospective victim. Yet all the while, out of one corner of his eyes, Joseph was aware of his brother's approach, the approach of a handsome young animal filled with a fury of anger. He was aware, too, of Daisy leaning far out of her swivel-chair, watching David's progress with a nervous alarm.

David spoke instantly and quickly, lest his words take fright before they were uttered and remain unsaid. "You—you damn fool! What d'ya mean keeping your store open like this on a Jewish holiday? Don't you know it's Yom Kippur? You're a fine one, you are!" David possessed a husky, resonant voice. There was strength in his lungs that his words were audible all over the store.

Joseph went even whiter and stretched out an impatient arm as if to shove his younger brother away. "Where do you think you are? . . . Who do you think you're talking to?" He made a movement as though to strike David, and then hesitated and turned to his customer who was looking at the brothers with wide, startled eyes.

It was David who closed the gap. He stood over Joseph like a great bear, and his eyes were blazing fire. He had now completely lost control of his temper, and Joseph was no longer a brother and not even an acquaintance. He was merely an exasperating worm who had somehow got in his path and who must somehow be shown his place. "A fine one you are! And all that papa has done for you, too! I'd be ashamed to look a decent man in the face . . . Every other Jew in town is closed up, and here you are . . . shoving in money so that your wife can get fat . . . and eat more ham . . . afraid you'll lose a little business!"

They stood facing one another, almost touching, one a strong, handsome animal, the other like a worried, petulant gnat. Joseph's anger was bottled up, tensely, tightly, and drew all the color of his face within him until he was seething with a poison of emotions. "Get out of here!" he whispered furiously. "What right have you got to come in here anyway? You've got nothing to do with me. I'll throw you out! I'll throw you out like the dog you are!"

The customer who was buying the suit stepped aside and looked on. He had forgotten that he was worried about the length of the sleeves. That, in itself, was something of an event in his life. He was a poor man and it was not often that he bought a new suit. For weeks his wife had been pestering him. "You look a perfect fright in that old suit of yours. It's about time you bought a new outfit. I saw something in the window of The Hub . . . Now don't come home tonight and tell me you forgot all about it. I'm sick and tired . . ." He had left his wife feeling shabby and out of sorts. Now he was in The Hub about to purchase a new suit, a rare event, and the sleeves had been rather short. But he could not think of sleeves as he looked as Joseph and David.

"Why don't you throw me out then?" asked David. He did not wait for an answer and brought the palm of his hand against Joseph's face. It was a sharp, painful blow, and when he withdrew his hand, he could see where he had left a dark red imprint on his brother's face. The finger prints fascinated him. He could not move his eyes from the dark red marks with the intensely white spaces in between. He even forgot that he had struck Joseph. There seeemed neither rhyme nor reason to it all. There was only that imprint, somehow horrible and shameful.

For a moment, Joseph stared at his brother. Tiny crystals appeared in the corners of his eyes, but they were tears of astonishment rather than of grief. Suddenly, he lost control of his tightly packed passions. It was as though the cork that had been bottling up the poison had given way to a sharp, explosive pressure and blown off, loosing the angry fumes within. He jumped at David, a snarling caricature of himself, and the two brothers became intricately mad, aiming a tempest of blows at one another, most of which failed in their aim. Joseph's impact forced David against a movable clothing rack; the rack swayed from side to side and finally fell to the floor and the two young men fell on top of it, becoming involved in sleeves and trousers. They finally struggled fiercely in this maze while customers and clerks surrounded them, shouting, imploring, fascinated at the unexpected show. Then, a woman pushed her way through the gaping spectators. It was Daisy, white and desperate.

A coil of her hair had come loose and straggled down her neck to her shoulder, so that she looked like an easy woman from down on Galena Street. "Pull them apart!" she screamed to one of the clerks. "Don't stand there lookin' at 'em. What do you think we're paying you for?" The clerk looked at her helplessly, as if saying, Well, I know what you're paying me for, but it's not for this. As he hesitated, Daisy bent over and with all her strength clutched at David's shoulders. Her entrance into the tangle was the signal for the clerk to do likewise; while she held firmly to David, the clerk pinned Joseph's arms behind him and jerked him to his feet. The two brothers subsided almost as abruptly as they had begun. David looked frantically about for his hat that had been knocked off his head during the battle. It was crushed out of shape and covered with dust. He stood creasing it nervously for perhaps a minute, and then started on his way to the outer door.

He was nearing his objective when he felt someone clutching at his sleeve. He turned about, and it seemed as though Daisy's eyes were boring through him, blue daggers, sharp and pointed, twisting in his sickened consciousness. "You hit him," she gasped. "You struck your own brother, and he's older than you. I'll always hold this against you. Barbarian! Don't think I'll ever for-

get it. There was no reason . . . I could have the police on you . . . I could send you to the penitentiary . . . as God is my witness. . . ." And always he felt the eyes, like blue needles, stabbing him through and through.

He shook off her grasp, impatiently, yet he was full of sadness. He could not understand why, all of a sudden, he should be so unutterably sorry, so full of loathing for himself, for everyone. "You're to blame!" he cried out, and his eyes were brimming over with tears. "If it hadn't been for you there'd be no trouble. But it's because you changed him. Since he's known you. . . ."

"I can never forgive you for this," she went on breathlessly, as though she feared that her strength would leave her before all her words were said. "It's like you was hitting me. You're like a criminal. But wait! You'll come to a bad end. You'll be in a bad fix some day and we'll—spit on you! Coming around here—the idea . . . before all our customers . . . Do you think I'll ever forget this? Some things burn in me. I'm a sensitive woman. If it wasn't that God's truth was in me I'd . . . But wait . . . you'll be punished. . . ."

"Aw, let me go!" He shook off her grasp and walked on, but she continued to follow him, over the threshold, to the sidewalk, clinging to him while passers-by looked over their shoulders. Many of them nodded to her, for by this time she was well known in the town. "Joe Singermann's wife . . . she ain't nobody's fool . . ." Many of them stopped, but the look in her eyes bade them keep a respectful distance. "Go tell your father that I never want to look at him again. Every day I was in his hell of a store he made me suffer . . . insulting me . . . and now that God has provided us with our own business, he sends you to pester us. But nothin' can harm us because God is our strength. . . ."

"Let me go!" said David gruffly, and walked away from her, but she stood looking after him for a long time. He could feel her eyes stabbing through his back until he turned the corner. And even when he knew that she could no longer see him, he felt her presence like a plague in his body.

"Get back to your customers," Joseph ordered his clerks, and flicked the dust off his trousers with his hands. His necktie had come undone and he drew it tight under his collar. He smoothed his hair and wiped the dust and perspiration off his face. "Where's Daisy? Tell her to get back to the cash register. Where does she think she is, standing like that out on the sidewalk? Call her back there, you—I mean you. I'm not paying you to look at me. . . ." He turned to the customer who had been trying on the suit. "That's brothers for you," and he

forced a weak, wretched smile. "That guy was my brother . . . Would you believe it? . . . I want you to excuse me, friend. How's the fit?" And he began pressing his agile, nervous hands down the back of the coat, patting the collar, the shoulders. "You couldn't get a better-looking suit made to order." Already he had forgotten David. Once more he was intensely concentrated in the suit, the customer, the necessity of making a sale. "Turn around. See how it lays in the back?"

The customer was embarrassed; he tried to interest himself in the suit, but all the time he kept thinking of the two brothers, one like a great, enraged animal, the other like a gnat, restless, spasmodic. "Kind of bad tempered, that brother of yours, ain't he? Hurt you? He's bigger'n you. But you put up a great battle. How much is the suit? . . . Yaa, I'll take it. It's a good thing your wife separated the both o' you. Plucky woman, Mrs. Singermann . . . How are you, Mrs. Singermann? Thirty-five dollars. Yaa. My wife kept pesterin' me to get a suit, an' now I got one, an' I hope she's satisfied . . .You said it! They always want you to be dolled up like a million dollars. Say! That brother-in-law o' yours, he ain't to be trifled with . . . Hit your husband a nasty one. I just stood there. I'm neutral. Ha! Ha! Naw, I wasn't a bit inconvenienced, Mrs. Singermann. Just forget about it. Them boys they're just like the old man. I used to do all my buyin' across the street until Joe opened this place. Always like Joe to wait on me. He treats me square. But I like the old man. He's a proper old devil. The boys is just like him. Once they get mad! . . . Thanks, Mrs. Singermann. I will come in again, thanks. You got my whole pay roll, now. Ha! Some fight that was. . . ."

David strode along back to the synagogue. It was growing dark now. The smelter smokestack south of the town was lifting its plume of fire into the sky, as though the devil were lying in there on his back breathing defiance to the heavens. There was a hard, vicious beauty about it, unconscious and unpremediated. David lifted his eyes to this burning splendor, but its beauty was a blankness in his mind. He had that sadness in him, that deep loathing of himself and of everyone. What a fight that had been! What ever made him do it? What was the use of it all? He should never have gone to the store. If Joseph wanted to keep open on Yom Kippur, if he were sinning, why he'd be punished, that's all. Sinning! thought David bitterly. What did sinning have to do with it? They were getting the money while all the other Jewish stores were closed tighter than drums. They were too damn smart. Well,

he'd got one on the nose just the same. Maybe it'll teach him a lesson. "I'll never speak to you again." Well, Mrs. Daisy Singermann, I should worry whether you do or whether you don't.

David's thoughts ran on: That woman! She's the cause of it all. If only she'd be decent and let somebody else have a chance . . . the greedy snake . . . Aw, I guess I shouldn't have hit him. The way my hand looked on his face . . . He's not so strong. What did she mean when she said that some day I'd be in a fix? What's she pokin' her nose . . . aw, I shouldn't have hit him. But what the hell? What right has he to keep his store open on Yom Kippur when it is the law to fast and pray?

It was dark when he reached the synagogue and he could see the dim light within reflected through the colored glass. There were a hundred or more voices raised in that piercing agonizing song so full of blood and tears. They were singing Kol Nidre. David stood out there in the darkness and a peace came over him, a quietness. If that piercing, ecstatic song, broken by deep sobs, significant pauses, could go on forever! But the song ends, thought David. The song ends and prayers are forgotten, and you struggle blindly and work yourself to the bone . . . And at night you seek diversion in those dives, those cheap cribs. Where is Kol Nidre then? Where are the thoughts of Moses, Abraham, and Solomon? And David turned into the syna-gogue. And the candlelight was soft and kindly to his eyes.

Questions for Analysis and Discussion

This is the story of a fist fight between two brothers.

1. The narrator of the story involves himself in its events by making judgments about the characters. With which characters does he sympathize? How do you know? Notice the difference in the narrator's descriptions of David and Joseph. What do the descriptions of David and Joseph tell you of the narrator's beliefs and values?

2. Why was it a sacrifice for the Jewish storekeepers of Silver Bow, Montana, to keep their stores closed on Saturdays? What economic problem was created when the Day of Atonement fell on Saturday? Where did the Singermann family come from? How had living in America changed their customs? What customs remained?

3. Moses Singermann was the patriarch of his family. Why was Joseph absent from the synagogue service? Why was this an embarrassment to his father? David says people are cursing the Singermanns behind their backs. Is this true? Do the Jews of Silver Bow feel sorry for Moses or are they angry at him? The narrator says that this was one occasion when David sympathized with his father's attitude. What are we to infer from this? On what subjects were the father and son likely to disagree? Both Moses and David blame Daisy, Joseph's wife, for Joseph's "apostasy." Are they honest in this view? With what does David equate his brother's scorning of the faith of their father? What is David's opinion of his brother?

4. In the presence of Joseph, David felt inferior. Why? Joseph believed that even in a family it should be "each man for himself." Who do you imagine fostered such a belief? David had come unconsciously to be jealous of his brother and to hate him. How had this feeling grown in him? Who was responsible—he, Joseph, or their father? What was David's reason for his anger against his brother? What in your view was the real reason? What additional information would you want to have to understand the source of David's anger?

5. What psychological reason, if any, caused David to blame Daisy for Joseph's scorning of his religion? What position did Daisy occupy in her husband's store? What causes the violent fight between the brothers? How is the fight stopped? After the fight, as David tries to leave the store, Daisy stops him. What does she say to him? This fight will bring about a rift between Joseph and his family. Daisy will see to it. Is she justified? How has the family treated her? Was she in any way to blame for their attitude toward her? What reputation did Daisy have in the town?

6. This next series of questions deals with one aspect of the author's technique. During the quarrel between the two brothers, the narrator stops to describe the reactions of a particular customer who was in the store. What purpose does the narrator have in introducing this aside? Does it belong in the action of the story? After the fight, the narrator introduces a long speech by the same customer. Does this speech belong in the narrative of the quarrel between the brothers? Why do you think the author introduced it at that point?

7. Joseph recovers quickly after the fight and sells his customer the suit. What does this tell you about him? The narrator tells you what thoughts run through David's mind. Why doesn't he tell you what Joseph was thinking or what Daisy was thinking?

Suggested Activities

1. Invite a Rabbi from the community to discuss with the class the nature and the major observances of the Jewish New Year (Rosh Hashanah) and the Day of Atonement (Yom Kippur). A knowledgeable teacher, resident, or student may be able to do this if a Rabbi is not available.

2. To dramatize the contributions of German-Jewish immigrants to American life, read Chapter 3 of Oscar Handlin's *Adventure in Freedom* and Chapter 5 of Rufus Learsi's *The Jews in America* and report to the class how the Jewish peddlers plied their trade, how they developed into merchants, and what they contributed to the communities in which they settled.

3. The focus of *Day of Atonement* is on David. The author tells us what goes on in his mind during his fight with his brother. Write

a "stream of consciousness" account of what goes on in Joseph's mind after David leaves the store. Be sure to include thoughts about his relationship with his wife Daisy, his feelings about his father, the break with his tradition, and his anger toward his brother David.

4. Write a dialogue between Joseph and Daisy at home, after they have closed their store, in which they discuss the events of the day; or write a dialogue between David and his father at home after the synagogue service in which David tells his father of his fight with his brother Joseph; or write the thoughts that run through the mind of David's mother when she learns of the fight between her two sons. Will the mother feel the same antagonism toward Daisy that her husband and younger son feel?

5. Write a conversation between two friends of Moses Singermann, one Jewish and one non-Jewish, in which they discuss Joseph's actions in opening a store in competition with his father and in keeping the store open on the Day of Atonement.

6. If you were a psychologist and Moses Singermann came to ask you what kind of relationship he should maintain with his son Joseph, what advice would you give him and what reasons would you give for this advice?

7. *Day of Atonement* deals with German-American Jews who were beginning to establish themselves as a community concerned with maintaining two forms of identity—one with their people, its history and customs, and the other with America, the nation that had accepted them so hospitably and had offered them the freedom to live where they wished, to worship God according to their beliefs, to engage in any work or business they chose, and to join the mainstream of American life and culture. You may be interested in studying the growth of a typical German-American community in the United States. Read Stephen Birmingham's *Our Crowd* and report to the class on how the community was organized, what philanthropic enterprises it engaged in, what it did to help fellow Jewish immigrants feel at home, how its members related to their non-Jewish neighbors, what it contributed to the development of the nation.

Amalgamated Clothing Workers of America, New York. Courtesy of American Jewish Archives, Hebrew Union College, Jewish Institute of Religion.

By Leo Litwak

The Oath

Introduction: **Strife in the Labor Movement**

The Jews in Russia and Poland lived in ghettos and were prevented by decree from getting a secular education. Most of them lived in poverty and found compensation for the misery of their lives in observing the rituals of their faith and in the study of their holy books.

In the latter part of the nineteenth century a movement begun earlier in Western Europe called the Haskalah *(Enlightenment) reached Russian Jews. One of the forms it took was an attempt on the part of scholarly and artistic young Jews to break away from purely Jewish learning and to join Russian intellectual circles in the study of literature, art, and science. These young scholars made every effort to gain admission into the secular schools of the country and to pursue knowledge that would lead to careers in the professions or the arts.*

Their dreams were shattered by the anti-Semitic outrages against their people which followed the assassination of Czar Alexander II in 1881. They turned from a devotion to Russian culture to causes that they hoped would remedy the plight of their people. One such cause was Zionism. They reasoned that if the Jewish people were to attain any dignity in a world that so often turned against them, they needed a homeland, a country which was theirs where they would not be a tolerated and persecuted minority.

A second cause was socialism. It was in these years, in the 1860s and 1870s, that Russia moved toward industrialization. Iron and steel mills and textile factories were built, and within a short time the country had a sizable labor force, among whom were many Jewish workers.

Many of the political-minded Jews of the period were attracted by the theories of Karl Marx. As members of an impoverished people, they saw in the theories of socialism the possibility of setting up a society in which the wealth of production would be more equitably distributed, and which would also be free of anti-Semitism. They were stimulated also by the long Jewish tradition regarding treatment of the worker dating back to Biblical times: a worker with a grievance against an employer could even have the holiest service in the synagogue stopped to air his grievance.

The anti-Semitic excesses in Russia and other parts of Eastern Europe and the promise of a new life in America led hosts of Jews to emigrate to the New World. For most of them, at first, America was not the dreamt of "golden land." Seeking any kind of livelihood, a great number of the new immigrants found jobs in clothing factories and sweatshops where they were cruelly exploited. This was a world that was ripe for socialist movements, for organizing unions, for calling strikes, and for improving the lot of the worker. A number of young intellectual Jews became leaders in the movement. One of these was Abraham Cahan in New York City who founded a Yiddish newspaper called The Forward. Articles in this publication educated the Jewish worker and helped him understand his rights.

The first attempts at union organization and the calling of strikes created many dangers for the strikers and their leaders. The factory owners had the support of the city authorities, and the police were often called in to break up the lines of pickets. In addition, the bosses sometimes called in gangsters and hoods to beat up the leaders and the more militant strikers. They sought in this way to frighten them into surrender.

These were harsh times, and many people suffered, but owing largely to the efforts of outstanding Jewish community leaders like Louis Marshall and lawyers like Louis Dembitz Brandeis, who later became a Justice of the U.S. Supreme Court, peace was attained. The result was the establishment of two large unions in the New York City clothing business—the International Ladies Garment Workers Union and the Amalgamated Clothing Workers of America—which became models for unions in other industries in different parts of the country.

Similar struggles took place in Chicago. In the struggle in Chicago for the improvement of working conditions, three groups were formed. There were the employers who wished to maintain the status quo; the union organizers who sought to persuade the workers to form a vigorous union that would strike for better salaries and working conditions if bargaining failed; and the burly, stupid hoods among the population who were hired by the factory owners to use violence to frighten the leaders of the workers and to prevent the workers from succeeding in their efforts. This is the background of Leo Litwak's The Oath.

THERE WAS in our old Detroit neighborhood a restaurant called the Cream of Michigan, famous for its barley soup and delicatessen. It was a humble place, in a humble neighborhood, planted among haberdasheries and grocery stores. The Cream of Michigan didn't confine its service to the cream. It's true that you could find affluent gents from the suburbs with monogrammed hankies in the breast pockets of English-cut tweed jackets who sought the corn bread and barley soup of their youth. But the Cream of Michigan was mainly patronized by neighborhood people, men of the working class. It was also the special preserve of the Jewish toughs, our hoods, who occupied the counter and the front tables. When we passed behind them and glimpsed a rear view we saw bulls at a feeding trough with enormous backs and necks and jowls. They wore fedoras on small domes.

We knew a man who was a doctor to these hoods. This doctor entered the Cream of Michigan one day. He heard a quarrel and turned to look. A behemoth descended from his stool, grabbed a little guy who had irritated him, and with a twist and a twirl heaved him through the plate-glass window. The little guy crawled to the streetcar tracks where, as the doctor put it, "He exsanguinated." That was a new style for our people, our own hoods and killers. And after all the pretty talk is pared away, who were Arthur and his Knights? The cowboys of the West? Stenka Razin? Robin Hood? Admired butchers. It wasn't a style Jake cared for. The Jewish hoods were killing Jews, not dragons. It's not that they lacked sentiment. The jukebox at the rear of the Cream of Michigan played *Meine Yiddische Momma*, among other fine pieces, and these hulks grieved for mothers. Yet they could blot the tears, honk their noses, get down from their stools, and heave you through plate-glass windows. While you exsanguinated they finished their barley soup. My Pa, Jake Gottlieb, scorned these bums. He had no quarrel with sentiment. In memory of his own mother he could also weep. These oxen, though, when they were finished weeping were ready to pound your head with fists like boulders. They struck without sentiment; not even with hard feelings, and resumed slurping their soup. The incident with the exsanguinating man was rare since most of the damage they inflicted was off the premises.

There was one among our hoods, Happy Weinberg, whom we kids most admired. Weinberg had a sunny disposition and a freckled red face as tubby as the moon. When Happy grinned you saw white and gold. He had a laugh that was so exuberant you had to join in. He was fond of children; he let them hang around while he played pool. He probably got a boost out of the appreciation of children. I wouldn't have been surprised to find Happy watching cowboy movies on Saturday afternoon. I don't mean to represent him as a moron who happened to be a hood by accident—a buffoon first, secondly a bruiser. That isn't my intention. Because that big sunny face with the merry eyes might very well be focused on a brutal scene such as a girl being teased while her cowed escort is invited to be a bystander. . . . Happy could unloose that infectious laugh while some frightened tailor was being slapped around. It was a good laugh, a real "ho-ho" that used all two hundred and fifty pounds of Happy. He was able to laugh at how absurd men look when they are being tormented. We kids didn't despise him for that. Weren't we instructed to be cool when murder was done? I'm speaking, of course, of our other models, Tom Mix and Buck Jones and Bob Steele and the Manassa Mauler and Achilles and Joshua and Sgt. York, not to mention Mickey Mouse and that crowd. His cool meanness, his cheerful sadism made Happy all the more admirable to us kids. Not to Jake Gottlieb, however.

Jake walked past the counter at the Cream of Michigan as if the hoods didn't exist. He wasn't about to surrender a first-rate delicatessen because hoodlums shared his appetite for good barley soup. With my brother Ernie and me in tow he marched to the tables in back and let people know that Gottlieb was around. He ridiculed the hoods. His comments were loud and clear.

We often accompanied Jake to the Cream of Michigan, even in the summer when we were on vacation. On a rainy day we welcomed the chance to get away from our tent at the lake and take a trip to Detroit to have some restaurant food. But the prospect of Jake offending Happy and his cohorts scared me. These men needed little cause to heave you through plate-glass windows. Ernie made no effort to disguise his anguish. Happy Weinberg had an unpredictable sense of humor. He might laugh off Jake's abuse. He might even enjoy our nervy Pa. But he had a buddy, Whitey Spiegelman, who was dangerously sensitive. This Spiegelman wasn't to be teased. Ernie feared that Jake was ignorant of Spiegelman's possibilities. Such ignorance was a threat to us all. Spiegelman resembled a clerk. He was scrawny and bald and doughy-nosed. If a defined chin is evidence of power, he would be classed as timid and meek, for he had no chin. Yet, despite appearances, he was a dangerous man. We heard stories of sudden furies, provoked by trivialities. He swarmed over his opposition, flailing like a windmill, not stopping until his tantrum had run its course. He may have lacked Weinberg's heft, but he was relentless. He had exceptionally skillful hands. We saw him perform card tricks. We watched him move around a pool table, bending, sighting, then stroking quickly. It was foolish to provoke such a man.

One Sunday when our appetite for vacation ebbed, a succession of gray days, bickering, the tent closing in on us, we accepted Jake's offer of a drive into Detroit for a meal at the Cream of Michigan.

Again we had to listen to Jake's daring abuse, and I wished I was back at the lake. Better the dullness of our tent. But when nothing came of Jake's ridicule—the restaurant was crowded and every kid's pa had a big voice and every table had someone putting on a show—I relaxed and ate. I felt wonderful relief and became sassy myself.

We loaded up with delicatessen as we left. We were outside the restaurant when Happy Weinberg summoned Jake. He was waiting at the curb, leaning against the open door of a new Hudson. Spiegelman was at the wheel.

"Gottlieb, you old bastard. Say hello to a friend." It was an exuberant, high-pitched voice, a friendly tone that offered no threat.

Jake handed one package to Ernie and another to me and faced Weinberg with folded arms. "Do I know you? We've been introduced?"

"You're Gottlieb, the laundryman, OK? You work for Kravitz at Atlas Linen. Meet my pal Whitey Spiegelman." He leaned into the car and explained to Whitey Spiegelman that Jake Gottlieb was a friend. Spiegelman didn't seem impressed.

"I'm no friend of yours," Jake declared. It was clear that he offered a statement of policy, not merely a fact. Did he take that strong line because his sons were present? We knew that Jake's tone was always pitched to an audience. Couldn't he, out of concern for us, have retreated on this occasion? I have a photo of Jake taken about that time, an impressive profile, a face that would attract a sculptor who wants to make something of a coarse-grained stone. A heavy face, a big chin, the short neck making a firm pedestal for the large head.

Happy bent down and faced me at eye level. "I see you boys around, don't I? You're Vic, right?" I was thrilled that he knew my name. "And this here is Ernie who hangs out with Lenny Mitchell. Lenny Mitchell is my buddy, do you know that? I take care of Lenny Mitchell. Well, you boys got some daddy. What big ideas he got. Don't be surprised if one of these days you find out that me and your Pa are in business. Weinberg and Gottlieb. How's that for a team?"

Jake said, "I got no business with you."

Happy straightened up and clapped Jake's shoulder, a good swat. "Don't be in such a rush, Gottlieb. I can do you favors."

"Why should you do me favors?"

"We got mutual friends."

"What friends?"

"Hy Kravitz."

"He's no friend."

"He speaks nice about you."

"By the time I'm finished with Kravitz," Jake said, "either he'll be out of business or he'll be paying us a living wage. You go tell that to Kravitz."

"It would be a special favor to me, Jake, if you talk nice to Kravitz. A friend of Kravitz is a friend of Happy Weinberg."

He only asked that Jake be reasonable and talk to Kravitz.

"You making threats?" Jake asked.

Happy appealed to us. "Did you hear me say anything, kiddies? What a touchy pa you got."

If Jake wanted to demonstrate that he didn't fear the most dangerous hoods on Twelfth Street, he had proved his point. What he said next made me dizzy.

"Listen, bums, with such arms and shoulders you should be standing in the front lines, breaking Nazi skulls. Instead, you specialize in old tailors. Tell Kravitz if he wants to speak to Jake Gott-

lieb, he can talk to him face to face. He don't have to use third parties."

Weinberg didn't need to make threats. His reputation made threats for him. If he greeted you, you were threatened. His tone of voice was irrelevant. I knew my Pa had been threatened and I trembled.

"We hear stories about them," Ernie told Jake as we left the Cream of Michigan. "You don't fool around with Weinberg and Spiegelman. They can do terrible things."

We were under the spell of Weinberg's threat when Jake pulled us into the doorway of a closed Woolworth's.

"Listen, organizing a union is dangerous work. I don't hide that from you. Those bums mean me no good. But I assure you, boys, it doesn't give me a second of worry. I have been banged on the head; I have been hit in the face. No one intimidates your Pa, Jake Gottlieb."

"These guys are serious," Ernie said. "Nothing is beyond them. Anything goes."

Jake clapped our shoulders. He fixed us solemnly. It was an occasion he meant us to remember. I felt, as I'm sure Ernie did, that this was one of Jake's stagy moments.

"Boys, if anything happens to me, Kravitz will be responsible. Remember that."

Ernie asked, "What do you

mean, 'Remember'?"

"Remember what I told you. Act according to your conscience. Never forget you are the sons of Jake Gottlieb."

Ernie was almost ready to explode. "Of course we won't forget. What a thing to ask."

"And act accordingly."

"Act? What do you expect us to do?"

"I shouldn't have to say more." Did he imagine himself the Papa of Mafiosos? "I only ask that you remember," he said. "Take an oath. Swear that you will do your duty by your Pa."

We stood among the Woolworth displays, sales on swim suits, suntan lotions, mosquito repellent, bug sprays, picnic utensils—reminded of the common pleasures of ordinary life at Walled Lake—and Jake demanded that we take an oath appropriate to the barren hills of Sicily or ancient Israel, but not Twelfth Street.

"Swear!" he ordered. "If something happens to your Pa, swear that you'll remember."

"What could happen? What?"

"You heard what this bum Weinberg said."

"It's foolish," Ernie said. "I won't swear."

Why was Ernie so obstinate? All he had to do was swear and Jake would be pacified. He insisted that we swear. He wouldn't budge from the spot until we did. However reluctantly given, he wanted our oaths. He wanted guarantees that his two sons would follow in his tracks and accept the consequences of his acts.

We squabbled in the doorway of Woolworth's. The threat of Weinberg no longer oppressed us. We fought each other.

"It's stupid. It's false! It's just melodrama!"

"Swear!"

We ignored inquisitive looks from passers-by.

Finally I said, "Yes, Pa. I swear." I said it to give him pleasure. Yet what wonderful relief after I swore to remember. That was always Jake's effect on me. He oppressed me; then he liberated me.

So Ernie also agreed. "OK. I will."

"You'll what?"

"I swear."

"Get Kravitz!"

We swore that if anything happened to Jake Gottlieb we would hold Kravitz to blame. The next time that Jake faced Kravitz and was threatened, Jake would warn him, "Anything that happens to me, happens to you. My boys will see to it."

He hadn't won Ernie's good will and so he wasn't satisfied. He stopped the car before turning into the camp. Again he gripped our shoulders and held us tight.

"I hide nothing from you. You are of an age to be men and you got obligations. Your Pa now speaks to you as men. You can see from our meeting with these hoodlums that I have enemies. They are dangerous and they have no affection for Jake Gottlieb. That suits me. That's my pleasure. I don't want their affection. Not a tiny bit. Such enemies give me no trouble. Not when I got two sons to take up my cause. So pay attention. I want you to swear an oath. If anything happens to your Pa, remember that Hyman Kravitz is the man. Get Kravitz."

We took the oath. We swore and not for the last time. Jake was in a risky business and he wanted guarantees of our loyalty. "Who knows how long I'll be around? Can you blame me if I want your attention?"

Ernie blamed him.

How could we take the oath seriously? Our Pa often assumed histrionic poses. Ernie swore, and then tried to put the oath out of mind.

"It's foolish," he told me. "He hams it up too much."

We numbed ourselves to what Jake asked. Did he set himself against Happy Weinberg? That was no match. Happy Weinberg at two hundred and fifty outweighed Jake by seventy pounds or more. Happy Weinberg, every day of his life, every hour of every day—including the night hours when he had bad dreams—plotted the most brutal use of his two hundred and fifty pounds. He was familiar with guns, brass knuckles, knives, pipes, blackjacks, bare hands. He saw all the world's furnishings as possible weapons. He studied each man he met with the obsession of a general who must consider any terrain he enters as a potential battlefield. Men were Happy Weinberg's battlefield. As for Jake, I never imagined his massive arms and his barrel chest to be tools of war. He dreamed of the day when the lion would be couched with the lamb. He couldn't sustain his ferocity. He only had moments. If he conquered you, he assumed your burdens.

Jake let everyone know about his meeting with Happy Weinberg.

"They have me marked," he boasted. "Spiegelman, Weinberg, the whole Cream of Michigan crowd. If they didn't know I had a big mouth and sons to avenge me, I'd long ago be planted in a wooden box."

Listening to him you could lose respect for his achievement. "Why doesn't he keep it to himself?" Ernie asked. "Why do we have to be told? What does he expect from us?"

"Shouldn't we share his troubles?"

"Even Weinberg and Spiegelman have their pride. There's no reason to insult them."

Jake believed in a homeric style of history and told whoppers in the manner of the Greeks. It didn't bother me. It was a respectable tradition. Didn't Achilles boast each night at the campfire? Didn't the heroes proclaim their pedigrees, cite their credits, advertise their power before launching spears? Despite the bragging, spears were launched; the glory merited. It wasn't a style for those raised in the laconic tradition of Gary Cooper whose silences, by the way, I always thought hammier and stagier than the bragging of more natural men. Jake's style suited me, if not Ernie.

I had terrible dreams. I woke up and saw Ernie in the cot opposite mine evidently in the same fix. Our nightmares had the same source. Jake made us swear and the oaths lay on our hearts like hot brands.

I remember a dream that Ernie and I must have shared. I dreamt that I rowed behind swimmers, crossing the lake. Jake was in the lead, flinging himself far ahead of the others. I rowed desperately to keep up. Fog closed us in. I thrashed the oars trying to keep Jake in view. I lost him. I rowed on and saw him floundering. He was stiffened with cramps. His enormous chin stretched to keep above the water. His eyes rolled. He grasped the side of the boat and tried to enter. He didn't have the strength. I couldn't reach him. He said to me, "Don't worry yourself, Sonny. It's all right." Then he went under.

It was not me, but Ernie whose shout woke up our tent. I jerked up, ready to yell and saw Ernie hanging over the edge of his cot, clutching for the man who sank in my dream.

Jake tried to comfort us when he showed up at the lake. He invited us to accompany him down to the beach.

"Your Ma tells me you have bad dreams."

The machinery of his arms and shoulders and chest was ponderous, as if sweaty effort was needed to get it under way.

"She says you wake up at night."

Ernie didn't want any inquiry into his dreams. He said his dreams were his own business.

"If our talk the other day has given you problems, I want you to forget about it. Put it out of your mind altogether. It wasn't my intention, boys, to give you worries."

"Of course that was your intention," Ernie said. "How can you say it wasn't? How can you ask us to take such an oath and then tell us not to worry?"

"I'll tell you what," Jake said. "Put it out of your mind. Forget it altogether."

"It's too late," Ernie said.

"I exaggerate. It's my nature. You know your Pa, boys. He gets excited."

I didn't want to be let off. I knew the reputation of the Cream of Michigan crowd as well as Ernie did. They were interested in Jake and we ought to be worried.

Ernie said, "If only I could understand why you were so rude to Happy after he says that he admires you. Did you have to be so insulting when you could have turned him down in a nice way?"

"I should be a gentleman, you mean. You picked the wrong Pa, Sonny. Your Pa, Jake Gottlieb, speaks his mind. His tongue don't go around in circles."

Though they both may have had good intentions, they marched inexorably into conflict. Jake said that it wasn't his policy to stick his head in the ground in the face of danger. He feared no man. He dared Weinberg to do his worst. "This Weinberg you admire so much, this bum you call 'Happy,' this ignorant hoodlum, is nothing. I don't negotiate with this pig. He's nothing; I offer him nothing. He gets no respect from me. I treat him like he belongs in the wild woods or the pigsty. Nothing; a cipher. What someday you got to understand is that it's your Pa, Jake Gottlieb, who is something. Don't go looking so far from home if you want someone to respect. Try respecting your own Pa."

Ernie wanted to speak what would be most damaging; he also wanted to restrain himself from speaking. He said finally, "Why don't you let someone else blow your horn?"

Jake stopped and caught Ernie's arm. "Who?" he asked. "Who will do it for me? My sons? Can I rely on my sons to speak up for their Pa? There's no one else to do the job, so Jake Gottlieb advertises himself. Otherwise he would never be heard from."

"Why should anyone be heard from? I don't want to be heard from."

Jake shook him. "I worry about you. You got no sense. I'm worried that you'll bury yourself. You'll smother because you didn't have the nerve to fight." Jake shook him. "If you hide your talents who will see you? No one will come looking. Don't count on the generosity of strangers when you can't depend on your own children. Men will step on you just to be rid of the competition. They'll pretend they didn't know you were underfoot. You better make a sound. Yell out. Tell everyone who you are. You got plenty to brag about, a strong, intelligent boy like you, Gottlieb's son."

My brother said, "I'm nothing. I got nothing to brag about." He made nothing of himself in order to torment Jake.

"You're plenty. You're Gottlieb's son."

"A man shouldn't have to boost himself."

Advice poured in from every quarter, Jake observed. Employers advised him to drop dead. Cops advised him to go back to Russia. Now even beardless kids got into the act. "Everybody in the world has an idea how Jake Gottlieb should behave. I'd love to pay attention but my hearing ain't so hot. It's my tough luck to have a bad character that I grew up with. Now I'm stuck with it. You don't divorce your character like it's your wife."

He said to me afterward, "Your brother got no respect."

"He worries for you, Pa."

"My worst enemy don't show such contempt."

"He boasts about you. He feels terrible after an argument."

"I leave you no fortune. I got nothing in the bank. I invest everything in a reputation. All I leave you is the honor of being Gottlieb's son."

What more could he give? It was true about his character. He had been fashioned in fires so intense that all of the easily worked material had been consumed and only what was fiercely tempered and unworkable remained in his construction. He was reconciled to himself. That was the source of his enthusiasm and his energy. He wanted to be no one but Jake Gottlieb. He thought Jake Gottlieb as splendid a character as there was on the scene, adequate to any war, ready to assume the station he deserved but which was denied him by men and history. He wanted Ernie to acknowledge, despite the smallness of his achievement, his true size. I saw my Pa Jake as monumental. You could get your bearings by sighting him. He commanded us to remember him. Ernie wanted to hold out, but he took the oath. I'll never let Ernie forget. We swore, more than once.

Questions for Analysis and Discussion

This story deals with the relationship between a father and his sons and presents a portrait of a union organizer.

1. What is the world of this story? What was the Cream of Michigan? Why was it famous? How does the narrator describe the hoods who frequented the Cream of Michigan? Why was Happy Weinberg admired by the kids? Why was he feared by the adults? What was there about this world that it bred men like Happy Weinberg and Whitey Spiegelman? What was there about this world that it also bred men like Jake Gottlieb?

2. Many American Jewish writers tell their stories through narrators who recall experiences of their childhood. Is this an effective way to tell a story? Why does the narrator refer to his father as Jake Gottlieb rather than as my father? Why was Jake not afraid of Happy Weinberg nor of any of the hoods that infested the neighborhood near where he lived? Why did the boy believe that his father should fear the hoods? Why was Jake a thorn in Kravitz's flesh? The narrator records a conversation between Jake and Weinberg. Weinberg is conciliatory; Jake is aggressive and insulting. Why is Jake so belligerent? What is the reason for Jake's anger against the hoods? How is Kravitz using the hoods?

3. What oath does Jake want his sons to take? How does Ernie view his father? Does he believe his father is in the wrong? Why does he take the oath? What about his father does the narrator admire?

4. What nightmare do the sons have about the father? In what way does the nightmare reveal what is going on in their minds? The father, when he learns the boys are troubled, tells them to put the oath out of their minds. Why can't they do this? Ernie asks his father, "Why don't you let someone else blow your horn?" What is Jake's answer? What is Jake's philosophy of life? Do you agree with him or do you agree with Ernie who seems to prefer the quiet, uninvolved life?

5. The story is a portrait of the narrator's father. The son says that he saw his father as monumental. What did he mean? What was Jake fighting for? Why was he the enemy of men like Kravitz and Weinberg? What was noble and heroic about him? "Ernie represents the East European, quiet, scholarly Jew who seeks peace at any cost,

and Jake is like the Israeli Jew who will protest and fight if his independence, freedom, and sense of justice are threatened." What is your reaction to this view? Weinberg and Spiegelman are portrayed as renegade Jews, the betrayers of all the Jews hold sacred. Do you agree with this characterization?

6. What in your view was the author's purpose or intention in writing this story? Does the story fulfill the author's purpose?

Suggested Activities

1. Of the many plays dealing with employer-worker conflicts two pertinent ones may be discussed in class to understand the unrest in industry in the early days of unionization and the suffering created by attempts to organize workers and to win for them improvement in working conditions and better compensation for their work. These are John Galsworthy's *Strife* and Clifford Odet's *Waiting for Lefty*. Enact key scenes from these plays in class; or report on these plays, stressing those elements that are related to the themes of *The Oath*.

2. Suppose Jake had been beaten up by Happy Weinberg. Write a scene in which the brothers are standing in the hospital corridor outside their father's room discussing what had happened and trying to determine what they can do to avenge this attack upon Jake.

3. Write a speech that Ernie makes at a meeting of workers in which he urges them to use violence to stop the attacks against workers and the organizers of the union. Remember that Ernie is basically a peaceful young man who abhors violence and that his decision to fight back comes hard.

4. Report on the careers and activities of such outstanding labor leaders as Samuel Gompers, Sidney Hillman, David Dubinsky, Walter Reuther, and others. Have these leaders helped or hindered America's economic growth?

5. Set up in the classroom a meeting of workers with the men who are trying to organize them. Have them discuss whether it is wise to organize, and then how to deal with the gangsters who are trying

to frighten them into submission and the police who are supporting the employers by breaking up picket lines. Also have them discuss ways and means of winning the support of the populace for their efforts.

6. Many of the Jewish people of the lower East Side read a Yiddish newspaper called *The Forward*. There was a feature in it called "A Bintel Brief" (a bundle of letters). The newspaper published letters from the readers who asked advice and guidance from the editor. *A Bintel Brief* has been published in a paperback edition. Read through it and select letters that deal with working conditions and the need for workers to organize. Summarize your findings and report these to the class.

Warren Dickerson. *New York City-East Side*. Los Angeles County Museum of Natural History.

By Yaacov Luria

My Medical Career

Introduction: **The Lower East Side in New York City**

Many of the tens of thousands of Jews who came to America from East Europe between 1880 and 1914 settled in a small area of Manhattan which came to be known as the Lower East Side. Here they crowded together in tenements and sought to earn a livelihood. They took whatever jobs were available and worked very hard for small wages. Many entered the clothing industry; others became peddlers and sold their wares from pushcarts on the streets; still others opened small stores. A few were mechanics, building workers, or artisans, and they made their living doing repair work.

Their religious and cultural interests and activities compensated most of these immigrants for the hardships of their lives. Many spent time in the synagogue, and gave an aura of beauty to their holiday observances. Many met friends in the cafeterias to discuss current events. They read their newspapers avidly, listened to famous cantors, attended plays, and discussed books.

With time, a few of the luckier and more ambitious ones became well-to-do. They moved away from the crowds, the dirt, and the clutter of the East Side to better neighborhoods. They tried to become Americanized faster and to assume the speech and manners of their affluent neighbors. Some even began to look down upon their less fortunate brethren. But a sense of guilt or a sting of memory kept them contributing from a distance to causes that might help their underprivileged fellow Jews. They supported day nurseries, religious schools, charity funds, and free loan societies for the poor.

East Side Jews were people of spirit and action. Poverty turned a few to crime. But most of them respected education as a way of escaping poverty and regaining dignity. Parents wanted better lives *for their children, and the children responded to the challenge of America. They worked hard to achieve their ambitions. Putting a child through school as far as he would go was a responsibility a family took seriously. Mothers and brothers and sisters worked if necessary. In fact, working one's way through school became an honored tradition. By dint of dream and effort, a generation of professionals—scholars, teachers, doctors, lawyers—emerged from the ghetto.*

Hopes and ambition were often thwarted by tragedy. People lost jobs or fell victims to illness or accident. But it was the rare family that didn't manage to rise above disaster and push towards its goals.

My Medical Career is a fictional account of a boy, living in poverty in New York's Lower East Side, who was offered an opportunity to study medicine. How he makes a vital choice is the basis for this story.

FOR AT least one day during the summer of 1928, when I was thirteen, I was headed toward a medical career. I missed my opportunity by, quite literally, a few hairs.

That summer was an unhappy one for my family. The older of my two sisters had lost her husband after being married little more than a year, and she was forced to return to our small Jackson Street flat, on the East Side, with her six-week-old baby. This pathetic homecoming made me suddenly see the world as full of random, inexplicable cruelty. Visitors pushed their way into our living room, with its drawn shades, and I fled from them, because it seemed to me that they were there less to share our grief than to enjoy it. For hours at a time, I would stay in my little boxlike room, simply staring out the window at the narrow, crowded street below. My behavior so disturbed Mother that she finally decided to do something she had never done before—send me to visit my father's brother, Uncle Pincus.

My father had died in the influenza epidemic of 1919. At the end of the First World War, after many years of near poverty as a junk dealer, Uncle had gone into building construction and quickly became rich. He could then afford two large houses. His town house, a fourteen-room, white mansion of Colonial style with colonnades that rose a full three stories, was in Harrisburg, Pennsylvania. His summer house was an affected rustic cottage near the beach at Longport, a few miles below Atlantic City. It was there my mother planned to send me. After my father's death, Uncle Pincus had made a point of dropping in on us during his occasional trips to New York. He would pinch my cheek affectionately each time he arrived, and would stay for perhaps a quarter of an hour, nervously stroking his full red mustache while he talked with my mother. Just before standing up to leave, he would pull a thin, pale-gold watch from his vest pocket and look at it, as if he had an important appointment to keep. My mother said he came to ease his conscience. After all, she said, we *were* his brother's children.

Mother sent me to visit Uncle Pincus merely on the strength of his telling her every so often to "send the children sometime," and it never occurred to her to notify him or his wife, my Aunt Deborah, in advance. So when I rang the doorbell of the cottage one Thursday evening, wearing faded trousers and an old shirt and carrying a few extra clothes wrapped in brown paper, and with my usual long hair cut, I received a rather equivocal welcome. Aunt Deborah opened the door. Pale and worn-looking, she kissed me and said, "Look, it's Anna's boy, Jack," but Uncle Pincus, who stood beside her, instead of pinching my cheek gave me an indifferent pat on the shoulder. Then he and Aunt Deborah, and Gertrude, who was thirty and the oldest of their three children, took me to the kitchen. My older cousins, Herb, who was seventeen, and Julius, who was a year younger, had gone to a movie, Aunt

Deborah said. While I was having a makeshift supper of rice pudding and milk, Gertrude asked me, "How long are you staying?" She was a thin woman, whose eyes were magnified by thick, horn-rimmed glasses. When she married, a few years before, my mother had speculated on whether her husband would be able to soften her severe tongue. She always spent the summer in Longport, while her husband stayed on in Trenton, where he worked.

"The child just comes," Aunt Deborah said to her, "and you already ask him when he's going."

"Aunt Anna might have taken the trouble to let us know," Gertrude said. "We don't exactly run a boarding house."

Ingenuously, I said, "I'm not staying very long. Only until you send me home."

Uncle Pincus laughed, and said I was a clever boy. "Don't you think so, Deborah?" Then he pinched my cheek, as though to make up for his tepid welcome.

Directly after supper, I was shown to a large upstairs room, across the hall from one occupied by Herb and Julius. The bed was soft and comfortable, and for an hour or so that night, the first I had ever spent away from my family, I lay awake wishing my Jackson Street friends could see me in such luxury. Except for a few visits to Coney Island, this was my first time at the seashore.

At Coney, it was hard to distinguish the sound of the sea from that of the crowds, but in this quiet room, with the windows opened to the fresh salt air, I could plainly hear the steady roar of the surf. It gave me a strange feeling—a kind of delight mixed with a faint thrill of fear. All at once, I was appalled by the dinginess and meanness of my surroundings at home. My second year at high school wasn't due to begin for ten days, and I prayed silently that I might be allowed to stay at my uncle's until the last second. I was just falling asleep when Herb and Julius came noisily up the stairs. They stood for a moment in the doorway of my room, but I pretended to be asleep. I was in too exalted a mood to talk to anyone.

At breakfast the next morning, Uncle Pincus told me to hurry, for I was to go with him in his car to Atlantic City. When we arrived there, he rushed me to a men's-clothing store on Atlantic Avenue. He didn't take long to have me outfitted with a gray herringbone suit, a plaid tie, and three white shirts. The shirts and tie I took with me; the suit needed alterations, which would require a day or so. "Now," Uncle Pincus said when we emerged from the store, "take the trolley back to Longport and get a haircut. In my house, you can't wear your hair over your eyes that way. It looks terrible. Get a good, short

haircut—do you hear?" He spoke so sternly his red mustache quivered.

I nodded, but I knew that I couldn't obey my uncle completely. The boys on Jackson Street were strongly against short haircuts. Wearing one's hair long and bushy was a sign of maturity, like long trousers. Only pre-school kids had cropped hair. So when I got back to Longport, I told the barber to give me a *very* light trim, and when he was finished, I was pleased to see in the mirror that my hair seemed hardly cut at all.

When I reached the house, Gertrude, who was sitting on the back porch, which faced the sea, put down a magazine she was reading and looked at me in surprise. "Didn't Papa tell you to get a haircut?" she asked.

"I got one," I said.

"*I* can't see any difference," she said. "He'll be good and mad."

"I can wear my hair as I please," I said. "I'm not a baby."

"Well, just wait until Papa sees you," she said, and picked up the magazine.

I walked down to the beach, where I found Herb and Julius. They hadn't paid much attention to me at breakfast, but now they said I might play ball with them, and we played a game in which the two of them tossed the ball back and forth, and I tried to intercept it. I soon became weary of this, especially as they were beginning to mimic my East Side speech. When I had stood them as long as I could, I went off by myself and gathered starfish and hermit crabs.

After lunch, Herb and Julius announced to me the great and special event for the afternoon— an exhibition baseball game between the Atlantic City team and the Philadelphia Athletics, who that season were involved in a race for the pennant. I had never seen a professional team play, and when I told my cousins this, on the way to the ballpark, they seemed overcome with amazement.

"Say," Herb asked, "how long since you came off the ship?"

"I was born here," I said.

"My sister says people on the East Side are all greenhorns," Julius said. "She told me they use their bathtubs to make pickles."

"We do not. We're as American as you are."

"Then how come you've never seen a real ball game?" Herb asked.

"Because it takes money to go to the Yankee Stadium," I replied.

"You don't call *that* money, do you?" Herb asked.

"That's just pocket money," Julius said. "I don't even have to ask my dad for that kind of money."

I didn't answer. My poverty had now become a shameful matter, and I walked beside my cousins resenting them and hating myself. It was hard to keep back the tears, and when we reached the gate to the ballpark, I suddenly said, "I don't want to go," and ran from them.

In the evening, after it had grown dark, I sat by myself on the backporch steps and watched the play of moonlight on the water. I heard the voices of Gertrude and my uncle in the kitchen, but I didn't listen closely to what they were saying until I realized they were talking about me. Gertrude seemed angry.

"But they *were* taking him," she said. "He just turned and ran away. They wouldn't lie."

"Never mind 'he ran away.' They must have been fresh to him. With an orphan and such a poor child, you have to be kind," my uncle said.

"Well, he's a fresh kid, too," she said. "You told him to have his hair cut short, and he came back looking exactly the same."

"Where is he, anyway?" my uncle asked, and he called, "Jack! Jack!"

I didn't care whether they guessed I'd been listening to them, and I went slowly up the steps and into the kitchen. They were sitting by the table. My uncle leaned forward and pinched my cheek heartily, and said, "Sit down, Jack. Sit by me for a minute." He tugged at the ends of his mustache. "Jack," he asked, "what class are you in at school?"

"I'll be going into the third term."

"You're already in high school?" he said in surprise. "Well, that certainly proves you're a smart boy." Then he was silent, as though thinking deeply. At last, he said, "Do you want to go to college?"

"I think so," I said, "but—"

"But where will the money come from—isn't that what bothers you? Well, I've been thinking, and I don't see why money has to stand in your way. You're the son of my brother." He tapped the edge of the table slowly with his fingers. "How would you like to be a doctor, Jack?"

"I don't know," I said. "I guess I would someday."

Even at thirteen, I understood that one of the biggest things that could ever happen to me would be to become a doctor. Herb and Julius, of course, being the sons of a man of wealth, could be what they liked—doctors, lawyers, dentists, or partners in his business— but only luck or extreme sacrifice by Mother and me could ever bring me a professional career. This kind of elevation in the world, so rare among the people in my neighborhood, had always seemed beyond my hopes. My uncle, aware of all this, was probably more amused than annoyed by my apparent lack of enthusiasm.

"The boy don't know," he said to Gertrude. "He *guesses* he would. Well, good enough. Tonight is Shabbos, and we shouldn't

be talking of these things now. But I'll just say, boy, that if you want to be a doctor I'll support you through."

I didn't reply, and now my uncle did seem irritated. "Look here," he said. "If you want this, you're going to have to be a real person, someone who won't disgrace me. You'll have to *obey*. That's how you get somewhere, knowing when someone knows better than you. Tomorrow, go back to that barber and tell him I said he should give you a short haircut." He grabbed my bushy hair with one hand and gave it a jerk. "Short—do you understand? Now go to bed."

The next day being Saturday, a day of rest, I spent the morning around the house, and in the afternoon walked down to the beach. When I came back, about five o'clock, I passed Herb's and Julius's room, and noticed they were getting into their best clothes. "Going somewhere?" I couldn't help asking.

"A party," Julius said. "Tonight. At a girl's house."

"Feel like coming?" Herb asked offhandedly. "Dad says we should take you."

"I don't need your parties," I said.

"He'll only run away again," Julius said.

I started to walk on, but Herb called out, "For God's sake, can't you ever take a joke?"

"What joke?" I said.

"Now, look," Herb said. "Get off your high horse, get a haircut like Dad asked you, put on the new suit, and we'll go to the party. Good enough?"

"O.K.," I said, a little grudgingly, and went to my room. There on the bed was the new suit. It had been delivered while I was at the beach. I tried it on and looked at myself in the mirror. Just then my uncle stopped at the door and reminded me, "The barbershop is still open. Remember what you're supposed to do. The boys will be waiting for you."

I nodded and left the house, but I couldn't make myself go to the barbershop right away. I decided that there wasn't any real hurry, as there was still some time before supper, and I walked along the beach for a while. I thought that if I should have my hair cut, it would grow long enough in a week's time to be suitable for Jackson Street, and if cutting my hair was all my uncle wanted from me, I supposed there was no harm in it. But I still wasn't satisfied with myself when I finally went into the barbershop. While I was waiting my turn, I caught sight of myself in the mirror. It was not just my hair, I thought, it was myself he was trying to change. What right had anyone to do that? Suddenly, my uncle loomed in my mind as a strange, inhuman grownup who wanted to demonstrate his power over me.

"Next," one of the barbers said, looking my way.

"Never mind," I said, and hurried from the shop. I walked up and down the beach, and it was well after dark when I returned to the house. It was empty. Herb and Julius had doubtless left for the party, and I supposed the others had gone to a movie, but I didn't mind being alone. I went straight to my room, closed the door, and got in bed.

My uncle said nothing at all to me about the haircut when he saw me at Sunday-morning breakfast. He didn't even bother to greet me. I wasn't hurt so much as disappointed that he didn't give me a chance to tell him why I had disobeyed him. I fished with the boys in the morning, and somehow got along better with them than before. I was able to take their sarcasm about again running off, and was equally sarcastic myself. It was making my stand that had done this for me, I told myself.

At lunch, my uncle still ignored me, but near the end of the meal he said in a heavy, judgelike manner, "It seems to me that disobedient children are like my grandmother's cow. I would bring her a pail of fodder—something to eat, mind you—and what would she do? She would kick the pail over. A big body," he added, lifting his finger and wagging it, "and no brain."

This was a public reprimand. Everyone knew he was referring to me. I was silent, but my face must have been red as I got up and went upstairs. I packed my clothes in the same brown paper I'd brought them in, came down to the dining room, and told Aunt Deborah I was going back home. She was genuinely distressed, and tried to persuade me to change my mind.

"I want to go home," I insisted.

"Is it that we haven't treated you well?" she asked, glancing at my uncle. "You don't care for my food?"

"I just have to go home," I said.

"He'll go back to his mother and tell her what terrible people we are," Gertrude said sarcastically.

"I won't tell her anything," I said, and started toward the dining-room door.

"All right," Uncle Pincus said. "All right. No more arguments. The boy wants to go home, let him go home. Get in the car, Jack, and I'll drive you to the station."

"No," I said. "I can take the trolley."

"Where is the new suit? You're not leaving the suit?" Aunt Deborah asked pleadingly, and she came over and put her arms around me. I felt myself weakening, but then I broke away from her.

The last thing I heard my uncle say as I shut the front door behind me was something about my being the kind of boy who wouldn't be happy unless he kicked over the pail.

My mother, naturally, was surprised to see me when I knocked at our door late that evening. We walked from the front hall into the living room, where my sister was sewing. The apartment was hot and muggy. Mother anxiously asked me a lot of questions, but I only answered that I liked it better at home.

"With all that," Mother said to my sister, "the ocean, a palace of a house, fresh air, he still likes it better here." She was so pleased that tears came to her eyes. "Maybe the rich are not blessed."

Before I went to bed, I walked out to the little waterfront park near my house. The oily damp of the East River lay heavy on the night air. Sitting down on the grass, I watched the multitude of people, my neighbors. I felt closer to them than I ever had before. I even felt that we had in common a kind of pride and independence.

My uncle visited us a week later and brought my new suit with him. He said nothing about paying for a medical career, or any other kind of career, for me, nor did he pinch my cheek. But when he stood up to leave, I looked him full in the eyes and we shook hands.

Questions for Analysis and Discussion

This is a fictional account of a personal experience.

1. What do you learn about the narrator from the first two paragraphs? From what perspective is he recounting an experience he had at the age of thirteen? How effective is the first paragraph?

2. Why does Jack's mother decide to send him to visit his Uncle Pincus? Jack says that it seemed to him that the people who came to visit his sad home came not to share his family's grief but to enjoy it. Is there any psychological truth in this observation? If it is true that people who visit bereaved families "enjoy" the visit, what is the nature of the "enjoyment"? Why didn't Jack's mother notify Uncle Pincus that she was sending Jack for a visit?

3. What does the reader learn about Uncle Pincus? How did Uncle Pincus show his concern for his dead brother's family? How does the narrator, telling this story of a childhood experience, feel toward Uncle Pincus and his family?

4. How is Jack received at his uncle's summer home? Describe Jack's impressions of his cousin Gertrude. Describe his feelings in bed the first night of his visit.

5. Uncle Pincus decides to make a gentleman of his nephew. How does he go about it? Why does Jack find it impossible to allow the barber to cut his hair short? After playing ball for a while with his cousins Jack goes off by himself. Why?

6. Jack's cousins decide to take him to see an exhibition baseball game. Why did Jack run away from his cousins and refuse to see the game? What are Herb and Julius really like?

7. Uncle Pincus wants to help his brother's son. Why is Jack so unenthusiastic about his uncle's offer? The "haircut" becomes a symbol in the story. What does it symbolize to Jack? What is its importance to Uncle Pincus?

8. The climax of the story occurs in the barbershop. What prompts Jack's decision to refuse to have his hair cut short? What do you learn about the narrator from his account of this boyhood experience?

What is the position of the aunt in the household? Why doesn't she speak up or interfere?

9. Jack's visit has been a learning experience for both him and his uncle. In what ways?

10. Look back at the story now and "brainstorm" it. What insight into yourself or other people does it lead you to?

Suggested Activities

1. The world of the Jewish ghetto of the East Side during the early years of this century was exotic and unique. It should be interesting to study. Get a copy of Hutchens Hapgood's noted book, *The Spirit of the Ghetto*. After you have read it, report to the class what you learned about Jewish ghetto existence in New York City.

2. The Jewish people in the ghetto had all kinds of problems, many of them personal. When deeply troubled, some sought advice by writing to the editor of one of the Yiddish newspapers called *The Forward*. He answered these letters in a column called "A Bintel Brief," (a bundle of letters). Not long ago, a selection of these letters in translation was published in paperback with the same title. Get a copy and report to the class on the different problems faced by the ghetto Jews. Discuss how poverty affected the lives of these people and what they did to rise above their lot.

3. You may be interested in learning something of the language spoken by the Jews of the East Side ghetto. It was called Yiddish, a Germanic language written in Hebrew letters. About thirty percent of the language was Hebrew and there were root words from other languages as well—Latin, French, Russian, Polish, and so forth. See if you can find any Yiddish words that have become part of the English language. Ask someone in your community who knows the language to tell your class something of its history and quality. There are a number of recent books that will give you information about the language: Maurice Samuel's *In Praise of Yiddish* and Leo Rosten's *The Joys of Yiddish*.

4. There are two or three Yiddish plays that have become classics in world literature. The most popular of these is *The Dybbuk* by S. Ansky. Read the play and discuss in class what it reveals of Jewish

beliefs and values. (Incidentally, the play is about the exorcism of a troubled spirit who controls the mind of a maiden, a theme popular in literature today.)

5. Some of the quality of the old East Side still remains. If you live in New York City, and you wish to have an interesting experience, visit Orchard Street on the lower East Side on a Sunday afternoon. Write a descriptive essay recounting what you saw and felt.

6. Write an autobiographical sketch about a time you visited one of your relatives in a place different from where you lived. It could have been a happy and pleasant visit, or one that brought disappointment and unhappiness. Try to get some description and dialogue into your account and see if your sketch can make some comment about the nature of people.

Educational Alliance. Yivo Institute for Jewish Research.

By Grace Paley

The Loudest Voice

Introduction: **Public Schools in the Jewish Ghettos**

The Jewish people who came to America from East Europe came with hopes and dreams. In this land where there were no Czars and no pogroms, and where secular education was available to everyone, they felt it was possible through work and schooling to rise above poverty. One had to go to school; or if that were impossible, one needed to send one's children to school.

In the first two decades of the present century, the typical Jewish child went to two schools: the public school, with a variety of subjects and activities and frequently warm and pleasant though strict teachers, and the heder or religious school, which was crowded and drab, and in most cases devoted exclusively to a one-method study of the prayerbook, the Five Books of Moses, and portions of the other books of the Scripture. Many parents employed private tutors instead of sending their children to the heder.

The administrators and teachers of the public schools, mostly Christians, had established an Anglo-American environment, and their goal was to shape the Jewish children in their care into Americans whose lives were governed by a code of values and manners then prevalent in Protestant American circles.

Assemblies always began with a salute to the flag, the singing of "The Star-Spangled Banner," the reading of a passage from the Bible, and the singing of a Protestant hymn, the most popular one being "Abide with Me." Assemblies concluded with the singing of the first and last stanzas of "America." Many of the programs contained recitations by pupils of passages from the great oratorical classics of American history. There were also gayer programs, such as performances of scenes from Pinafore, The Pirates of Penzance, *and* The Mikado.

Classes were large and seats were fixed in rows on the floor. Pupils were taught frequently to sit at attention with hands folded on their desks so that teachers could get clerical work done without interruption. But there were compensations. Mornings and afternoons were broken up when the windows were thrown open, pupils rose and moved into the aisles, inhaled and exhaled the fresh air as the teacher counted, and went through a series of calisthenics to bring back a readiness for further learning. The learning had variety, especially when the afternoons were devoted to lessons in music and drawing.

The teachers taught their pupils more than subject matter. They taught them cleanliness and manners. The tidiest pupils—those with neatly combed hair and clean ears, those wearing clean shirts and a tie or neat dresses—were paraded before the class. Pupils were admonished to brush their teeth, not to pick their noses, to stop biting their nails, and to eat like ladies and gentlemen. The boys were taught to respect girls and women, and all pupils were taught to respect elderly people and to be polite at all times. Teachers tried also to get their pupils to discard the foreignisms in their English speech.

One sad result of this Americanization process was that many of the children became ashamed of their parents who, in the hardworking ghetto world, either never learned to speak English or spoke English with a heavy accent—one that came to be the subject of comedy in books, plays, and cartoons. Many of the teachers sought to counteract this sense of shame by extolling the virtues of the immigrant parents and by treating fathers and mothers, when they visited the school, with the utmost respect; but it did not always work.

The busy parents were pleased by the achievements of their children. Most were unaware of the Christian content of the Bible reading and of the Protestant hymns. But almost all were troubled by the Christmas celebrations. Their children acted in Christmas plays, often performing the story of the gifts of the Magi. They learned and sang Christmas carols, and they decorated their classrooms with Christmas designs and symbols. However, the parents did nothing about it. Their ambition for their children, their happiness that America provided free education, overcame their fears. They accepted the Christmas celebration in public school as a necessary element in the reach for learning and success. They were reassured by the belief that the Jewish education their children were receiving and the Jewish holiday observances in which their children participated at home and in the synagogue would cancel any harmful effects of the Christmas spirit.

In The Loudest Voice, *Grace Paley treats this problem with sensitivity and humor.*

THERE IS a certain place where dumb-waiters boom, doors slam, dishes crash; every window is a mother's mouth bidding the street shut up, go skate somewhere else, come home. My voice is the loudest.

There, my own mother is still as full of breathing as me and the grocer stands up to speak to her. "Mrs. Abramowitz," he says, "people should not be afraid of their children."

"Ah, Mr. Bialik," my mother replies, "if you say to her or her father 'Ssh,' they say 'In the grave it will be quiet.'"

"From Coney Island to the cemetery," says my papa, "It's the same subway; it's the same fare."

I am right next to the pickle barrel. My pinky is making tiny whirlpools in the brine. I stop a moment to announce, "Campbell's Tomato Soup, Campbell's Vegetable Beef Soup, Campbell's S-c-otch Broth . . ."

"Be quiet," the grocer says, "the labels are coming off."

"Please, Shirley, be a little quiet," my mother begs me.

In that place the whole street groans: Be quiet! Be quiet! but steals from the happy chorus of my inside self not a tittle or a jot.

There, too, just around the corner, is a red brick building that has been old for many years. Every morning the children stand before it in double lines which must be straight. They are not insulted. They are waiting anyway.

I am usually among them. I am, in fact, the first, since I begin with an "A."

One cold morning the monitor tapped me on the shoulder. "Go to Room 409, Shirley Abramowitz," he said. I did as I was told. I went in a hurry up a down staircase to Room 409, which contained sixth-graders. I had to wait at the desk without wiggling until Mr. Hilton, their teacher, had time to speak.

After five minutes, he said, "Shirley?"

"What?" I whispered.

He said, "My! My! Shirley Abramowitz! They told me you had a particularly loud, clear voice and read with lots of expression. Could that be true?"

"Oh, yes," I whispered.

"In that case, don't be silly; I might very well be your teacher some day. Speak up, speak up."

"Yes," I shouted.

"More like it," he said. "Now, Shirley, can you put a ribbon in your hair or a bobby pin? It's too messy."

"Yes," I bawled.

"Now, now, calm down." He turned to the class. "Children, not a sound. Open at page 39. Read till 52. When you finish, start again." He looked me over once more. "Now, Shirley, you know, I suppose, that Christmas is coming. We are preparing a beautiful play. Most of the parts have been given out. But I still need a child with a strong voice, lots of stamina. Do you know what stamina is? You do? Smart kid. You know, I heard you read 'The Lord is my shepherd' in Assembly yesterday. I was very impressed. Wonderful delivery. Mrs. Jordan, your teacher, speaks highly of you. Now listen to me, Shirley Abramowitz, if you want to take the part and be in the play, repeat after me, 'I swear to work harder than I ever did before.' "

I looked to heaven and said at once, "Oh, I swear." I kissed my pinky and looked at God.

"That is an actor's life, my dear," he explained. "Like a soldier's, never tardy or disobedient to his general, the director. Everything," he said, "absolutely everything will depend on you."

That afternoon, all over the building, children scraped and scrubbed the turkeys and the sheaves of corn off the schoolroom windows. Goodbye Thanksgiving. The next morning a monitor brought red paper and green paper from the office. He made new shapes and hung them on the walls and glued them to the doors.

The teachers became happier and happier. Their heads were ringing like the bells of childhood. My best friend Evie was prone to evil, but she did not get a single demerit for whispering. We learned "Holy Night" without an

error. "How wonderful!" said Miss Glacé, the student teacher. "To think that some of you don't even speak the language!" We learned "Deck the Halls" and "Hark! The Herald Angels". . . . They weren't ashamed and we weren't embarrassed.

Oh, but when my mother heard about it all, she said to my father: "Misha, you don't know what's going on there. Cramer is the head of the Tickets Committee."

"Who?" asked my father. "Cramer? Oh yes, an active woman."

"Active? Active has to have a reason. "Listen," she said sadly, "I'm surprised to see my neighbors making tra-la-la for Christmas."

My father couldn't think of what to say to that. Then he decided: "You're in America! Clara, you wanted to come here. In Palestine the Arabs would be eating you alive. In Europe you had pogroms. Argentina is full of Indians. Here you got Christmas. . . . Some joke, ha?"

"Very funny, Misha. What is becoming of you? If we came to a new country a long time ago to run away from tyrants, and instead we fall into a creeping pogrom, that our children learn a lot of lies, so what's the joke? Ach, Misha, your idealism is going away."

"So is your sense of humor."

"That I never had, but idealism you had a lot of."

"I'm the same Misha Abramowitz. I didn't change an iota. Ask anyone."

"Only ask me," says my mama, may she rest in peace. "I got the answer."

Meanwhile the neighbors had to think of what to say too.

Marty's father said: "You know, he has a very important part, my boy."

"Mine also," said Mr. Sauerfeld.

"Not my boy!" said Mrs. Klieg. "I said to him no. The answer is no. When I say no, I mean no!"

The rabbi's wife said, "It's disgusting!" But no one listened to her. Under the narrow sky of God's great wisdom she wore a strawberry-blond wig.

Every day was noisy and full of experience. I was Right-Hand Man. Mr. Hilton said: "How could I get along without you, Shirley?"

He said: "Your mother and father ought to get down on their knees every night and thank God for giving them a child like you."

He also said: "You're absolutely a pleasure to work with, my dear, dear child."

Sometimes he said: "For God's sake, what did I do with the script? Shirley! Shirley! Find it."

Then I answered quietly: "Here it is, Mr. Hilton."

Once in a while, when he was very tired, he would cry out: "Shirley, I'm just tired of screaming at those kids. Will you tell Ira Pushkov not to come in till Lester points to that star the second time?"

Then I roared: "Ira Pushkov, what's the matter with you? Dope! Mr. Hilton told you five times already, don't come in till Lester points to that star the second time."

"Ach, Clara," my father asked, "what does she do there till six o'clock she can't even put the plates on the table?"

"Christmas," said my mother coldly.

"Ho! Ho!" my father said. "Christmas. What's the harm? After all, history teaches everyone. We learn from reading this is a holiday from pagan times also, candles, lights, even Chanukah. So we learn it's not altogether Christian. So if they think it's a private holiday, they're only ignorant, not patriotic. What belongs to history, belongs to all men. You want to go back to the Middle Ages? Is it better to shave your head with a secondhand razor? Does it hurt Shirley to learn to speak up? It does not. So maybe someday she won't live between the kitchen and the shop. She's not a fool."

I thank you, Papa, for your kindness. It is true about me to this day. I am foolish but I am not a fool.

That night my father kissed me and said with great interest in my career, "Shirley, tomorrow's your big day. Congrats."

"Save it," my mother said. Then she shut all the windows in order to prevent tonsillitis.

In the morning it snowed. On

the street corner a tree had been decorated for us by a kind city administration. In order to miss its chilly shadow our neighbors walked three blocks east to buy a loaf of bread. The butcher pulled down black window shades to keep the colored lights from shining on his chickens. Oh, not me. On the way to school, with both my hands I tossed it a kiss of tolerance. Poor thing, it was a stranger in Egypt.

I walked straight into the auditorium past the staring children. "Go ahead, Shirley!" said the monitors. Four boys, big for their age, had already started work as propmen and stagehands.

Mr. Hilton was very nervous. He was not even happy. Whatever he started to say ended in a sideward look of sadness. He sat slumped in the middle of the first row and asked me to help Miss Glacé. I did this, although she thought my voice too resonant and said, "Show off!"

Parents began to arrive long before we were ready. They wanted to make a good impression. From among the yards of drapes I peeked out at the audience. I saw my embarrassed mother.

Ira, Lester, and Meyer were pasted to their beards by Miss Glacé. She almost forgot to thread the star on its wire, but I reminded her. I coughed a few times to clear my throat. Miss Glacé looked around and saw that everyone was in costume and on line waiting to play his part. She whispered, "All right . . ." Then:

Jackie Sauerfeld, the prettiest boy in the first grade, parted the curtains with his skinny elbow and in a high voice sang out:
"Parents dear
We are here
To make a Christmas play in time.
It we give
In narrative
And illustrate with pantomime."
He disappeared.

My voice burst immediately from the wings to the great shock of Ira, Lester, and Meyer, who were waiting for it but were surprised all the same.

"I remember, I remember, the house where I was born . . ."

Miss Glacé yanked the curtain open and there it was, the house —an old hayloft, where Celia Kornbluh lay in the straw with Cindy Lou, her favorite doll. Ira, Lester, and Meyer moved slowly from the wings toward her, sometimes pointing to a moving star and sometimes ahead to Cindy Lou.

It was a long story and it was a sad story. I carefully pronounced all the words about my lonesome childhood, while little Eddie Braunstein wandered upstage and down with his shepherd's stick, looking for sheep. I brought up lonesomeness again, and not being understood at all except by some women everybody hated. Eddie was too small for that and

Marty Groff took his place, wearing his father's prayer shawl. I announced twelve friends, and half the boys in the fourth grade gathered round Marty, who stood on an orange crate while my voice harangued. Sorrowful and loud, I declaimed about love and God and Man, but because of the terrible deceit of Abie Stock we came suddenly to a famous moment. Marty, whose remembering tongue I was, waited at the foot of the cross. He stared desperately at the audience. I groaned, "My God, my God, why hast thou forsaken me?" The soldiers who were sheiks grabbed poor Marty to pin him up to die, but he wrenched free, turned again to the audience, and spread his arms aloft to show despair and the end. I murmured at the top of my voice. "The rest is silence, but as everyone in this room, in this city —in this world—now knows, I have life eternal."

That night Mrs. Kornbluh visited our kitchen for a glass of tea.

"How's the virgin?" asked my father with a look of concern.

"For a man with a daughter, you got a fresh mouth, Abramovitz."

"Here," said my father kindly, have some lemon, it'll sweeten your disposition."

They debated a little in Yiddish, then fell in a puddle of Russian and Polish. What I understood next was my father, who said, "Still and all, it was certainly a beautiful affair, you have to admit, introducing us to the beliefs of a different culture."

"Well, yes," said Mrs. Kornbluh. "The only thing . . . you know Charlie Turner—that cute boy in Celia's class—a couple others? They got very small parts or no part at all. In very bad taste, it seemed to me. After all it's their religion."

"Ach," explained my mother, "what could Mr. Hilton do? They got very small voices; after all, why should they holler? The English language they know from the beginning by heart. They're blond like angels. You think it's so important they should get in the play? Christmas . . . the whole piece of goods . . . they own it."

I listened and I listened until I couldn't listen any more. Too sleepy, I climbed out of bed and kneeled. I made a little church of my hands and said, "Hear, O Israel . . ." Then I called out in Yiddish, "Please, good night, good night. Ssh."

My father said, "Ssh yourself," and slammed the kitchen door.

I was happy. I fell asleep at once. I had prayed for everybody: my talking family, cousins far away, passers-by, and all the lonesome Christians. I expected to be heard. My voice was certainly the loudest.

Questions for Analysis and Discussion

Many stories by American Jewish writers deal with the problem faced by the Jewish immigrant in acquiring his education in a school system whose values and content were largely Anglo-American.

1. The prevailing tone of *The Loudest Voice* is comic. How is the comedy helped by the fact that the narrator is Shirley Abramowitz? What is the nature of the humor of this story? Does it arise from exaggeration, incongruity, and/or the unexpected? Select a passage that you consider humorous and explain why you think it funny. Try reading this passage aloud to your classmates. Does it sound comic?

2. Describe Shirley Abramowitz. How does her "talent" embarrass her mother? Why doesn't it embarrass her father? What other abilities does Shirley have? What opportunity is offered Shirley? How does Shirley describe Mr. Hilton? What is Shirley's view of her mother? Does she respect her? What is her view of her father? Does she respect him?

3. How is the school being prepared for the celebration of Christmas? Mrs. Abramowitz is upset by the great to-do in school over Christmas. She discusses it with her husband. Why is Mr. Abramowitz not disturbed by the fuss in school over Christmas? Why does Mrs. Abramowitz say he is losing his idealism? How do you feel about the celebration of Christmas in secular schools? How do your Jewish neighbors feel about it?

4. Can you judge from the conversations in the story between Shirley's father and mother whether their relationship was a good one? Is Shirley happy in her home? If you think she is, what elements in the home are responsible for her well being? Support your conclusions with references from the text. What are Mr. Abramowitz's rationalizations for accepting the Christmas celebrations in school? Do you agree or disagree with his views? Why?

5. How did Shirley's neighbors try to avoid the contamination of the Christmas tree on the street corner? Do you agree with Shirley that the tree was a "stranger in Egypt"? What do you think of this metaphor? Does it suggest that Shirley was learning tolerance, or that she was captivated by the colorful aspects of Christmas and thereby

beginning to lose her Jewish identity? What do you think was the author's intention in having Shirley make such a comparison?

6. Shirley became Mr. Hilton's "right hand man." What qualities made her a successful stage manager and a poor promoter? Why is Shirley's account of the performance humorous? What was ironic about the performance of the play? Why did Mr. Hilton use Jewish youngsters almost exclusively in the play?

7. Before Shirley goes to sleep, she prays for everybody, including all the lonesome Christians. What in your view is the author's purpose in writing this story? Is she concerned with the problem of tolerance in American society? Is she depicting the Jewish family as a closely knit group facing the experiences of living in America with acceptance and humor? Is she describing the pleasures of growing up in a world where there are security and things to do? Does she suggest that American education may undermine Jewish identity? What do you think? Be sure to support your judgment with passages from the text. Is there danger that a uniform school system with a uniform program may remove the individual ethnic identity of pupils attending school?

Suggested Activities

1. Myra Kelly was an elementary school teacher of Irish birth who taught Jewish children in schools on the Lower East Side. She wrote stories about her experiences. Those were collected in *Little Citizens,* 1904, *Wards of Liberty,* 1907, and *Little Aliens,* 1910. Get a copy in the library of any one of these volumes and report to the class on one or two of the stories you like best.

2. Mary Antin was a young Jewish girl who immigrated with her parents from Russia to Boston in 1894 at the age of thirteen. She loved America because in this new world she was free from the persecutions and insults she had suffered in Russia. She wrote of her experiences in *The Promised Land.* Read those sections of the book that describe her school experiences and report to the class how Mary Antin adjusted to American education.

3. A gloomy description of the growing up of a young immigrant is to be found in a novel entitled *Call It Sleep* by Henry Roth. Find the passages in this book that describe David Schearl's experiences in the *heder* (religious school) and public school and describe these in a report to the class.

4. The story raises a question that can be debated in class. It concerns the celebration of Christmas in those public schools where there are Jewish students. There are three views that need to be examined and some conclusions reached about them.

    a. One view is that Christmas is not entirely a Christian holiday. In many respects it is a secular holiday like Thanksgiving which is celebrated by all Americans. If the emphasis is on the spirit of good will, on the colorful aspects of the holiday, the decorations, the gift-giving, and so forth, if no mention is made of the birth of Jesus in story or song, it may be acceptable in a secular school.

    b. A second view is that since the Jewish festival of Hanukkah comes at about the same time each year as Christmas, both holidays can be celebrated together. It provides an excellent experience for students in inter-cultural relations. Certain holidays of other ethnic groups, such as the Asians, could be celebrated also.

    c. The third position is that one of the basic elements of American democracy is separation of church and state—which means among other things that religious instruction and observance do not belong in the public school. There should therefore be neither Christmas nor Hanukkah celebrations in the school; in fact, there should be no activity related to a religious belief or custom.

5. As a student, Christian or Jewish, write an autobiographical sketch describing your participation in a school Christmas celebration. Tell what happened and how you participated in the event, and describe your feelings and possibly the feelings of your friends. Be honest. If you enjoyed the celebration, say so and describe what gave you the greatest pleasure. If you did not enjoy it, tell what it was that disturbed you about the event.

World War I, American Expeditionary Forces. New York Public Library Picture Collection.

By Irwin Shaw

Act of Faith

Introduction: **Anti-Semitism in the Thirties**

The years between 1929, the beginning of the Great Depression, and 1945, the end of World War II, were years of deep uncertainty, doubt, and fear for most of the Jewish citizens of America. Before 1929 there were anti-Semitic movements fostered by: 1) the appearance in sociological works of racial theories that relegated the Jew, along with other groups like the Slavs and Latins, to an inferior and unassimilable status; 2) the resentment among certain groups in the country toward the successes achieved by many Jews in business and the professions; 3) the conviction among restless and economically depressed masses of people that the government had sold out to special interests, and that certain minorities, such as the Italians, Irish, and Jews were in some ways responsible for their low status in society; and 4) the belief that the Jews had played a key role in the Russian Revolution, that they were basically radicals and anarchists and would bring a similar change in the government of the United States.

A major inspiration for anti-Semitic activity was The Protocols of the Elders of Zion, *a forged document produced by the Russian Czar's secret police, which recorded the alleged proceedings of a Jewish body planning to take over the Western world on behalf of international Jewry. This fantastic and libelous work managed to influence even people like Henry Ford.*

Adolf Hitler's accession to power in Germany in 1933 and the rampant anti-Semitism of his Nazi followers had repercussions in America. The German government financed the establishment of anti-Semitic groups, like the German-American Bund, which sought to spread the poisonous Nazi doctrines in America. The unrest of the depression caused many people to seek scapegoats, and the Jew became one of these. Dormant anti-Semitic groups, like the Ku Klux Klan, were revived. Some Catholics, who forgot that they had suffered bigotry and discrimination in America for many years, followed Father

Charles E. Coughlin in his Christian Front *movement against the Jews. Fundamentalist Protestants joined William Dudley Pelley's Silver Shirts or became the audience of such anti-Semitic rabble rousers as Gerald L. K. Smith. These and others threatened the security of America's Jewish citizens.*

It is small wonder, then, that the period between 1933 and 1939 was one of tension and distress for many of the Jews of America. They had found here, in this democracy, a haven from persecution where they had joined other oppressed minorities from abroad. Were they now again to face the attacks and the discrimination that had originally led them to flee to this country? They loved this land which had given them so much. Was America also to be tainted by the centuries of groundless hatred that had moved the peoples of Europe? Who were to be their friends and supporters if the enmity fostered by the extremist, lunatic groups erupted into general violence? Was America really different from Russia and Germany and the other places where, at certain periods in their history, the Jew had been treated as the enemy? These are the questions that color Irwin Shaw's Act of Faith.

"PRESENT IT in a pitiful light," Olson was saying, as they picked their way through the mud toward the orderly room tent. "Three combat-scarred veterans, who fought their way from Omaha Beach to—what was the name of the town we fought our way to?"

"Konigstein," Seeger said.

"Konigstein." Olson lifted his right foot heavily out of a puddle and stared admiringly at the three pounds of mud clinging to his overshoe. "The backbone of the Army. The non-commissioned officer. We deserve better of our country. Mention our decorations in passing."

"What decorations should I mention?" Seeger asked. "The marksman's medal?"

"Never quite made it," Olson said. "I had a cross-eyed scorer at the butts. Mention the bronze star, the silver star, the Croix de Guerre, with palms, the unit citation, the Congressional Medal of Honor."

"Gad, sir," Olson said with dignity, "do you think that one Southern military gentleman will dare doubt the word of another Southern military gentleman in the hour of victory?"

"I come from Ohio," Seeger said.

"Welch comes from Kansas," Olson said, coolly staring down a second lieutenant who was passing. The lieutenant made a nervous little jerk with his hand as though he expected a salute, then kept it rigid, as a slight superior smile of scorn twisted at the corner of Olson's mouth. The lieutenant dropped his eyes and splashed on through the mud. "You've heard of Kansas," Olson said. "Magnolia-scented Kansas."

"Of course," said Seeger. "I'm no fool."

"Do your duty by your men, Sergeant," Olson stopped to wipe the rain off his face and lectured him. "Highest ranking noncom present took the initiative and saved his comrades, at great personal risk, above and beyond the call of you-know-what, in the best traditions of the American Army."

"I will throw myself in the breach," Seeger said.

"Welch and I can't ask more," said Olson, approvingly.

They walked heavily through the mud on the streets between the rows of tents. The camp stretched drearily over the Rheims plain, with the rain beating on the sagging tents. The division had been there over three weeks by now, waiting to be shipped home, and all the meager diversions of the neighborhood had been sampled and exhausted, and there was an air of watchful suspicion and impatience with the military life hanging over the camp now, and there was even reputed to be a staff sergeant in C company who was laying odds they would not get back to America before July Fourth.

"I'm redeployable," Olson sang. "It's so enjoyable . . ." It was a jingle he had composed to no recognizable melody in the early days after the victory in Europe, when he had added up his points and found they came only to 63. "Tokyo, wait for me. . . ."

They were going to be discharged as soon as they got back to the States, but Olson persisted in singing the song, occasionally adding a mournful stanza about dengue fever and brown girls with venereal disease. He was a short, round boy who had been flunked out of air cadets' school and transferred to the infantry, but whose spirits had not been damaged in the process. He had a high, childish voice, and a pretty baby face. He was very good-natured, and had a girl waiting for him at the University of California, where he intended to finish his course at government expense when he got out of the Army, and he was just the type who is killed off early and predictably and sadly in motion pictures about the war, but he had gone through four campaigns and six major battles without a scratch.

Seeger was a large, lanky boy, with a big nose, who had been wounded at Saint Lô, but had come back to his outfit in the Siegfried Line, quite unchanged. He was cheerful and dependable and he knew his business and had broken in five or six second lieutenants who had been killed or wounded and the CO had tried to get him commissioned in the field, but the war had ended while the paperwork was being fumbled over at headquarters.

They reached the door of the orderly tent and stopped. "Be brave, Sergeant," Olson said. "Welch and I are depending on you."

"OK," Seeger said, and went in.

The tent had the dank, army-canvas smell that had been so much a part of Seeger's life in the past three years. The company clerk was reading a July 1945 issue of the *Buffalo Courier-Express*, which had just reached him, and Captain Taney, the company CO, was seated at a sawbuck table he used as a desk, writing a letter to his wife, his lips pursed with effort. He was a small, fussy man, with sandy hair that was falling out. While the fighting had been going on, he had been lean and tense, and his small voice had been cold and full of authority. But now he had relaxed, and a little pot belly was creeping up under his belt, and he kept the top button of his trousers open when he could do it without too public loss of dignity. During the war Seeger had thought of him as a natural soldier, tireless, fanatic about detail, aggressive, severely anxious to kill Germans. But in the past few months Seeger had seen him re-lapsing gradually and pleasantly into a small-town wholesale hardware merchant, which he had been before the war, sedentary and a little shy, and, as he had once told Seeger, worried, here in the bleak champagne fields of France, about his daughter, who had just turned twelve and had a tendency to go after the boys and had been caught by her mother kissing a fifteen-year-old neighbor in the hammock after school.

"Hello, Seeger," he said, returning the salute in a mild, off-hand gesture. "What's on your mind?"

"Am I disturbing you, sir?"

"Oh, no. Just writing a letter to my wife. You married, Seeger?" He peered at the tall boy standing before him.

"No, sir."

"It's very difficult," Taney sighed, pushing dissatisfiedly at the letter before him. "My wife complains that I don't tell her I love her often enough. Been married fifteen years. You'd think she'd know by now." He smiled at Seeger. "I thought you were going to Paris," he said. "I signed the passes yesterday."

"That's what I came to see you about, sir."

"I suppose there's something wrong with the passes." Taney spoke resignedly, like a man who never quite got the hang of army regulations and has had requisitions, furloughs, requests for court-martial returned for correction in a baffling flood.

"No, sir," Seeger said. "The passes're fine. They start tomorrow. Well, it's just . . ." He looked around at the company clerk, who was on the sports page. "This confidential?" Taney asked.

"If you don't mind, sir."

"Johnny," Taney said to the clerk, "go stand in the rain someplace."

"Yes, sir," the clerk said, and slowly got up and walked out.

Taney looked shrewdly at Seeger, spoke in a secret whisper. "You pick up anything?" he asked.

Seeger grinned. "No, sir, haven't had my hands on a girl since Strasbourg."

"Ah, that's good." Taney leaned back, relieved, happy he didn't have to cope with the disapproval of the Medical Corps.

"It's—well," said Seeger, embarrassed, "it's hard to say, sir—but it's money."

Taney shook his head sadly. "I know."

"We haven't been paid for three months, sir, and . . ."

"Damn it!" Taney stood up and shouted furiously. "I would like to take every bloody chair-warming old lady in the Finance Department and wring their necks."

The clerk stuck his head into the tent. "Anything wrong? You call for me, sir?"

"No," Taney shouted. "Get out of here."

The clerk ducked out.

Taney sat down again. "I suppose," he said, in a more normal voice, "they have their problems. Outfits being broken up, being moved all over the place. But it is rugged."

"It wouldn't be so bad," Seeger said. "But we're going to Paris tomorrow. Olson, Welch and myself. And you need money in Paris."

"Don't I know it." Taney wagged his head. "Do you know what I paid for a bottle of champagne on the Place Pigalle in September. . . ?" He paused significantly. "I won't tell you. You won't have any respect for me the rest of your life."

Seeger laughed. "Hanging," he said, "is too good for the guy who thought up the rate of exchange."

"I don't care if I never see another franc as long as I live." Taney waved his letter in the air, although it had been dry for a long time.

There was silence in the tent and Seeger swallowed a little embarrassedly, watching the CO wave the flimsy sheet of paper in regular sweeping movements. "Sir," he said, "the truth is, I've come to borrow some money for Welch, Olson and myself. We'll pay it back out of the first pay we get, and that can't be too long from now. If you don't want to give it to us, just tell me and I'll understand and get the hell out of here. We don't like to ask, but you might just as well be dead as be in Paris broke."

Taney stopped waving his letter and put it down thoughtfully. He peered at it, wrinkling his brow, looking like an aged bookkeeper in the single gloomy light that hung in the middle of the tent.

"Just say the word, Captain," Seeger said, "and I'll blow . . ."

"Stay where you are, son," said Taney. He dug in his shirt pocket and took out a worn, sweatstained wallet. He looked at it for a moment. "Alligator," he said, with automatic, absent pride. "My wife sent it to me when we were in England. Pounds don't fit in it. However . . ." He opened it and took out all the contents. There was a small pile of francs on the table in front of him. He counted them. "Four hundred francs," he said. "Eight bucks."

"Excuse me," Seeger said humbly. "I shouldn't have asked.

"Delighted," Taney said vigorously. "Absolutely delighted." He started dividing the francs into two piles. "Truth is, Seeger, most of my money goes home in allotments. And the truth is, I lost eleven hundred francs in a poker game three nights ago, and I ought to be ashamed of myself. Here . . ." he shoved the pile toward Seeger. "Two hundred francs."

Seeger looked down at the frayed, meretricious paper, which always seemed to him like stage money, anyway. "No, sir," he said. "I can't take it."

"Take it," Taney said. "That's a direct order."

Seeger slowly picked up the money, not looking at Taney. "Some time, sir," he said, "after we get out, you have to come over to my house and you and my father and my brother and I'll go on a real drunk."

"I regard that," Taney said, gravely, "as a solemn commitment."

They smiled at each other and Seeger started out.

"Have a drink for me," said Taney, "at the Cafe de la Paix. A small drink." He was sitting down to write his wife he loved her when Seeger went out the tent.

Olson fell into step with Seeger and they walked silently through the mud between the tents.

"Well, *mon vieux?*" Olson said finally.

"Two hundred francs," said Seeger.

Olson groaned. "Two hundred francs! . . . That miserable, penny-loving Yankee!"

"He only had four hundred," Seeger said.

"I revise my opinion," said Olson.

They walked disconsolately and heavily back toward their tent.

Olson spoke only once before

they got there. "These raincoats," he said, patting his. "Most ingenious invention of the war. Highest saturation point of any modern fabric. Collect more water per square inch, and hold it, than any material known to man. All hail the quartermaster!"

Welch was waiting at the entrance of their tent. He was standing there peering excitedly and shortsightedly out at the rain through his glasses, looking angry and tough, like a big-city hack driver, individual and incorruptible even in the ten-million collored uniform. Every time Seeger came ˈupón Welch unexpectedly, he couldn't help smiling at the belligerent stance, the harsh stare through the steel-rimmed GI glasses, which had nothing at all to do with the way Welch really was. "It's a family inheritance," Welch had once explained. "My whole family stands as though we were getting ready to rap a drunk with a beer glass. Even my old lady." Welch had six brothers, all devout, according to Welch, and Seeger from time to time pictured them standing in a row, on Sunday mornings in church, seemingly on the verge of general violence, amid the hushed Latin and Sabbath millinery.

"How much?" Welch asked loudly.

"Don't make us laugh," Olson said, pushing past him into the tent.

"What do you think I could get from the French for my combat jacket?" Seeger said. He went into the tent and lay down on his cot.

Welch followed them in and stood between the two of them, a superior smile on his face. "Boys," he said, "on a man's errand."

"I can just see us now," Olson murmured, lying on his cot with his hands clasped behind his head, "painting Montmartre red. Please bring on the naked dancing girls. Four bucks worth."

"I am not worried," Welch announced.

"Get out of here." Olson turned over on his stomach.

"I know where we can put our hands on sixty-five bucks." Welch looked triumphantly first at Olson, then at Seeger.

Olson turned over slowly and sat up. "I'll kill you," he said, "if you're kidding."

"While you guys are wasting your time," Welch said, "fooling around with the infantry, I used my head. I went into Reems and used my head."

"Rance," Olson said automatically. He had had two years of French in college and he felt, now that the war was over, that he had to introduce his friends to some of his culture.

"I got to talking to a captain in the Air Force," Welch said eagerly. "A little fat old paddle-footed captain that never got higher off the ground than the second floor of Com Z headquarters, and he told me that what he would admire to do more than anything else is to take home a nice shiny German Luger pistol with him to show to the boys back in Pacific Grove, California."

Silence fell on the tent, and Welch and Olson looked tentatively at Seeger.

"Sixty-five bucks for a Luger, these days," Olson said, "is a very good figure."

"They've been sellin' for as low as thirty-five," said Welch hesitantly. "I'll bet," he said to Seeger, "you could sell yours now and buy another one back when you got some dough, and make a clear twenty-five on the deal."

Seeger didn't say anything. He had killed the owner of the Luger, an enormous SS major, in Coblenz, behind some paper bales in a warehouse, and the major had fired at Seeger three time with it, once nicking his helmet, before Seeger hit him in the face at twenty feet. Seeger had kept the Luger, a long, heavy, well-balanced gun, very carefully since then, lugging it with him, hiding it at the bottom of his bedroll, oiling it three times a week, avoiding all opportunities of selling it, although he had been offered as much as a hundred dollars for it and several times eighty and ninety, while the war was still on, before German weapons became a glut on

the market.

"Well," said Welch, "there's no hurry. I told the captain I'd see him around eight o'clock in front of the Lion D'Or Hotel. You got five hours to make up your mind. Plenty of time."

"Me," said Olson, after a pause. "I won't say anything."

Seeger looked reflectively at his feet and the other two men avoided looking at him. Welch dug in his pocket. "I forgot," he said. "I picked up a letter for you." He handed it to Seeger.

"Thanks," Seeger said. He opened it absently, thinking about the Luger.

"Me," said Olson, "I won't say a bloody word. I'm just going to lie here and think about that nice fat Air Force captain."

Seeger grinned a little at him and went to the tent opening to read the letter in the light. The letter was from his father, and even from one glance at the handwriting, scrawly and hurried and spotted, so different from his father's usual steady, handsome, professional script, he knew that something was wrong.

"Dear Norman," it read, "sometime in the future, you must forgive me for writing this letter. But I have been holding this in so long, and there is no one here I can talk to, and because of your brother's condition I must pretend to be cheerful and optimistic all the time at home, both with him and your mother, who has never been the same since Leonard was killed. You're the oldest now, and though I know we've never talked very seriously about anything before, you have been through a great deal by now, and I imagine you must have matured considerably, and you've seen so many different places and people. . . . Norman, I need help. While the war was on and you were fighting, I kept this to myself. It wouldn't have been fair to burden you with this. But now the war is over and I no longer feel I can stand up under this alone. And you will have to face it some time when you get home, if you haven't faced it already, and perhaps we can help each other by facing it together. . . ."

"I'm redeployable," Olson was singing softly, on his cot. "It's so enjoyable, In the Pelilu mud, With the tropical crud. . . ." He fell silent after his burst of song.

Seeger blinked his eyes, at the entrance of the tent, in the wan rainy light, and went on reading his father's letter, on the stiff white stationery with the University letterhead in polite engraving at the top of each page.

"I've been feeling this coming on for a long time," the letter continued, "but it wasn't until last Sunday morning that something happened to make me feel it in its full force. I don't know how much you've guessed about the reason for Jacob's discharge from the Army. It's true he was pretty

badly wounded in the leg at Metz, but I've asked around, and I know that men with worse wounds were returned to duty after hospitalization. Jacob got a medical discharge, but I don't think it was for the shrapnel wound in his thigh. He is suffering now from what I suppose you call combat fatigue, and he is subject to fits of depression and hallucinations. Your mother and I thought that as time went by and the war and the army receded, he would grow better. Instead, he is growing worse. Last Sunday morning when I came down into the living room from upstairs he was crouched in his old uniform, next to the window, peering out. . . ."

"What the hell," Olson was saying, "if we don't get the sixty-five bucks we can always go to the Louvre. I understand the Mona Lisa is back."

"I asked Jacob what he was doing," the letter went on. "He didn't turn around. 'I'm observing,' he said. 'V-1's and V-2's. Buzz-bombs and rockets. They're coming in by the hundreds.' I tried to reason with him and he told me to crouch and save myself from flying glass. To humor him I got down on the floor beside him and tried to tell him the war was over, that we were in Ohio, 4,000 miles away from the nearest spot where bombs had fallen, that America had never been touched. He wouldn't listen.

'These're the new rocket bombs,' he said, 'for the Jews.'"

"Did you ever hear of the Pantheon?" Olson asked loudly.

"No," said Welch.

"It's free."

"I'll go," said Welch.

Seeger shook his head a little and blinked his eyes before he went back to the letter.

"After that," his father went on, "Jacob seemed to forget about the bombs from time to time, but he kept saying that the mobs were coming up the street armed with bazookas and Browning Automatic rifles. He mumbled incoherently a good deal of the time and kept walking back and forth saying, 'What's the situation? Do you know what the situation is?' And he told me he wasn't worried about himself, he was a soldier and he expected to be killed, but he was worried about Mother and myself and Leonard and you. He seemed to forget that Leonard was dead. I tried to calm him and get him back to bed before your mother came down, but he refused and wanted to set out immediately to rejoin his division. It was all terribly disjointed and at one time he took the ribbon he got for winning the Bronze star and threw it in the fireplace, then he got down on his hands and knees and picked it out of the ashes and made me pin it on him again, and he kept repeating, "This is for when they are coming for the Jews.'"

"The next war I'm in," said Olson, "they don't get me under the rank of colonel."

It had stopped raining by now, and Seeger folded the unfinished letter and went outside. He walked slowly down to the end of the company street, and facing out across the empty, soaked French fields, scarred and neglected by various armies, he stopped and opened the letter again.

"I don't know what Jacob went through in the army," his father wrote, "that has done this to him. He never talks to me about the war and he refuses to go to a psychoanalyst, and from time to time he is his own bouncing, cheerful self, playing in tennis tournaments and going around with a large group of girls. But he has devoured all the concentration camp reports, and I have found him weeping when the newspapers reported that a hundred Jews were killed in Tripoli some time ago.

"The terrible thing is, Norman, that I find myself coming to believe that it is not neurotic for a Jew to behave like this today. Perhaps Jacob is the normal one, and I, going about my business, teaching economics in a quiet classroom, pretending to understand that the world is comprehensible and orderly, am really the mad one. I ask you once more to forgive me for writing you a letter like this, so different from any letter or conversation I've ever had with you. But it is crowding me, too. I do not see rockets and bombs, but I see other things.

"Wherever you go these days—restaurants, hotels, clubs, trains, you seem to hear talk about the Jews, mean, hateful murderous talk. Whatever page you turn to in the newspapers you seem to find an article about Jews being killed somewhere on the face of the globe. And there are large, influential newspapers and well-known columnists who each day are growing more and more outspoken and more popular. The day that Roosevelt died I heard a drunken man yelling outside a bar, 'Finally, they got the Jew out of the White House.' And some of the people who heard him merely laughed, and nobody stopped him. And on V-E Day, in celebration, hoodlums in Los Angeles savagely beat a Jewish writer. It's difficult to know what to do, whom to fight, where to look for allies.

"Three months ago, for example, I stopped my Thursday night poker game, after playing with the same men for over ten years. John Reilly happened to say the Jews were getting rich out of this war, and when I demanded an apology, he refused, and when I looked around at the faces of the men who had been my friends for so long, I could see they were not with me. And when I left the house, no one said good night to me. I know the poison was spreading from Germany before the war and during it, but I had not realized it had come so close.

"And in my economics class, I find myself idiotically hedging in my lectures. I discover that I am loathe to praise any liberal writer or any liberal act, and find myself somehow annoyed and frightened to see an article of criticism of existing abuses signed by a Jewish name. And I hate to see Jewish names on important committees, and hate to read of Jews fighting for the poor, the oppressed, the cheated and hungry. Somehow, even in a country where my family has lived a hundred years, the enemy has won this subtle victory over me—he has made me disenfranchise myself from honest causes by calling them foreign, Communist, using Jewish names connected with them as ammunition against them.

"And, most hateful of all, I find myself looking for Jewish names in the casualty lists and secretly being glad when I discover them there, to prove that there at least, among the dead and wounded, we belong. Three times, thanks to you and your brothers, I have found our name there, and, may God forgive me, at the expense of your blood and your brother's life, through my tears, I have felt that same twitch of satisfaction. . . .

"When I read the newspapers and see another story that Jews are still being killed in Poland, or Jews requesting that they be given back their homes in France, or that they be allowed to enter some country where they will not be murdered, I am annoyed with them, I feel they are boring the rest of the world with their problems, they are making demands on the rest of the world by being killed, they are disturbing everyone by being hungry and asking for the return of their property. If we could all fall through the crust of the earth and vanish in one hour, with our heroes and poets and prophets and martyrs, perhaps we would be doing the memory of the Jewish race a service. . . .

"This is how I feel today, son. I need some help. You've been to the war, you've fought and killed men, you've seen the people of other countries. Maybe you understand things that I don't understand. Maybe you see some hope somewhere. Help me. Your loving father."

Seeger folded the letter slowly, not seeing what he was doing because the tears were burning his eyes. He walked slowly and aimlessly across the dead autumn grass of the empty field, away from the camp.

He tried to wipe away his tears, because with his eyes full and dark, he kept seeing his father and brother crouched in the old-fashioned living room in Ohio and hearing his brother, dressed in the old, discarded uniform, saying, "These're the new rocket bombs. For the Jews."

He sighed, looking out over the bleak, wasted land. Now, he thought, now I have to think about it. He felt a slight, unreasonable twinge of anger at his father for presenting him with the necessity of thinking about it. The Army was good about serious problems. While you were fighting, you were too busy and frightened and weary to think about anything, and at other times you were relaxing, putting your brain on a shelf, postponing everything to that impossible time of clarity and beauty after the war. Well, now, here was the impossible, clear, beautiful time, and here was his father, demanding that he think. There are all sorts of Jews, he thought, there are the sort whose every waking moment is ridden by the knowledge of Jewishness, who see signs against the Jew in every smile on a streetcar, every whisper, who see pogroms in every newspaper article, threats in every change of the weather, scorn in every handshake, death behind each closed door. He had not been like that. He was young, he was big and healthy and easy-going, and people of all kinds had seemed to like him all his life, in the Army and out. In America, especially, what was going on in Europe had seemed remote, unreal, unrelated to him. The chanting, bearded old men burning in the Nazi furnaces, and the dark-eyed women screaming prayers in Polish and Russian and German as they were pushed naked into the gas chambers had seemed as shadowy and almost as unrelated to him as he trotted out onto the stadium field for a football game, as they must have been to the men named O'Dwyer and Wickersham and Poole who played in the line beside him.

They had seemed more related in Europe. Again and again in the towns that had been taken back from Germany, gaunt, gray-faced men had stopped him humbly, looking searchingly at him, and had asked, peering at his long, lined, grimy face, under the anonymous helmet, "Are you a Jew?" Sometimes they asked it in English, sometimes French, or Yiddish. He didn't know French or Yiddish, but he learned to recognize the phrase. He had never understood exactly why they had asked the question, since they never demanded anything from him, rarely even could speak to him, until, one day in Strasbourg, a little bent old man and a small shapeless woman had stopped him, and asked, in English, if he was Jewish.

"Yes," he said, smiling at them.

The two old people had smiled widely, like children. "Look," the old man had said to his wife. "A young American soldier. A Jew. And so large and strong." He had touched Seeger's arm reverently with the tips of his fingers, then had touched the Garand he was carrying. "And such a beautiful rifle . . ."

And there, for a moment, although he was not particularly sensitive, Seeger got an inkling of why he had been stopped and questioned by so many before. Here, to these bent, exhausted old people, ravaged of their families, familiar with flight and death for so many years, was a symbol of continuing life. A large young man in the uniform of the liberator, blood, as they thought, of their blood, but not in hiding, not quivering in fear and helplessness, but striding secure and victorious down the street, armed and capable of inflicting terrible destruction on his enemies.

Seeger had kissed the old lady on the cheek, and she had wept, and the old man had scolded her for it, while shaking Seeger's hand fervently and thankfully before saying goodby.

And, thinking back on it, it was silly to pretend that, even before his father's letter, he had been like any other American soldier going through the war. When he had stood over the huge SS major with the face blown in by his bullets in the warehouse in Coblenz, and taken the pistol from the dead hand, he had tasted a strange little extra flavor of triumph. How many Jews, he'd thought, has this man killed, how fitting it is that I've killed him. Neither Olson nor Welch, who were like his brothers, would have felt that in picking up the Luger, its barrel still hot from the last shots its owner had fired before dying. And he had resolved that he was going to make sure to take this gun back with him to America, and plug it and keep it on his desk at home, as a kind of vague, half-understood sign to himself that justice had once been done and he had been its instrument.

Maybe, he thought, maybe I'd better take it back with me, but not as a memento. Not plugged, but loaded. America by now was a strange country for him. He had been away a long time, and he wasn't sure what was waiting for him when he got home. If the mobs were coming down the street toward his house, he was not going to die singing and praying.

While he was taking basic training he'd heard a scrawny, clerk-like-looking soldier from Boston talking at the other end of the PX bar, over the watered beer. "The boys at the office," the scratchy voice was saying, "gave me a party before I left. And they told me one thing. 'Charlie,' they said, 'hold onto your bayonet. We're going to be able to use it when you get back. On the Yids.'"

He hadn't said anything then, because he'd felt it was neither possible nor desirable to fight against every random overheard voice raised against the Jews from one end of the world to another. But again and again, at odd moments, lying on a barracks cot, or stretched out trying to sleep on the floor of a ruined French farmhouse, he had heard that voice, harsh, satisfied, heavy with hate and ignorance, saying above the beery grumble of apprentice soldiers at the bar, "Hold onto your bayonet. . . ."

And the other stories—Jews collected stories of hatred and injustice and inklings of doom like a special, lunatic kind of miser. The story of the naval officer, commander of a small vessel off the Aleutians, who, in the officers' wardroom, had complained that he hated the Jews because it was the Jews who had demanded that the Germans be beaten first and the forces in the Pacific had been starved in consequence. And when one of his junior officers, who had just come aboard, had objected and told the commander that he was a Jew, the commander had risen from the table and said, "Mister, the Constitution of the United States says I have to serve in the same Navy with Jews, but it doesn't say I have to eat at the same table with them." In the fogs and the cold, swelling Arctic seas off the Aleutians, in a small boat, subject to sudden, mortal attack at any moment. . . .

And the two young combat engineers in an attached company on D-Day, when they were lying off the coast before climbing down into the landing barges. "There's France," one of them had said.

"Like every place else," the first one had answered. "The Jews've made all the dough during the war."

"Shut up!" Seeger had said, helplessly thinking of the dead, destroyed, wandering, starving Jews of France. The engineers had shut up, and they'd climbed down together into the heaving boat, and gone into the beach together.

And the million other stories. Jews, even the most normal, and best adjusted of them, became living treasuries of them, scraps of malice and bloodthirstiness, clever and confusing and cunningly twisted so that every act by every Jew became suspect and blameworthy and hateful. Seeger had heard the stories, and had made an almost conscious effort to forget them. Now, holding his father's letter in his hand, he remembered them all.

He stared unseeingly out in front of him. Maybe, he thought, maybe it would've been simpler to have been killed in the war, like Leonard. Simpler. Leonard would never have to face a crowd coming for his mother and father. Leonard would not have to listen

and collect those hideous, fascinating little stories that made of every Jew a stranger in any town, on any field, on the face of the earth. He had come so close to being killed so many times, it would have been so easy, so neat and final.

Seeger shook his head. It was ridiculous to feel like that, and he was ashamed of himself for the weak moment. At the age of twenty-one, death was not an answer.

"Seeger!" It was Olson's voice. He and Welch had sloshed silently up behind Seeger, standing in the open field. "Seeger, *mon vieux*, what're you doing—grazing?"

Seeger turned slowly to them. "I wanted to read my letter," he said.

Olson looked closely at him. They had been together so long, through so many things, that flickers and hints of expression on each other's faces were recognized and acted upon. "Anything wrong?" Olson asked.

"No," said Seeger. "Nothing much."

"Norman," Welch said, his voice young and solemn. "Norman, we've been talking, Olson and me. We decided—you're pretty attached to that Luger, and maybe —if you—well . . ."

"What he's trying to say," said Olson, "is we withdraw the request. If you want to sell it, OK. If you don't, don't do it for our sake. Honest."

Seeger looked at them, standing there, disreputable and tough and familiar. "I haven't made up my mind yet," he said.

"Anything you decide," Welch said oratorically, "is perfectly all right with us. Perfectly."

They walked aimlessly and silently across the field, away from camp. As they walked, their shoes making a wet, sliding sound in the damp, dead grass, Seeger thought of the time Olson had covered him in the little town outside Cherbourg, when Seeger had been caught going down the side of a street by four Germans with a machine gun on the second story of a house on the corner, and Olson had had to stand out in the middle of the street with no cover at all for more than a minute, firing continuously, so that Seeger could get away alive. And he thought of the time outside Saint Lô when he had been wounded and had lain in a minefield for three hours and Welch and Captain Taney had come looking for him in the darkness and had found him and picked him up and run for it, all of them expecting to get blown up any second.

And he thought of all the drinks they'd had together, and the long marches and the cold winter together, and all the girls they'd gone out with together, and he thought of his father and brother crouching behind the window in Ohio waiting for the rockets and the crowds armed with Browning Automatic rifles.

"Say," he stopped and stood facing them. "Say, what do you guys think of the Jews?"

Welch and Olson loked at each other, and Olson glanced down at the letter in Seeger's hand.

"Jews?" Olson said finally. "What're they? Welch, you ever hear of the Jews?"

Welch looked thoughtfully at the gray sky. "No," he said. "But remember, I'm an uneducated fellow."

"Sorry, Bud," Olson said, turning to Seeger. "We can't help you. Ask us another question. Maybe we'll do better."

Seeger peered at the faces of his friends. He would have to rely upon them, later on, out of uniform, on their native streets, more than he had ever relied on them on the bullet-swept street and in the dark minefield in France. Welch and Olson stared back at him, troubled, their faces candid and tough and dependable.

"What time," Seeger asked, "did you tell that captain you'd meet him?"

"Eight o'clock," Welch said. "But we don't have to go. If you have any feeling about that gun . . ."

"We'll meet him," Seeger said. "We can use that sixty-five bucks."

"Listen," Olson said, "I know

how much you like that gun, and
I'll feel like a heel if you sell it."

"Forget it," Seeger said, starting

to walk again. "What could I use
it for in America?"

Questions for Analysis and Discussion

The narrator of this story is omniscient. He knows all about his characters, their personalities, backgrounds, and experiences. He tells this story about three soldiers in the American army just after the defeat of the Germans because he has a purpose in mind. What his purpose is we will discover later after we have analyzed some of the elements that make up the story.

1.   How do we know that the three soldiers—Sergeant Seeger and Privates Olson and Welch—are friends? What experiences, mentioned by the narrator, cemented this friendship? What do we learn about the personalities and backgrounds of the three men? Is there anything in the story to suggest that these men could have been friends even if they had not been in the army together? Would they have been friends, for example, if they had worked on the same job or in the same business? What qualities did they have in common? What made them good soldiers?

2.   Where were these soldiers stationed at this time? Why does the narrator introduce the fact that it is raining heavily and that the soldiers, when they walk from place to place, tread in deep mud? Does introducing the bad weather serve any purpose? Does it show that even in defeat of the enemy, war is hell? Would the story have suffered if the weather had been pleasant?

3.   Seeger borrows some money from his captain so he and his friends can have a holiday in Paris. But the money is insufficient. What kind of man is Captain Taney? Why does Seeger respect him? Why does Captain Taney respect Seeger? What in the character of these two men made it possible for Seeger to invite Taney to visit him and his family after the war?

4.   Since there is not enough money for the visit to Paris, Welch suggests that Seeger sell his German Luger. Why don't the soldiers have enough money for their furlough? How did Seeger get the

Luger? Why is the Luger so valuable an object to him? The narrator apparently wishes the reader to see the Luger as a symbol. At this point in the story what does the Luger symbolize? Why would Seeger hesitate to part with it? What information that we get later tells us what the Luger means to Seeger?

5. At what point in the story do we learn that Seeger is a Jew? What purpose does the narrator have in keeping from the reader, until Seeger reads the letter from his father, that Seeger is Jewish? Who gives Seeger the letter from his father? This fact, too, highlights a relationship the narrator has taken some trouble to establish. What relationship?

6. Why is Seeger's father writing to him? Why is the father unable to cope with the problem he describes in his letter to his son? Why does the narrator interrupt the continuity of the letter with comments, conversation, and singing by Olson and Welch? Why is the substance of the letter juxtaposed against the friendship of the two men for Seeger? In what way does this "foreshadow" the climax of the story? What do we learn from the letter about what is troubling Seeger's brother, Jacob? Seeger's father writes that he does not know the reasons for Jacob's neurotic behavior. He doesn't know, he says, what happened to Jacob in the army. Read the letter carefully. Is there enough information given you to explain sufficiently that a sensitive young man like Jacob could conclude that the Jews in America faced a danger similar to that faced by the Jews of Germany? Seeger's father says that it is possible that Jacob is normal and that he, going about his business as a teacher of economics, is the mad one because he is oblivious to the danger faced by the Jews of America. What dangers to the Jews does Seeger's father see in American life? Do you think he was right? Evaluate the place of the Jew in American life as you see it today. Are there extremist groups in America today that are antagonistic to Jews and other minority groups?

7. Does the narrator agree with the analysis of the situation of the Jew in America as defined by Seeger's father? On what does the narrator pin his hopes for a future for all minority groups in America? What relationship is there between the fears defined by Seeger's father and the purpose which the narrator had in mind when he told this story? What are the narrator's purposes in telling this story? What is the central theme of the story?

8. What memories did his father's letter awaken in Seeger? How do these memories reveal Seeger's Jewish consciousness? Do we

understand now why the Luger was so important to Seeger? What is meant symbolically by Seeger's decision to sell the Luger so that he and his friends may enjoy their holiday in Paris? Olson and Welch show their feelings for Seeger. The narrator thereby indicates that America is different from Germany. Does he succeed? Is it likely that Olson and Welch will deny Seeger? What had Olson done for Seeger? Would he do this again if Seeger were in danger in America?

9. The letter from his father evokes in Seeger memories of many stories in which Jews are insulted and reviled. The narrator suggests that in every Jew, as in every member of a minority group, there is a self-consciousness about his ethnic identity. If this is true, what can the Jew in America do to overcome this sensitivity? Seeger even envies his brother Leonard who died in battle and who thereby avoided the problem of returning to face anti-Semitism in America. Is this an exaggeration by the narrator? Is it believable that Seeger who was so outgoing, friendly, and so popular with his fellow soldiers, would feel this way? How had Olson, Welch, and Taney shown their friendship for him? The narrator says that Seeger realized he would have to rely on his friends if a movement against Jews ever developed in America. Was Seeger's faith in his friends justified? What does the narrator believe? What is the significance of the title, "Act of Faith"? Whose was the act of faith?

10. Fiction is often tendentious; that is, it is written to reveal to the reader what the author conceives to be an injustice or an evil. The incidents and relationships in such works are frequently "arranged" to support the author's view. This need not necessarily affect the quality of the author's literary effort. Some outstanding works of literature—*The Jungle, The Grapes of Wrath, An American Tragedy, The Invisible Man, The Victim*—were written to expose evils. Evaluate "Act of Faith." Has the author "arranged" events and relationships to such an extent that the story lacks artistic integrity? Or has he presented his case in such honest, truthful, and human terms as to produce a fine work of literature?

Suggested Activities

1. Make a study of conditions in the military during World War II to determine the extent of prejudice toward minority groups that prevailed in the army, navy, and air force. An interesting project would be to analyze conditions in the armed forces as revealed in the following works:

> James Jones   *From Here to Eternity*
> Philip Roth   *Defender of the Faith*
> Norman Mailer   *The Naked and the Dead*
> John Hersey   *A Bell for Adano*
> Herman Wouk   *The Caine Mutiny*
> Joseph Heller   *Catch-22*
> Irwin Shaw   *The Young Lions*

2. Many Jews were prominent during the presidency of Franklin Delano Roosevelt, among them Felix Frankfurter, Sidney Hillman, Benjamin V. Cohen, Samuel Rosenman, Henry Morgenthau, Jr. Investigate the life of one of these men to determine what part he played in the program of the New Deal.

3. Make a study of the conditions in America that led to racist agitation against Jews between 1933 and 1945. Why were Jews attacked as radicals, international bankers, and warmongers? Why was Roosevelt referred to by racists as President Rosenfeld? Why did the anti-Semitic groups in America fail? Investigate the dangers of scapegoating, of stereotyping, and of forming broad generalizations about a people from the actions of a few.

4. Pretend that you are Seeger. Write the answer to his father's letter.

5. Pretend that you are Taney. Write the letter to his wife in which he tells her about some of the men in his regiment.

6. Analyze the attitude toward war that is revealed in this story. Is the narrator critical, patriotic, neutral? What do you think? If you have read Shaw's *The Young Lions,* is the attitude toward war in that novel different from the one in this story? What is your view of the narrator's reactions to the war? Write an essay recording the results of your analysis.

7. Translate "Act of Faith" into a radio play. Use one performer to serve as narrator to introduce the story and fill in narrative gaps. Another performer could read the letter Seeger's father sent him. The story provides most of the dialogue.

8. Read *It Can't Happen Here* written by Sinclair Lewis in 1935. Report to the class how Lewis envisioned the rise of fascism in America. Consider the following questions in your report.

a. Is America really different? Can the concentration camps and death camps happen here?

b. Can there ever be real security and peace in the world as long as even one small group of people is threatened?

c. What makes people hate one another? Can prejudice and discrimination be eradicated?

Ben Shahn. *Saturday in Louisiana.* 1935. U.S. Resettlement Administration.

By Jack Ansell

The Only One in Town

Introduction: **The Small Community in the South**

The first Jews to come to the South as a group were forty-one Jews from England. They came to Georgia in 1733 and were allowed to land by Colonel James Oglethorpe, a soldier, who sought to help the unhappy prisoners in English jails. Some of these unfortunate people were in jail because they could not pay their debts. Oglethorpe received permission from George II to establish a new colony in a tract of land that came to be called Georgia. The voyage of the Jewish immigrants was financed by wealthy English Jews who believed that this was a good way to help those of their compatriots who had recently arrived in London from other parts of Europe, many of them without any means of support.

These Jewish immigrants soon became active members of the colony, and most of them joined the Revolutionary forces in the struggle for independence. Two Southern Jews won fame as leaders in the war: Mordecai Sheftall, who served as commissary general for Georgia's militia and Continental troops, and Francis Salvador, who sat in the rebel provincial congress and who lost his life in a punitive expedition against enemy Indians. Salvador has been referred to by some historians as the "Southern Paul Revere."

During the nineteenth century, German Jews came to America seeking freedom and many settled in the South. They, too, in time, became active members of the communities in which they lived and contributed to their growth. They were joined in the latter nineteenth and early twentieth century by new immigrants from East Europe.

Most of the Jews who came to the South settled in the large cities. A few, however, went into the rural areas, and it was not surprising to find one or two Jewish storekeepers in the small towns of Georgia, Alabama, and the Carolinas with populations of from two to five thousand.

The Jews of the South were caught up in the conflicts of slavery and civil rights. During the Civil War almost all of them supported the Confederacy, and many of their sons died, defending the Confederacy. Judah P. Benjamin, a Jew, was Jefferson Davis's secretary of state. Though only a few Jews were plantation owners, and a few were merchants who bought and sold slaves, many well-to-do Jewish families had black household slaves. They had come over the years to accept the values and culture of their white neighbors. There were exceptions, however, as in the case of the famous Judah Touro of New Orleans, who publicly freed his slaves.

Although changes in attitude occurred during the years of movements to give civil rights to the blacks, the fears persisted. On the one hand, Jews were expected by the whites who were their neighbors and customers to join the white citizens' councils in actions against the blacks and their supporters. On the other hand, they were subjected to the harassment of fanatic groups like the Ku Klux Klan whose antagonism extended to blacks, Catholics, and Jews alike. Most Jews recognized the justice of the cause of the blacks, but they feared to become involved. Some of their religious leaders spoke out, and brought the wrath of white fanatics upon the Jewish community. People were threatened; temples were bombed; and Jewish communities became tense and worried.

Their insecurity was compounded when groups of Northern sympathizers came South to join in the civil rights movement. Once, for example, when nineteen Rabbis came South to join Martin Luther King, Jr., in protest against police violence in Birmingham, Alabama, the Jewish community was vexed. Its leaders finally persuaded the nineteen Rabbis to leave and let them deal with the problem in their way.

Others, however, came South and remained to join Martin Luther King, Jr., and his supporters in their marches for equal rights for black citizens. Two young Jewish lawyers with a black assistant, working in Mississippi to encourage black citizens to vote, were murdered by white fanatics who sought this way to stem the tide of the movement.

The Jews in the urban communities could unite in protest against violence directed against them. They could win the support of the

Christian clergy, the business community, and the press. It was the Jews in the outlying areas, in the small towns with highly bigoted populations, who faced serious problems of morality, principle, and conscience. This is the background of The Only One in Town *by Jack Ansell.*

THE TOWN of Twosboro is easy to miss, if you are driving more than thirty miles an hour along Highway 25. There is a small oak arrow on the left side of the road, and just below it the words, TWOSBORO 2 MILES. But there has been so much rain in the north-central areas of Louisiana lately that the *w*, the *s*, and the *b*, and the *r* have faded sadly, and are just now barely distinguishable. A speeding eye sees only *T O O O*, which has been mistaken for everything from a new kind of traffic sign to an advertisement for Toololoo's liver remedy, which is very popular in this part of the world. They have been so busy in Twosboro lately that no one has had time to repaint the wooden arrow.

Until last week there were one thousand seven hundred thirty-nine residents in Twosboro. Marcus and Lillian Greenbaum were the only Jews. They owned and operated one of the two clothing and dry-goods stores on Lacey Street, the seven-block business section of Twosboro, as had Marcus's father, Abram Greenbaum, before him. The firm of A. Greenbaum and Son was sixty-seven years old last week. Marcus was forty-six on Monday.

It started on Tuesday, just before noon. Marcus and his wife, Lillian, were stacking levis on the open counter to the right of the store's new all-glass door when Daniel Culp, the manager of the only supermarket in Twosboro, lumbered in. Daniel Culp always lumbers in, just as he always lumbers out. Daniel is a tall, rangy, candle-limbed man with a pallid face at once so round and so sad that it seems forever to be begging a return to the right body. Daniel never says hello or goodbye. He stares at you from baby's eyes until you feel guilty of some small neglect, then with an innocence so artless it turns you to marble, he says laconically what he has come to say. He said what he came to say on Tuesday.

"Marcus. We was some of us noticin' only a hour so ago how you was the only man in Twosboro not to been signed up by the White Citizens Council." He paused with a hint of forbearance. "We think you better do that little thing, Marcus."

Marcus Greenbaum, whose hair was thinning, ran his thick stubby fingers through the random strands along his forehead. "I told Chet Tulley when he came around last week I wasn't interested in joining anything, Daniel." he said. His wife, Lillian, looked down at the levis. Her eyes were anxious slits.

Daniel Culp's soft, high voice never changed its level. His voice is popular in Twosboro at the semi-annual Baptist revivals. "I tell you somethin', Marcus. Man's sure got a privilege of changin' his mind one week to the next. This week ain't last week. I ain't Chet Tulley, neither."

Marcus, who is a full head-and-a-half shorter, and considerably broader, looked slowly up. "You don't need me, Daniel. One member more or less doesn't make or break the Citizens Council."

"We need you, Marcus. Know what I mean? We need you. We got to have you, Marcus. Okay I send Chet back around?"

Marcus' lips were pale and pursed. "No need to, Daniel," he said.

Daniel leaned imperceptibly forward but he appeared to Marcus like a man toppling from stilts. "You got a love on for niggers, Marcus?" His brown infant's eyes were black.

Lillian Greenbaum's head jerked up like a frightened fowl's. The veins were heavy in Marcus's neck. "There's no need for that kind of talk between us, is there, Daniel?" It sounded less a question than a soliloquy. Marcus, who had never found a particular joy in talking, often sounded as though he were talking to himself.

Daniel Culp smiled. "Nobody means to be rude or nothin', Marcus, and we've knowed each other most all our lives I reckon, but it ain't hard in a town size of Twosboro for a Jew and a nigger to wind up in the same stall. I don't like bein' outspoken like that, Marcus, an' I'm only sayin' it for your own good. You an' your good folks been fine citizens since Twosboro come into bein' awmost, but this thing's big, Marcus, it's got everbody all worked up in nearbouts ever town around here. There's durn near as many niggers as there are whites in Pachatoula Parish, Marcus, and we got to be organized a hundred per cent proper. Why, them coons could get theirselves organized faster'n jackrabbits the way this NAACP thing's goin'. No matter what else you may of got wind of, all the Council's set out to do is see none of them radical notions starts stirrin' em up. An' maybe if any one of them black boogers starts yappin' 'bout his rights, sort of show him what his rightful place is. Lestways in Twosboro. Reckon you better sign up, Marcus. I'll tell ole Chet to drop back by. Nice to seen you, Lillian."

When Daniel Culp had lumbered out, candle-limber and candle-sallow, Lillian Greenbaum turned a plaintive face, and her voice was shrill. "You lost your head, Marcus? Have you gone and lost your senses, Marcus?

This goddern summertime heat got to you? It's not enough to be the only Jewish people in this town? You have to be God yet, too?"

Marcus seemed not to hear her. He didn't answer. A curious smile started to mingle with the return of color to his lips. He always smiled like that when he was hurt, or lonely. He began arranging the levis in small neat stacks again, studying his edged precision with a heavy, slow respect. He knew how it irritated Lillian, this terrible detachment he assumed now with such cruel deliberateness. But he couldn't do otherwise. There was no talking to Lillian anymore. He only ended up in some inarticulate corner, desperately stuttering the pathetic explanations for what he had yet to explain to himself.

His thick plodding fingers paralleled his thoughts. For the hundredth time since Chet Tulley had come by the store last week he asked himself what he was doing. He found no answer, not even the thinnest solace of pride. He was too small a man, he knew, to experience pride which somehow wasn't wanted or shared. He was alone, and he wasn't certain why.

It was strange. He was not a very smart man, and certainly not a brave man, and scarcely a man stirred to the bowels by the plights of whole races and creeds. If anything, he was a dismal, diffi-

dent man. These things he knew, or thought he knew. He was too simple a man to understand the maze of social consciousness, much less rear up to defend it. But when Chet Tulley had held out the small white card, itself so oddly anonymous, he had said "no" without pause or inflection. And all because of some confused chemistry in which he—who in Twosboro so often forgot he was a Jew—had suddenly, near shatteringly, remembered that he was. It was nothing he could turn into a convincing word, not even to Lillian. He recalled with a painful flush how he had said to her after Chet Tulley left the store, "I think maybe the first time in my life I'm near to knowing what it is to be a Jew," only to have her glower back as she might to a child or a fool. He had stayed to himself for hours after that, thinking about himself, and about Twosboro, and about being a Jew. He had known so few Jewish families in his life, outside his own and Lillian's. They went to nearby Mannerville or to Lillian's home in Vicksburg for the High Holy Days, but the rest of the year they were Jews in name only —in Twosboro, speaking the Twosboro tongue, thinking the Twosboro thought. And now for the first time in that life he was apart from the only people, the only home, he had ever really known. And no one to understand it, least of all himself. Here again, as always, his mind reached its stale dead end. His hands reached by rote for another stack of levis.

Lillian was raging on, as she had since last week. "What's a name on a piece of paper, Marcus? Nothing. Absolutely nothing. Lord! These people are our friends here, Marcus, they're the people we play gin with and watch television with. They're our customers, Marcus. Are you forgetting that, too? They're our *customers*. Do we play gin rummy with the *shvartsahs*? Are we living up north somewhere? This is the south, Marcus, it's Twosboro, we live right down here in Twosboro . . ."

Marcus heard her, and pretended he didn't; and he felt neither guilty nor noble; and he knew, almost dumbly, that the fear in her voice was not false.

On Wednesday, Chet Tulley—the only sober barber in Twosboro and an unkempt, faltering man—came by again, and held out the white card with calloused fingers and guarded eyes. Marcus said, as gently as he was able, "I'm sorry, Chet, but I just won't do it." Lillian's eyes moved heavenward, and for a moment glazed stunningly mad.

Daniel Culp returned on Thursday, bringing with him the president of the Pachatoula Bank and Trust, Adam Sanders, who is a quiet and prosperous man, and whose family in the early days of Twosboro had made it possible for Abram Greenbaum to settle there. Daniel Culp said little, while the benign banker—noted in Twosboro for licking the wounds which others have made—assured both Marcus and Lillian that they were two of the most highly respected people in the whole of Pachatoula Parish, as were Abram and Sarah Greenbaum before them, God rest their beloved souls, and that the only thing the good citizens of Twosboro were asking was that some nominal allegiance be given where allegiance was so assuredly due. Marcus, almost mesmerized by the deep honeyed drawl, thought for an instant he was actually agreeing to everything the ingratiating little man was saying, but when Daniel Culp said sharply, "We give you ever chance there is to give, Marcus. Don't blame us none whatever gits set loose now." He realized that a voice he could not rightly call his own had again managed the unqualified no.

That afternoon three Negro customers, to whom they had been selling for years and even used for odd jobs around the house, came into the store, and Lillian turned away from them with accusing abruptness, while Marcus waited on them with the dull familiarity of a lifetime, and tried—dispassionately—to bring them into some kind of balance with himself, and with Daniel Culp, and with Lillian and with Twosboro. And couldn't. They were colored and he was white. They were Negroes and he was . . . a Jew. He felt suddenly as implausibly ancient as he felt curiously unborn. He wished for a single exquisite second he might feel that what he was doing he was doing out of great wisdom or reason or truth. It seemed so simple to feel simple humanity. It seemed so barren to have to think, again and again, I cannot put my name to this injustice because I am a Jew. It seemed so foolish and so foreign in Twosboro. He wondered—as he watched the undaunted colored people laugh themselves like children out of the new glass door—what his father might have done in his place. But his image of his father was as dim as his own tired question. He was tired to his soul.

On Friday morning he and Lillian walked the ten short blocks from their house to the store, and it was almost as if he had expected to find exactly what he found. A. Greenbaum and Son was a jarring cavity in the center of Lacey Street. The glass window and door had been totally shattered, and there was nothing inside but overturned counters and racks, and random pieces of soiled material and torn clothing which looked foolishly like cast-offs at the end of a masquerade. Marcus gazed upon the scene as hollowly as it upon him; and although he was faintly aware of the deep gurgling noise in Lillian's throat, which sounded peculiarly as though she were drowning, he could not lift an arm to comfort her nor find the voice for anger.

They left Twosboro that night, saying little to themselves or each other. They drove to Mannerville, some fifty miles to the north, where he had a cousin, and only once during the still dark drive did a word pass between them. That was when Lillian, her head pressed against the plastic seat cover of the car, said between closed teeth, "Not even one of precious *shvartsahs* to tell us good-bye." But the words were merely a natural lining to the emptiness that clothed him. There was no one and nothing to fight. It was as if something had been ordered, something ordained, and he but its helpless purveyor.

Somebody remarked in Twosboro yesterday that since everybody in town is now solidly behind the Council it wouldn't hurt them any to get the sign on Highway 25 repainted. There are one thousand seven hundred and thirty-seven residents now of course, although Daniel Culp's wife, Mary Alice, is expecting another next month. There are six hundred and sixty-three Negroes and one thousand seventy-four whites. There are no Jews in Twosboro.

Questions for Analysis and Discussion

This is the story of a man struggling between the demands of earn-
ing a livelihood and the demands of principle and conscience.

1. What does the first paragraph tell you about the town of Twosboro, near New Orleans? What technique does the narrator use to
characterize the town? How large a town was it? How did Marcus and
Lillian Greenbaum come to be living in Twosboro? The narrator begins the second paragraph with the phrase "Until last week . . . ."
What is suggested by the phrase?

2. How does the narrator describe Daniel Culp? What was the
relationship between Daniel and the Greenbaums? Why does Daniel
want Marcus to join the White Citizens Council? The narrator tells
his story in the past tense, but once in a while, when he describes a
character, he uses the present tense. What in your view is his purpose
in doing this? Is it effective? What is Marcus's response to Daniel's
request that he join the White Citizens' Council?

3. The narrator moves into Marcus's mind. What are his thoughts?
How does Marcus see himself? What has his being Jewish to do with
his refusal, when Chet Tulley asked him, to join the White Citizens
Council?

4. Marcus's wife, Lillian, is appalled and frightened by his refusal.
Why? What are her arguments to persuade Marcus to join the
Council? Why is Marcus unable to answer her?

5. Adam Sanders joins Daniel Culp in an attempt to win Marcus
over. How does the narrator describe Adam? How is Marcus indebted
to him? What arguments does Adam use to persuade Marcus to join
the Council? What threats does Daniel use? Why is Marcus unmoved?

6. Again, the narrator lets us look into Marcus's mind. He is waiting on three black customers to whom he had been selling for years.
What are his thoughts? What are the reasons why he cannot join the
white people of Twosboro in their organization "to keep the blacks
in their place"?

7. How did the white community show its anger against Marcus?
Why did the Greenbaums leave Twosboro? Why didn't Marcus stay
and sue for damages? How did Lillian reproach Marcus? Do you

regard Marcus as heroic or foolish? Comment on the effectiveness of the last paragraph. The story is simply and sparsely written. It is objective and dispassionate. Do these qualities help to make it a good story? How?

Suggested Activities

1. Organize the class into a group, Christian and Jewish, representative of a southern community. The community has learned that a delegation of northern clergymen—Protestant, Catholic, and Jewish —is scheduled to arrive in their town to join in a protest against school segregation. Discuss plans on how to receive and deal with the delegation from the North.

2. Read Chapters 19, 20, and 21 in Eli N. Evans' *The Provincials* and Chapter 13 in Mark H. Elovitz's *A Century of Life in Dixie* (published by the University of Alabama Press). Report to the class your findings concerning the Jewish community's experience with white southern attitudes toward blacks and the moral dilemma faced by southern Jews when confronted with black militancy on behalf of civil rights.

3. Write a conversation between Daniel Culp and Adam Sanders about the refusal of Marcus Greenbaum to join the White Citizens Council of Twosboro. Would they be facing a moral dilemma in deciding to order the destruction of Marcus' store? Daniel was a friend and classmate of Marcus. They played together as children. Adam was a friend of Marcus' father. Would these facts make them hesitate about their decision?

4. Many blacks were Marcus' customers. Lillian believes that the blacks did not care that Marcus' business was ruined and that she and her husband were forced to leave town. Do you agree? Create a scene in the home of one of the blacks. Have him discuss with his wife and young son (an adolescent) what had happened to the Greenbaums. They might express regrets that a new storekeeper is not likely to extend credit to them or treat them so well. They might express surprise that Marcus acted as he did. In other words, determine how the blacks at Twosboro reacted to what happened to Marcus and

record it in dialogue. You might also include, if you wish, some reference to NAACP materials that they may have read.

5. Write an editorial for a newspaper which is read in Twosboro in which you comment on the treatment the Greenbaums received at the hands of their white neighbors. You might criticize Marcus for his stubbornness and foolishness. You might criticize the whites for their bigotry and cruelty. You might comment on Marcus' heroism. In other words, express your view concerning the events in Twosboro recorded in the story.

6. Read the passage in Eli N. Evans' *The Provincials* which describes the activities of Harry Golden, a New York East Side Jew, who moved to Charlotte, North Carolina, and published a newspaper called *The Carolina Israelite* (pages 315–317). (The articles in the newspaper served Golden well for they were the grist for the many books he wrote on the Jewish experience in America. You may be interested in reading his book about the southern Jewish experience called *Our Southern Landsman.*) Prepare an oral report on Golden's humorous plans for dealing with segregation. In your report comment on whether in your view these "plans" are or are not effective in "poking holes in southern segregation."

Via Della Reginella. Courtesy of Leni Sonnenfeld.

By Arthur Miller

Monte Sant' Angelo

Introduction: **Identity**

In The Secret Jews *Joachim Prinz mentions unusual customs that were observed in Catholic homes in different parts of the world. The people who observed the customs or performed the rituals did not know why they did these things, only that it was a tradition with them handed down from the past. In one home in a remote village in Brazil an ancient parchment called* Mizrach *hung on the eastern wall to indicate the direction one must face when praying. In another home, the father would wrap himself once a year in the fall in a white sheet with black stripes, pray from a special book, and not eat from sundown on one day to sundown of the next. Without knowing it, he was observing Yom Kippur, the Day of Atonement. In Rio de Janeiro, wealthy women of a certain class would stop activities on Friday afternoons, get home before sunset, spread a white cloth on their dining room table, and light candles. Without knowing it and without reciting prayers, they were celebrating the arrival of the Jewish Sabbath.*

In the history of the Jewish people, many attempts were made to convert them to the prevailing religion of the country. Not all Jews remained loyal to their faith. Frequently, those who converted under threat of death or expulsion secretly retained as many of the customs and rituals as were possible. As time went by some of the observances remained though the reasons for them were forgotten.

During the time of the Spanish Inquisition, large numbers of Jews converted. They became known as conversos *or* marranos. *They had hoped to attain security as converted Catholics, but this was not to be. They were spied upon, and when it was discovered that they practiced a Jewish custom in secret, they were denounced to the Inquisition and suffered the tortures of interrogation and punishment for heresy. In fear and desperation, many left the country, going to the newly founded colonies in South America or to countries in Europe which were not so fanatic. Away from the excessively diligent spies and inquisitors, some openly identified themselves as Jews. Others, however, reverted to Jewish ways without relinquishing their newly adopted Catholicism. That is why in some Catholic homes in South America and Europe—even in Spain, France, and Italy, the centers of Catholicism—remnants of Jewish practice may be found. For the Jew who encounters them it often provides a link to his past and a reminder of the cruel treatment his people have had to endure. At times, it strengthens his sense of Jewish identity.*

THE DRIVER, who had been sitting up ahead in perfect silence for nearly an hour as they crossed the monotonous green of Foggia, now said something. Appello quickly leaned forward in the back seat and asked him what he had said.

"That is Monte Sant' Angelo before you."

Appello lowered his head to see through the windshield of the rattling little Fiat. Then he nudged Bernstein, who awoke resentfully, as though his friend had intruded. "That's the town up there," Appello said. Bernstein's annoyance vanished, and he bent forward. They both sat that way for several minutes, watching the approach of what seemed to them a comically situated town, even more comic than any they had seen in the four weeks they had spent moving from place to place in the country. It was like a tiny old lady living on a high roof for fear of thieves.

The plain remained as flat as a table for a quarter of a mile ahead. Then out of it, like a pillar, rose the butte; squarely and rigidly skyward it towered, only narrowing as it reached its very top. And there, barely visible now, the town crouched, momentarily obscured by white clouds, then appearing again tiny and safe, like a mountain port looming at the end of the sea. From their distance they could make out no road, no approach at all up the side of the pillar.

"Whoever built that was awfully frightened of something," Bernstein said, pulling his coat closer around him. "How do they get up there? Or do they?"

Appello, in Italian, asked the driver about the town. The driver, who had been there only once before in his life and knew no other who had made the trip—despite his being a resident of Lucera, which was not far away —told Appello with some amusement that they would soon see how rarely anyone goes up or comes down Monte Sant' Angelo. "The donkeys will kick and run away as we ascend, and when we come into the town everyone will come out to see. They are very far from everything. They all look like brothers up there. They don't know very much either." He laughed.

"What does the Princeton chap say?" Bernstein asked.

The driver had a crew haircut, a turned-up nose, and a red round face with blue eyes. He owned the car, and although he spoke like any Italian when his feet were on the ground, behind his wheel with two Americans riding behind him he had only the most amused and superior attitude toward everything outside the windshield. Appello, having translated for Bernstein, asked him how long it would take to ascend. "Perhaps three quarters of an hour—as long as the mountain is," he amended.

Bernstein and Appello settled back and watched the butte's approach. Now they could see that its sides were crumbling white stone. At this closer vantage it seemed as though it had been struck a terrible blow by some monstrous hammer that had split its structure into millions of seams. They were beginning to climb now, on a road of sharp broken rocks.

"The road is Roman," the driver remarked. He knew how much Americans made of anything Roman. Then he added, "The car, however, is from Milan." He and Appello laughed.

And now the white chalk began drifting into the car. At their elbows the altitude began to seem threatening. There was no railing on the road, and it turned back on itself every two hundred yards in order to climb again. The Fiat's doors were wavering in their frames; the seat on which they sat kept inching forward onto the floor. A fine film of white talc settled onto their clothing and covered their eyebrows. Both together began to cough. When they were finished Bernstein said, "Just so I understand it clearly and without prejudice, will you explain again in words of one syllable, why the hell we are climbing this lump of dust, old man?"

Appello laughed and mocked a punch at him.

"No kidding," Bernstein said, trying to smile.

"I want to see this aunt of mine, that's all." Appello began taking it seriously.

"You're crazy, you know that? You've got some kind of ancestor complex. All we've done in this country is look for your relatives."

"Well, Jesus, I'm finally in the country, I want to see all the places I came from. You realize that two of my relatives are buried in a crypt in the church up there? In eleven hundred something."

"Oh, is this where the monks come from?"

"Sure, the two Appello brothers. They helped build that church. It's very famous, that church. Supposed to be Saint Michael appeared in a vision or something."

"I never thought I'd know anybody with monks in his family. But I still think you're cracked on the whole subject."

"Well, don't you have any feeling about your ancestors? Wouldn't you like to go back to Austria or wherever you come from and see where the old folks lived? Maybe find a family that belongs to your line, or something like that?"

Bernstein did not answer for a moment. He did not know quite what he felt and wondered dimly whether he kept ragging his friend a little because of envy. When they had been in the country courthouse where Appello's grandfather's portrait and his great-grandfather's hung—both renowned provincial magistrates; when they had spent the night in Lucera where the name Appello meant something distinctly honorable, and where his friend Vinny was taken in hand and greeted in that intimate way because he was an Appello—in all those moments Bernstein had felt left out and somehow deficient. At first he had taken the attitude that all the fuss was childish, and yet as incident after incident, landmark after old landmark, turned up echoing the name Appello, he gradually began to feel his friend combining with this history, and it seemed to him that it made Vinny stronger, somehow

less dead when the time would come for him to die.

"I have no relatives that I know of in Europe," he said to Vinny. "And if I had they'd have all been wiped out by now."

"Is that why you don't like my visiting this way?"

"I don't say I don't like it," Bernstein said and smiled by will. He wished he could open himself as Vinny could; it would give him ease and strength, he felt. They stared down at the plain below and spoke little.

The chalk dust had lightened Appello's black eyebrows. For a fleeting moment it occurred to Appello that they resembled each other. Both were over six feet tall, both broad-shouldered and dark men. Bernstein was thinner, quite gaunt and long-armed. Appello was stronger in his arms and stooped a little, as though he had not wanted to be tall. But their eyes were not the same. Appello seemed a little Chinese about the eyes, and they glistened black, direct, and for women, passionately. Bernstein gazed rather than looked; for him the eyes were dangerous when they could be fathomed, and so he turned them away often, or downward, and there seemed to be something defensively cruel, and yet gentle there.

They liked each other not for reasons so much as for possibilities; it was as though they both had sensed they were opposites.

And they were lured to each other's failings. With Bernstein around him Appello felt diverted from his irresponsible sensuality, and on this trip Bernstein often had the pleasure and pain of resolving to deny himself no more.

The car turned a hairpin curve with a cloud below on the right, when suddenly the main street of the town arched up before them. There was no one about. It had been true, what the driver had predicted—in the few handkerchiefs of grass that they had passed on the way up the donkeys had bolted, and they had seen shepherds with hard mustaches and black shakos and long black cloaks who had regarded them with the silent inspection of those who live far away. But here in the town there was no one. The car climbed onto the main street, which flattened now, and all at once they were being surrounded by people who were coming out of their doors, putting on their jackets and caps. They did look strangely related, and more Irish than Italian.

The two got out of the Fiat and inspected the baggage strapped to the car's roof, while the driver kept edging protectively around and around the car. Appello talked laughingly with the people, who kept asking why he had come so far, what he had to sell, what he wanted to buy, until he at last made it clear that he was looking only for his aunt. When he said the name the men (the women remained at home, watching from the window) looked blank, until an old man wearing rope sandals and a knitted skating cap came forward and said that he remembered such a woman. He then turned, and Appello and Bernstein followed up the main street with what was now perhaps a hundred men behind them.

"How come nobody knows her?" Bernstein asked.

"She's a widow. I guess she stays home most of the time. The men in the line died out here twenty years ago. Her husband was the last Appello up here. They don't go much by women; I bet this old guy remembered the name because he knew her husband by it, not her."

The wind, steady and hard, blew through the town, washing it, laving its stones white. The sun was cool as a lemon, the sky purely blue, and the clouds so close their keels seemed to be sailing through the next street. The two Americans began to walk with the joy of it in their long strides. They came to a two-story stone house and went up a dark corridor and knocked. The guide remained respectfully on the sidewalk.

There was no sound within for a few moments. Then there was —short scrapes, like a mouse that started, stopped, looked about, started again. Appello knocked once more. The doorknob turned, and the door opened a foot. A pale little woman, not very old at all, held the door wide enough for her face to be seen. She seemed very worried.

"Ha?" she asked.

"I am Vincent Georgio."

"Ha?" she repeated.

"Vincenzo Giorgio Appello."

Her hand slid off the knob, and she stepped back. Appello, smiling in his friendly way, entered, with Bernstein behind him closing the door. A window let the sun flood the room, which was nevertheless stone cold. The woman's mouth was open, her hands were pressed together as in prayer, and the tips of her fingers were pointing at Vinny. She seemed crouched, as though about to kneel, and she could not speak.

Vinny went over to her and touched her bony shoulder and pressed her into a chair. He and Bernstein sat down too. He told her of their relationship, saying names of men and women, some of whom were dead, others whom she had only heard of and never met in this sky place. She spoke at last, and Appello could not understand what she said. She ran out of the room suddenly.

"I think she thinks I'm a ghost or something. My uncle said she hadn't seen any of the family in twenty-five years. I bet she doesn't think there are any left."

She returned with a bottle that had an inch of wine at the bottom of it. She ignored Bernstein and gave Appello the bottle. He drank. It was vinegar. Then she started to whimper and kept wiping the tears out of her eyes in order to see Appello. She never finished a sentence, and Appello kept asking her what she meant. She kept running from one corner of the room to another. The rhythm of her departures and returns to the chair was getting so wild that Appello raised his voice and commanded her to sit.

"I'm not a ghost, Aunty. I came here from America—" He stopped. It was clear from the look in her bewildered, frightened eyes that she had not thought him a ghost at all, but what was just as bad —if nobody had ever come to see her from Lucera, how could anybody have so much as thought of her in America, a place that did exist, she knew, just as heaven existed and in exactly the same way. There was no way to hold a conversation with her.

They finally made their exit, and she had not said a coherent word except blessing, which was her way of expressing her relief that Appello was leaving, for despite the unutterable joy at having seen with her own eyes another of her husband's blood, the sight was itself, too terrible in its associations, and in the responsibility it laid upon her to welcome him and make him comfortable.

They walked toward the church now. Bernstein had not been able to say anything. The woman's emotion, so pure and violent and wild, had scared him. And yet, glancing at Appello, he was amazed to see that his friend had drawn nothing but a calm sort of satisfaction from it, as though his aunt had only behaved correctly. Dimly he remembered himself as a boy visiting an aunt of his in the Bronx, a woman who had not been in touch with the family and had never seen him. He remembered how forcefully she had fed him, pinched his cheeks, and smiled and smiled every time he looked up at her, but he knew that there was nothing of this blood in that encounter; nor could there be for him now if on the next street corner he should meet a woman who said she was of his family. If anything, he would want to get away from her, even though he had always gotten along well with his people and hadn't even the usual snobbery about them.

As they entered the church he said to himself that some part of him was not plugged-in, but why he should be disturbed about it mystified him and even made him irritated with Appello, who was asking the priest where the tombs of the Appellos were.

They descended into the vault of the church, where the stone door was partly covered with water. Along the walls, and down twisting corridors running out of a central arched hall, were tombs so old no candle could illuminate most of the worn inscriptions. The priest vaguely remembered an Appello vault, but had no idea where it was. Vinny moved from one crypt to another with the candle he had bought from the priest. Bernstein waited at the opening of the corridor, his neck bent to avoid touching the roof with his hat. Appello, stooped even more than usual, looked like a monk himself, an antiquary, a gradually disappearing figure squinting down the long darkness of the ages for his name on a stone. He could not find it. Their feet were getting soaked. After an hour they left the church and outside fought off shivering small boys selling grimy religious postcards, which the wind kept taking from their fists.

"I'm sure it's there," Appello said with fascinated excitement. "But you wouldn't want to stick out a search, would you?" he asked hopefully.

"This is no place for me to get pneumonia," Bernstein said.

They had come to the end of a side street. They had passed shops in front of which pink lambs hung head down with their legs stiffly jutting out over the sidewalk. Bernstein shook hands with one and imagined for Vinny a scene for Chaplin in which a monsignor would meet him here, reach out to shake his hand, and find the cold lamb's foot in his grip, and Chaplin would be mortified. At the street's end they scanned the endless sky and looked over the precipice upon Italy.

"They might even have ridden horseback down there, in armor —Appellos." Vinny spoke raptly.

"Yeah, they probably did," Bernstein said. The vision of Appello in armor wiped away any desire to kid his friend. He felt alone, desolate as the dried-out chalk sides of this broken pillar he stood upon. Certainly there had been no knights in his family.

He remembered his father's telling of his town in Europe, a common barrel of water, a town idiot, a baron nearby. That was all he had of it, and no pride, no pride in it at all. Then I am an American, he said to himself. And yet in that there was not the power of Appello's narrow passion. He looked at Appello's profile and felt the warmth of that gaze upon Italy and wondered if any American had ever felt like this in the States. He had never in his life sensed so strongly that the past could be peopled, so vivid with generations, as it had been with Vinny's aunt an hour ago. A common water barrel, a town idiot, a baron who lived nearby. . . . It had nothing to do with *him*. And standing there he sensed a broken part of himself and wondered with a slight amusement if this was what a child felt on discovering that the parents who brought him up were not his own,

and that he entered his house not from warmth but from the street, from a public and disordered place. . . .

They sought and found a restaurant for lunch. It was at the other edge of the town and overhung the precipice. Inside, it was one immense room with fifteen or twenty tables; the front wall was lined with windows overlooking the plain below. They sat at a table and waited for someone to appear. The restaurant was cold. They could hear the wind surging against the window-panes, and yet the clouds at eye level moved serenely and slow. A young girl, the daughter of the family, came out of the kitchen, and Appello was questioning her about food when the door to the street opened and a man came in.

For Bernstein there was an abrupt impression of familiarity with the man, although he could not fathom the reason for his feeling. The man's face looked Sicilian, round, dark as earth, high cheekbones, broad jaw. He almost laughed aloud as it instantly occurred to him that he could converse with this man in Italian. When the waitress had gone, he told this to Vinny, who now joined in watching the man.

Sensing their stares, the man looked at them with a merry flicker of his cheeks and said, "*Buon giorno.*"

"*Buon giorno,*" Bernstein replied across the four tables between them, and then to Vinny, "Why do I feel that about him?"

"I'll be damned if I know," Vinny said, glad now that he could join his friend in a mutually interesting occupation.

They watched the man, who obviously ate here often. He had already set a large package down on another table and now put his hat on a chair, his jacket on another chair, and his vest on a third. It was as though he were making companions of his clothing. He was in the prime of middle age and very rugged. And to the Americans there was something mixed up about his clothing. His jacket might have been worn by a local man; it was tight and black and wrinkled and chalkdust-covered. His trousers were dark brown and very thick, like a peasant's, and his shoes were snubbed up at the ends and of heavy leather. But he wore a black hat, which was unusual up here where all had caps, and he had a tie. He wiped his hands before loosening the knot; it was a striped tie, yellow and blue, of silk, and no tie to be bought in this part of the world, or worn by these people. And there was a look in his eyes that was not a peasant's inward stare; nor did it have the innocence of the other men who had looked at them on the streets here.

The waitress came with two dishes of lamb for the Americans. The man was interested and looked across his table at the meat and at the strangers. Bernstein glanced at the barely cooked flesh and said, "There's hair on it."

Vinny called the girl back just as she was going to the newcomer and pointed at the hair.

"But it's lamb's hair," she explained simply.

They said, "Oh," and pretended to begin to cut into the faintly pink flesh.

"You ought to know better, signor, than to order meat today."

The man looked amused, and yet it was unclear whether he might not be a trifle offended.

"Why not?" Vinny asked.

"It's Friday, signor," and he smiled sympathetically.

"That's right!" Vinny said although he had known all along.

"Give me fish," the man said to the girl and asked with intimacy about her mother, who was ill these days.

Bernstein had not been able to turn his eyes from the man. He could not eat the meat and sat chewing bread and feeling a rising urge to go over to the man, to speak to him. It struck him as being insane. The whole place— the town, the clouds in the streets, the thin air—was turning into a hallucination. He knew this man. He was sure he knew him. Quite clearly that was impossible. Still, there was a thing beyond the impossibility of which he was drunkenly sure, and it was that if he dared he could start speaking Italian fluently with this man. This was the first moment since leaving America that he had not felt the ill-ease of traveling and of being a traveler. He felt as comfortable as Vinny now, it seemed to him. In his mind's eye he could envisage the inside of the kitchen; he had a startlingly clear image of what the cook's face must be like, and he knew where a certain kind of soiled apron was hung.

"What's the matter with you?" Appello asked.

"Why?"

"The way you're looking at him."

"I want to talk to him."

"Well, talk to him," Vinny smiled.

"I can't speak Italian, you know that."

"Well, I'll ask him. What do you want to say?"

"Vinny—" Bernstein started to speak and stopped.

"What?" Appello asked, leaning his head closer and looking down at the tablecloth.

"Get him to talk. Anything. Go ahead."

Vinny, enjoying his friend's strange emotionalism, looked looked across at the man, who was now eating with careful but immense satisfaction. "Scusi, signor."

The man looked up.

"I am a son of Italy from Amer-

ica. I would like to talk to you. We're strange here."

The man, chewing deliciously, nodded with his amiable and amused smile and adjusted the hang of his jacket on the nearby chair.

"Do you come from around here?"

"Not very far."

"How is everything here?"

"Poor. It is always poor."

"What do you work at, if I may ask?"

The man had now finished his food. He took a last long drag of his wine and got up and proceeded to dress and pull his tie up tightly. When he walked it was with a slow, wide sway, as though each step had to be conserved.

"I sell cloth here to the people and the stores, such as they are," he said. And he walked over to the bundle and set it carefully on a table and began untying it.

Bernstein's cheeks began to redden. From where he sat he could see the man's broad back, ever so slightly bent over the bundle. He could see the man's hands working at the knot and just a corner of the man's left eye. Now the man was laying the paper away from the two bolts of cloth, carefully pressing the wrinkles flat against the table. It was as though the brown paper were valuable leather that must not be cracked or rudely bent. The waitress came out of the kitchen with a tremendous round loaf of bread at least two feet in diameter. She gave it to him, and he placed it flat on top of the cloth, and the faintest feather of a smile curled up on Bernstein's lips. Now the man folded the paper back and brought the string around the bundle and tied the knot, and Bernstein uttered a little laugh, a laugh of relief.

Vinny looked at him, already smiling, ready to join the laughter, but mystified. "What's the matter?" he asked.

Bernstein took a breath. There was something a little triumphant, a new air of confidence and superiority in his face and voice. "He's Jewish, Vinny," he said.

Vinny turned to look at the man. "Why?"

"The way he works that bundle. It's exactly the way my father used to tie a bundle—and my grandfather. The whole history is packing bundles and getting away. Nobody else can be as tender and delicate with bundles. That's a Jewish man tying a bundle. Ask him his name."

Vinny was delighted. "Signor," he called with that warmth reserved in his nature for members of families.

The man, tucking the end of the string into the edge of the paper, turned to them with his kind smile.

"May I ask your name, signor?"

"My name? Mauro di Benedetto."

"Mauro di Benedetto. Sure!"

Vinny laughed, looking at Bernstein. "That's Morris of the Blessed. Moses."

"Tell him I'm Jewish," Bernstein said, a driving eagerness charging his eyes.

"My friend is Jewish," Vinny said to the man, who now was hoisting the bundle onto his shoulder.

"Heh?" the man asked, confused by their sudden vivacity. As though wondering if there were some sophisticated American point he should have understood, he stood there smiling blankly, politely, ready to join in this mood.

"*Judeo*, my friend."

"*Judeo?*" he asked, the willingness to get the joke still holding the smile on his face.

Vinny hesitated before this steady gaze of incomprehension. "*Judeo*. The people of the Bible," he said.

"Oh, yes, yes!" The man nodded now, relieved that he was not to be caught in ignorance. "*Ebreo*," he corrected. And he nodded to Bernstein and seemed a little at a loss for what they expected him to do next.

"Does he know what you mean?" Bernstein asked.

"Yeah, he said 'Hebrew,' but it doesn't seem to connect. Signor," he addressed the man, "why don't you have a glass of wine with us? Come, sit down."

"Thank you, signor," he replied appreciatively, "but I must be home by sundown and I'm already a little late."

Vinny translated, and Bernstein told him to ask why he had to be home by sundown.

The man apparently had never considered the question before. He shrugged and laughed and said, "I don't know. All my life I get home for dinner on Friday night, and I like to come into the house before sundown. I suppose it's a habit; my father—you see, I have a route I walk, which is this route. I first did it with my father, and he did it with his father. We are known here for many generations past. And my father always got home on Friday night before sundown. It's a manner of the family, I guess."

"*Shabbas* begins at sundown on Friday night," Bernstein said when Vinny had translated. "He's even taking home the fresh bread for the Sabbath. The man is a Jew, I tell you. Ask him, will you?"

"*Scusi*, signor," Vinny smiled. "My friend is curious to know whether you are Jewish."

The man raised his thick eyebrows not only in surprise but as though he felt somewhat honored by being identified with something exotic. "Me?" he asked.

"I don't mean American," Vinny said, believing he had caught the meaning of the man's glance at Bernstein. "*Ebreo*," he repeated.

The man shook his head, seeming a little sorry he could not oblige Vinny. "No," he said. He was ready to go but wanted to pursue what obviously was his most interesting conversation in weeks. "Are they Catholics? The Hebrews?"

"He's asking me if Jews are Catholics," Vinny said.

Bernstein sat back in his chair, a knotted look of wonder in his eyes. Vinny replied to the man, who looked once again at Bernstein as though wanting to investigate this strangeness further, but his mission drew him up and he wished them good fortune and said good-bye. He walked to the kitchen door and called thanks to the girl inside, saying the loaf would warm his back all the way down the mountain, and he opened the door and went out into the street and the sunshine, waving to them as he walked away.

They kept repeating their amazement on the way back to the car, and Bernstein told again how his father wrapped bundles. "Maybe he doesn't know he's a Jew, but how could he not know what Jews are?" he said.

"Well, remember my aunt in Lucera?" Vinny asked. "She's a school-teacher, and she asked me if you believed in Christ. She didn't know the first thing about it. I think the ones in these small towns who ever heard of Jews think they're a Christian sect of some kind. I knew an old Italian once who thought all Negroes were Jews and white Jews were only converts."

"But his name . . ."

"Benedetto is an Italian name too. I never heard of 'Mauro' though. 'Mauro' is strictly from the old sod."

"But if he had a name like that, wouldn't it lead him to wonder if. . . ?"

"I don't think so. In New York the name 'Salvatore' is turned into 'Sam.' Italians are great for nicknames; the first name never means much. 'Vicenzo' is "Enzo,' or 'Vinny' or even 'Chico.' Nobody would think twice about 'Mauro' or damn near any other first name. He's obviously a Jew, but I'm sure he doesn't know it. You could tell, couldn't you? He was baffled."

"But, my God, bringing home a bread for *Shabbas!*" Bernstein laughed, wide-eyed.

They reached the car, and Bernstein had his hand on the door but stopped before opening it and turned to Vinny. He looked heated; his eyelids seemed puffed. "It's early. If you still want to I'll go back to the church with you. You can look for the boys."

Vinny began to smile, and then they both laughed together, and Vinny slapped him on the back and gripped his shoulder as though to hug him. "Goddam, now you're starting to enjoy this trip!"

As they walked briskly toward the church the conversation returned always to the same point, when Bernstein would say, "I don't know why, but it gets me. He's not only acting like a Jew, but an Orthodox Jew. And doesn't even know—I mean it's strange as hell to me."

"You look different, you know that?" Vinny said.

"Why?"

"You do."

"You know a funny thing?" Bernstein said quietly as they entered the church and descended into the vault beneath it. "I feel like—at home in this place. I can't describe it."

Beneath the church, they picked their way through the shallower puddles on the stone floor, looking into vestibules, opening doors, searching for the priest. He appeared at last—they could not imagine from where—and Appello bought another candle from him and was gone in the shadows of the corridors where the vaults were.

Bernstein stood—everything was wet, dripping. Behind him, flat and wide, rose the stairway of stones bent with the tread of millions. Vapor steamed from his nostrils. There was nothing to look at but shadow. It was dank and black and low, an entrance to hell. Now and then in the very far distance he could hear a step echoing, another, then silence. He did not move, seeking the root of an ecstasy he had not dreamed was part of his nature; he saw the amiable man trudging down the mountains, across the plains, on routes marked out for him by generations of men, a nameless traveler carrying home a warm bread on Friday night—and kneeling in church on Sunday. There was an irony in it he could not name. And yet pride was running through him. Of what he should be proud he had no clear idea; perhaps it was only that beneath the brainless crush of history a Jew had secretly survived, shorn of his consciousness but forever caught by that final impudence of a Saturday Sabbath in a Catholic country; so that his very unawareness was proof, a proof as mute as stones, that a past lived. A past for me, Bernstein thought, astounded by its importance for him, when in fact he had never had a religion or even, he realized now, a history.

He could see Vinny's form approaching in the narrow corridor of crypts, the candle flame flattening in the cold draft. He felt he would look differently into Vinny's eyes; his condescension had gone and with it a certain embarrassment. He felt loose, somehow the equal of his friend—and how odd that was when, if anything, he had thought of himself as superior. Suddenly, with

Vinny a yard away, he saw that his life had been covered with an unrecognized shame.

"I found it! It's back there!" Vinny was laughing like a young boy, pointing back toward the dark corridor.

"That's great, Vinny," Bernstein said. "I'm glad."

They were both stooping slightly under the low, wet ceiling, their voices fleeing from their mouths in echoed whispers. Vinny held still for an instant, catching Bernstein's respectful happiness, and saw there that his search was not worthless sentiment. He raised the candle to see Bernstein's face better, and then he laughed and gripped Bernstein's wrist and led the way toward the flight of steps that rose to the surface. Bernstein had never liked anyone grasping him, but from this touch of a hand in the darkness there was no implication of a hateful weakness.

They walked side by side down the steep street away from the church. The town was empty again. The air smelled of burning charcoal and olive oil. A few pale stars had come out. The shops were all shut. Bernstein thought of Mauro di Benedetto going down the winding, rocky road, hurrying against the setting of the sun.

Questions for Analysis and Discussion

This story deals with identity, with the psychological necessity of people to see themselves as links in a chain of ethnic experiences that go into the past and give substance to their present.

1. Appello and Bernstein are close friends, even though one is Italian Catholic and the other Jewish. What information does the author give you to explain the basis of this friendship?

2. What is the author's attitude toward Appello and Bernstein? Does he show any sympathy, affection, or concern for them? Is he subjective, objective, or indifferent? How does he reveal his feelings for the characters he has created?

3. Is the situation a believable one? Would a young Jew accompany an Italian friend on a pilgrimage to Italy and join his friend in learning of his past and reestablishing contact with his relatives? What values could such an experience have for Bernstein? What satisfactions could two friends get traveling in Italy, if one of them spends time seeking out relatives or searching for tombs?

4. The author stops to describe the two friends. In what ways are they alike and in what ways different? Does the author make clear why the two were such close friends? Why is Bernstein uncomfortable when relatives greet Vinny in the warm, intimate way that one addresses members of one's family? Is he envious? What does he say about his own family? What has prevented him from establishing ties with his own family? He says to himself that "some part of him was not plugged in." What does he mean? What do you suppose separated Bernstein from emotional ties to his family? What seems to be the nature of the ignorance of his ancestry when one compares him to Appello? What memories does he have of the town his father came from?

5. What does the author tell you of the town of Monte Sant' Angelo? What does he tell you about the inhabitants? What do you learn of the customs and ways of the people? Does the author give you enough information? From your point of view, has he omitted anything you wanted to know? When the young men reach the center of town, only the men and boys come out to greet them. Where are the women? Why don't they, too, come out to greet the visitors?

6. How is Appello received by his aunt? Why does she ignore Bernstein? What social amenities does she observe? Why is she made so uncomfortable by the presence of her two visitors? Why isn't Appello disturbed by her incoherence when they are with her and by her relief when they leave?

7. What is Appello looking for in the vault of the church in Monte Sant' Angelo? Why are the tombs he is seeking important to him? Why does he give up his search? Do you consider Vinny's search for the tombs and later his visions of ancestors in armor as he and his friend look over the precipice upon Italy as sentimental and romantic? Do you admire Vinny's enthusiasm for his past or do you find it foolish?

8. A man enters the restaurant where Bernstein and Appello are having lunch. Bernstein feels an immediate affinity for this man. Is this believable? Have you met a stranger who struck you as someone you know and for whom you felt a sudden warmth? What in the man's manner and action made Bernstein conclude that he was Jewish? He asks Vinny to question the man. What does he learn about him? What is the stranger's name? What is his religion? Bernstein wants Vinny to ask the man whether he is Jewish. What is the man's response? What does Mauro di Benedetto know about Jews? Why does the meeting with Mauro exhilarate Bernstein? He is now ready to join Vinny in trying again to find the tombs of Vinny's ancestors. Who were these ancestors? Why in your view did Bernstein's meeting with Mauro give him a sense of pride?

9. What in your view was the author's purpose in writing this story? Do you find any distortions, exaggerations, or inaccuracies in the story which result from the author's straining to punctuate his purpose? What elements in the story, if any, do you find unreal or unbelievable?

10. What are the themes of the story? What incidents in the story support these themes? One of the themes of the story concerns itself with the need for identity in mankind. Is the theme effectively and dramatically presented?

Suggested Activities

1. The story lends itself to a number of possible creative writing exercises:

   a. Pupils might be asked to write about an experience in their lives when they first became aware of their ethnic identity. One of course knows that one is Irish, Italian, Jewish, or Greek. But there comes a moment when one keenly feels a tie with one's past. Such a moment might be the theme of an autobiographical sketch.

   b. Pupils might be asked to put themselves in the place of Appello or Bernstein and write a letter home to a relative or friend describing any of the dramatic experiences of the story or creating a new experience.

   c. Pupils might be asked to write an account of a visit of Appello and Bernstein to the home of Mauro di Benedetto on a Friday night at Mauro's invitation. This project would require imagination in determining the size of Mauro's family and the relationships among the members and research in learning where and how such families live in small Italian towns.

   d. Pupils might be asked to write the diary or an account of an experience of one of the priests in the church where Appello finds the tomb of his ancestors.

   e. Pupils might be asked to write the dialogue of a conversation between Bernstein and one of his older relatives in which Bernstein learns about his family and how they came to America.

2. Pupils with artistic ability might be asked to draw illustrations for the story: the town perched on a hill in Italy, the restaurant where Appello and Bernstein met Mauro, the town piazza, the dank stone vault of the church where the tombs are, a portrait of Appello's aunt, the huge loaf of bread.

3. Pupils might be asked to trace their family trees as far back as they can go, getting information from elderly relatives. Black pupils, for example, may be able to trace their line to an ancestor who was a

slave. The ancestors of Chinese, Japanese, or Chicano students should be of great interest to the class.

4.   The class should be encouraged to discuss and debate the importance or the necessity of having an identity that is related to one's people and one's past. Those people in our country who can trace their ancestry all the way back to the Revolution can go even beyond that time to ancestors who came from countries of Europe. There will be some who will believe that the past is a drag on their lives, that they are ready to start anew unhampered by the attitudes and values of a remote and alien ancestry. This should lead to lively debate in the classroom.

5.   It would be worthwhile to analyze the differences in the way the Inquisition functioned in Spain and in Italy. Apparently, the Italian Catholic hierarchy was not so fanatic as were the bishops and priests of Spain. What accounted for this? A committee of pupils could make such a study and report to the class.

6.   An outstanding novel dealing with Spanish life in the new world and with activities of the Inquisition is Thornton Wilder's *The Bridge of San Luis Rey*. A pupil may be asked to read the novel and report on it, stressing the reason why Brother Juniper was found guilty of heresy by the Inquisition.

7.   There is a description of an auto-da-fe in Voltaire's *Candide*. Have a pupil read the account and report on it in class, stressing Voltaire's satiric intent.

8.   Many *marranos* fled to other European lands. Some redeclared themselves as Jews when they came to the New World. A follow-up on these would be a good subject for research. See *The Secret Jews* by Joachim Prinz (New York: Random House, 1973).

By Stanley Ellin

The Crime of Ezechiele Coen

Introduction: **The Holocaust in Rome**

In order better to appreciate this story, it is necessary to know what happened to the Jewish community of Rome when the Nazis occupied the city.

In 1938 after Hitler had visited Mussolini and a pact between their two countries was signed, fascist Italy introduced anti-Jewish laws. As depicted in the film The Garden of Finzi-Continis, *Jews soon began to feel the effects of the discriminatory laws, but it was not until the fall of Mussolini and fascism in July 1943 and the movement of German troops into Italy that the plight of Italy's Jews became serious.*

The Nazis occupied Rome on September 11, 1943. At the time there were 12,000 Jews in Rome, the majority of whom lived in an area that had been a ghetto from 1555 (when a wall was built around the Jewish section by Pope Paul IV) until 1870 when Italy became unified and Rome secularized. The walls were then torn down, but most of the Jews continued to live in the area.

Except for a few rich and prominent members, the Roman Jewish community, like its East-European counterpart, was poor. The people lived in old, squalid tenements and most made their living from peddling, selling goods in small stores, or engaging in crafts of various kinds. The very poor were aided by a central community agency supported by the wealthier Jews of the city. The one structure Roman Jews were proud of was their handsome synagogue, where rich and poor gathered to pray.

Attempts to save the Roman Jewish community from the onslaught of the Nazis failed. However, fears and warnings had sent many of them into hiding. Others had been able to get out of the country. On Saturday, October 16, a Jewish Sabbath, the Nazis began to round up the Jews for transportation to Auschwitz, one of their most notorious extermination camps. They rounded up 1124 men, women, and children and crowded them into trains. Only fifteen returned to Rome from that death camp.

The hatred of the Italian population for the Nazis, formerly their friends and allies, now their conquerors and enemies, became progressively stronger. A partisan movement arose to drive the Nazis out of Italy. A number of partisan groups operated in and around Rome, harassing the enemy and waiting for the liberating allied forces. Among the members of these groups were many Jews.

What happened to the Jews of Rome happened on a massive scale to the Jews in the rest of Europe. When the horrors of the Holocaust made their first impress on the mind of the American Jew, he could not and would not comprehend it. He pushed it into the back of his mind, expecting that it would dissipate with time. But it haunted him, especially at poignant intervals when events brought sharp reminders. Eventually, he came to realize that a cataclysm of such proportions could not be buried; that, in fact, it was necessary, if mankind was to survive, for the evil story to be told over and over again, and never to be forgotten. And so, more and more, the Jewish catastrophe in Europe began to appear in works of literature, art, and music, even in a mystery story such as The Crime of Ezechiele Coen.

BEFORE THE disenchantment set in, Noah Freeman lived in a whirl of impressions. The chaotic traffic. The muddy Tiber. The Via Veneto out of Italian movies about *la dolce vita*. The Fountain of Trevi out of Hollywood. Castel Sant' Angelo out of *Tosca*. Rome.

"Rome?" Pop had said. "But why Rome? Such a foreign place. And so far away."

True. But to old Pop Freeman, even Rockland County, an hour from New York, was far away, and his two weeks of vacation there every summer an adventure. And, in fact, it was unlikely that Pop had been too much surprised at his son's decision to go journeying afar. After all, this was the son who was going to be a doctor—at the very least a teacher —and who had become, of all things, a policeman.

"A policeman in the family," Pop would muse aloud now and then. "A detective with a gun in the family like on TV. My own son. What would Mamma say if she ever knew, may she rest in peace?"

But, Noah had to admit, the old man had been right about one thing, Rome was far, far away, not only from New York, but also from the blood-quickening image of it instilled in young Noah Freeman when he was a schoolboy soaking himself in gaudy literature about Spartacus and Caesar and Nero. And the Pensione Alfiara, hidden away in an alley off Via Arenula, was hardly a place to quicken anyone's blood. It took an ill wind to blow an occasional American tourist there. In Noah's case, the ill wind was the cab driver who had picked him up at Fiumicino airport and who happened to be Signora Alfiara's brother-in-law.

It was made to order for disenchantment, the Pensione Alfiara. Granted that it offered bargain rates, its cuisine was monotonous, its service indifferent, its plumbing capricious, and its clientele, at least in early March, seemed to consist entirely of elderly, sad-eyed Italian villagers come to Rome to attend the deathbed of a dear friend. Aside from Signora Alfiara herself and the girl at the portiere's desk, no one on the scene spoke English, so communication between Noah and his fellow boarders was restricted to nods and shrugs, well meant, but useless in relieving loneliness.

Its one marked asset was the girl at the portiere's desk. She was tall and exquisite, one of the few really beautiful women Noah had yet encountered in Rome, because among other disillusionments was the discovery that Roman women are not the women one sees in Italian movies. And she lived behind her desk from early morning to late at night as if in a sad, self-contained world of her own, skillful at her accounts, polite, but remote and disinterested.

She intrigued him for more than the obvious reasons. The English she spoke was almost unaccented. If anything, it was of the clipped British variety, which led him to wonder whether she might not be a Briton somehow washed up on the Roman shore. And at her throat on a fine gold chain was a Mogen David, a Star of David, announcing plainly enough that she was Jewish. The sight of that small, familiar ornament had startled him at first, then had emboldened him to make a friendly overture.

"As a fellow Jew," he had said smilingly, "I was wondering if you—" And she had cut in with chilling politeness, "Yes, you'll find the synagogue on Lungotevere dei Cenci, a few blocks south. One of the landmarks of this part of Rome. Most interesting, of course"—which was enough to send him off defeated.

After that, he regretfully put aside hopes of making her acquaintance and dutifully went his tourist way alone, the guidebook to Rome in his hand, the Italian phrase book in his pocket, trying to work up a sense of excitement at what he saw, and failing dismally at it. Partly, the weather was to blame—the damp, gray March weather which promised no break in the clouds overhead. And partly, he knew, it was loneliness—the kind of feeling that made him painfully envious of the few groups of tourists he saw here and there, shepherded by an officious guide, but at least chattering happily to each other.

But most of all—and this was something he had to force himself to acknowledge—he was not a tourist, but a fugitive. And what he was trying to flee was Detective Noah Freeman, who, unfortunately, was always with him and always would be. To be one of those plump, self-satisfied, retired businessmen gaping at the dome of St. Peter's, that was one thing; to be Noah Freeman was quite another.

It was possible that Signora Alfiara, who had a pair of bright, knowing eyes buried in her pudding face, comprehended his state of mind and decided with maternal spirit to do something about it. Or it was possible that, having learned his occupation, she was honestly curious about him. Whatever the reason, Noah was deeply grateful the morning she sat down at the table where he was having the usual breakfast of hard roll, acid coffee, and watery marmalade, and explained that she had seen at the cinema stories about American detectives, but that he was the first she had ever met. Very interesting. And was life in America as the cinema showed it? So much shooting and beating and danger? Had he ever been shot at? Wounded, perhaps? What a way of life! It made her blood run cold to think of it.

The Signora was unprepossessing enough in her bloated shapelessness, her shabby dress and worn bedroom slippers; but at least she was someone to talk to, and they were a long time at breakfast settling the question of life in America. Before they left the table Noah asked about the girl at the portiere's desk. Was she Italian? She didn't sound like it when she spoke English.

"Rosanna?" said the Signora. "Oh, yes, yes, Italian. But when she was a little one—you know, when the Germans were here—she was sent to people in England. She was there many years. Oh, Italian, but *una Ebrea*, a Jew, poor sad little thing."

The note of pity rankled. "So am I," Noah said.

"Yes, she has told me," the Signora remarked, and he saw that her pity was not at all for the girl's being *una Ebrea*. More than that, he was warmed by the knowledge that the beautiful and unapproachable Rosanna had taken note of him after all.

"What makes her sad?" he asked. "The war's been over a long time."

"For some, yes. But her people will not let her forget what her father did when the Germans were here. There was the Resistance here, the partisans, you know, and her father sold them to the Germans. So they believe. Now they hate her and her brother because they are the children of a Judas."

"What do you mean, so they believe? Are they wrong about her father?"

"She says they are. To her, you understand, the father was like a saint. A man of honor and very brave. That might be. But when the Germans were here, even brave men were not so brave sometimes. Yet who am I to say this about him? He was the doctor who saved my life and the life of my first son when I gave birth to him. That is why when the girl needed work I paid back a little of my debt by helping her this way. A good bargain, too. She's honest, she works hard, she speaks other languages, so I lose nothing by a little kindness."

"And what about her brother? Is he still around?"

"You see him every day. Giorgio. You know Giorgio?"

"The cleaning man?"

"He cleans, he carries, he gets drunk whenever he can, that's Giorgio. Useless, really, but what can I do? For the girl's sake I make as much use of him as I can. You see the trouble with kindness? I wish to repay a debt, so now the windows are forever dirty. When you need that one, he is always drunk somewhere. And always with a bad temper. His father had a bad temper, too, but at least he had great skill. As for the girl, she is an angel. But sad. That loneliness, you know, it can kill you." The Signora leaned forward inquiringly, her bosom overflowing the table. "Maybe if you would talk to her —"

"I tried to," said Noah. "She didn't seem very much interested."

"Because you are a stranger. But I have seen her watch you when you pass by. If you were a friend, perhaps. If the three of us dined together tonight. . . ."

Signora Alfiara was someone who had her own way when she wanted to. The three of them dined together that night, but in an atmosphere of constraint, the conversation moving only under the impetus of questions the Signora aimed at Noah, Rosanna sitting silent and withdrawn as he answered.

When, while they were at their fruit and cheese, the Signora took abrupt and smiling leave of them with transparent motive, Noah said with some resentment to the girl, "I'm sorry about all this. I hope you know I wasn't the one to suggest this little party. It was the lady's idea."

"I do know that."

"Then why take out your mood on me?"

Rosanna's lips parted in surprise. "Mood? But I had no intention—believe me, it has nothing to do with you."

"What does it have to do with? Your father?" And seeing from her reaction that he had hit the mark, he said, "Yes, I heard about that."

"Heard what?"

"A little. Now you can tell me the rest. Or do you enjoy having it stuck in your throat where you can't swallow it and can't bring it up, one way or the other?"

"You must have a strange idea of enjoyment. And if you want the story, go to the synagogue, go to the ghetto or Via Catalana. You'll hear it there quick enough. Everyone knows it."

"I might do that. First I'd like to hear your side of it."

"As a policeman? You're too late, Mr. Freeman. The case against Ezechiele Coen was decided long ago without policemen or judges."

"What case?"

"He was said to have betrayed leaders of the Resistance. That was a lie, but partisans killed him for it. They shot him and left him lying with a sign on him saying 'Betrayer.' Yes, Mr. Freeman, Ezechiele Coen who preached honor to his children as the one meaningful thing in life died in dis-

honor. He lay there in the dirt of the Teatro Marcello a long time that day, because his own people —our people—would not give him burial. When they remember him now, they spit on the ground. I know," the girl said in a brittle voice, "because when I walk past them, they remember him."

"Then why do you stay here?"

"Because he is here. Because here is where his blackened memory—his spirit—remains, waiting for the truth to be known."

"Twenty years after the event?"

"Twenty or a hundred or a thousand. Does time change the truth, Mr. Freeman? Isn't it as important for the dead to get justice as the living?"

"Maybe it is. But how do you know that justice wasn't done in this case? What evidence is there to disprove the verdict? You were a child when all this happened, weren't you?"

"And not even in Rome. I was in England then, living with a doctor who knew my father since their schooldays. Yes, England is far away and I was a child then, but I knew my father."

If faith could really move mountains, Noah thought. "And what about your brother. Does he feel the way you do?"

"Giorgio tries to feel as little as he can about it. When he was a boy everyone said that someday he would be as fine a man and a doctor as his father. Now he's a drunkard. A bottle of wine makes it easy not to feel pain."

"Would he mind if I talked to him about this?"

"Why would you want to? What could Ezechiele Coen mean to you anyhow? Is Rome so boring that you must play detective here to pass the time? I don't understand you, Mr. Freeman."

"No, you don't," Noah said harshly. "But you might if you listen to what I'm going to tell you. Do you know where I got the time and money to come on a trip like this, a plain, ordinary, underpaid cop like me? Well, last year there was quite a scandal about some policemen in New York who were charged with taking graft from a gambler. I was one of them under charges. I had no part of that mess, but I was suspended from my job, and when they got around to it I was put on trial. The verdict was not guilty, I got all my back pay in one lump, and I was told to return to duty. Things must have looked fine for me, wouldn't you think?"

"Because you did get justice," Rosanna said.

"From the court. Only from the court. Afterward, I found that no one else really believed I was innocent. No one. Even my own father sometimes wonders about it. And if I went back on the force, the grafters there would count me as one of them, and the honest men wouldn't trust me. That's why I'm here. Because I

don't know whether to go back or not, and I need time to think, I need to get away from them all. So I did get justice, and now you tell me what good it did."

The girl shook her head somberly. "Then my father isn't the only one, is he? But you see, Mr. Freeman, you can defend your own good name. Tell me, how is he to defend his?"

That was the question that remained in his mind afterward, angry and challenging. He tried to put it aside, to fix on his own immediate problem, but there it was. It led him the next morning away from proper destinations, the ruins and remains italicized in his guidebook, and on a walk southward along the Tiber.

Despite gray skies overhead and the dismally brown, turbid river sullenly locked between the stone embankments below, Noah felt a quickening pleasure in the scene. In a few days he had had his fill of sightseeing. Brick and marble and Latin inscriptions were not really the stuff of life, and pictures and statuary only dim representations of it. It was people he was hungry to meet, and now that he had an objective in meeting them, he felt more alive than he had since his first day in Rome. More alive, in fact, than in all those past months in New York, working alongside his father in the old man's tailor shop. Not that this small effort to investigate the case of Ezechiele

Coen would amount to anything, he knew. A matter of dredging up old and bitter memories, that was about what it came to. But the important thing was that he was Noah Freeman again, alive and functioning.

Along Lungotevere dei Cenci construction work was going on. The shells of new buildings towered over slums battered by centuries of hard wear. Midstream in the Tiber was a long, narrow island with several institutional buildings on it. Then, facing it from the embankment, the synagogue came into view, a huge Romanesque marble pile.

There was a railing before the synagogue. A young man leaned at his ease against the railing. Despite the chill in the air he was in shirt sleeves, his tanned, muscular arms folded on his chest, his penetrating eyes watching Noah's approach with the light of interest in them. As Noah passed, the man came to attention.

"*Shalom.*"

"*Shalom,*" Noah said, and the young man's face brightened. In his hand magically appeared a deck of picture postcards.

"Postcards, hey? See, all different of Rome. Also, the synagogue, showing the inside and the outside. You are an *Americano Ebreo*, no? A *landsman?*"

"Yes," said Noah, wondering if only *American Ebreos* came this way. "But you can put away the pictures. I don't want any."

"Maybe a guidebook? The best Or you want a guide? The ghetto, Isola Tiberina, Teatro Marcello? Anywhere you want to go, I can show you. Two thousand lire. Ask anybody. For two thousand lire nobody is a better guide than Carlo Piperno. That's me."

"Noah Freeman, that's me. And the only place I want to go to is the rabbi's. Can I find him in the synagogue?"

"No, but I will take you to his house. Afterward we see the ghetto, Tiberina. . . ."

The rabbi proved to be a man of good will, of understanding; but, he explained in precise English, perhaps he could afford to be objective about the case of Ezechiele Coen because he himself was not a Roman. He had come to this congregation from Milan, an outsider. Yet, even as an outsider he could appreciate the depth of his congregation's hatred for their betrayer. A sad situation, but could they be blamed for that? Could it not be the sternest warning to all such betrayers if evil times came again?

"He's been dead a long time," said Noah.

"So are those whose lives he sold. Worse than that." The rabbi gestured at the shuttered window beyond which lay the Tiber. "He sold the lives of friends who were not of our faith. Those who lived in Trastevere across the river, working people, priests, who gave some of us hiding places when we needed them. Did the daughter of Ezechiele Coen tell you how, when she was a child, they helped remove her from the city at night in a cart of wine barrels, risking their lives to do it? Does she think it is easy to forget how her father rewarded them for that?"

"But why her?" Noah protested. "Why should your congregation make her an outcast? She and her brother aren't the guilty ones. Do you really believe that the sins of the fathers must be visited on the children?"

The rabbi shook his head. "There are sins, Signor Freeman, which make a horror that takes generations to wipe away. I welcome the girl and her brother to the synagogue, but I cannot wipe away the horror in the people they would meet there. If I wished to, I could not work such a miracle.

"Only a little while ago there was a great and flourishing congregation here, signor, a congregation almost as ancient as Rome itself. Do you know what is left of it now? A handful. A handful who cannot forget. The Jews of Rome do not forget easily. To this day they curse the name of Titus who destroyed the Temple in Jerusalem as they remember kindly the name of Julius Caesar who was their friend, and for whose body they mourned seven days in the Forum. And the day

they forgive Titus will be the same day they forgive Ezechiele Coen and his children and their children to come. Do you know what I mean, Signor Freeman?"

"Yes," said Noah. "I know what you mean."

He went out into the bleak cobblestone street, oppressed by a sense of antiquity weighing him down, of two thousand years of unrelenting history heavy on his shoulders, and not even the racketing of motor traffic along the river embankment, the spectacle of the living present, could dispel it. Carlo Piperno, the postcard vendor, was waiting there.

"You have seen the rabbi? Good. Now I show you Isola Tiberina."

"Forget Isola Tiberina. There's something else I want you to show me."

"For two thousand lire, anything."

"All right." Noah extracted the bank notes from his wallet. "Does the name Ezechiele Coen mean anything to you?"

Carlo Piperno had the hard, capable look of a man impervious to surprise. Nevertheless, he was visibly surprised. Then he recovered himself. "That one? *Mi dispiace, signor.* Sorry, but he is dead, that one." He pointed to the ground at his feet. "You want him, you have to look there for him."

"I don't want him. I want someone who knew him well. Someone who can tell me what he did and what happened to him."

"Everyone knows. I can tell you."

"No, it must be someone who wasn't a child when it happened. *Capisce?*"

"*Capisco.* But why?"

"If I answer that, it will cost you two thousand lire. Shall I answer?"

"No, no." Carlo reached out and dexterously took possession of the money. He shrugged. "But first the rabbi, now Ezechiele Coen who is in hell long ago. Well, I am a guide, no? So now I am your guide."

He led the way through a labyrinth of narrow streets to an area not far from the synagogue, a paved area with the remains of a stone wall girdling it. Beyond the wall were tenements worn by time to the color of the clay that had gone into their brick. Yet their tenants seemed to have pride of possession. In almost every window were boxes of flowers and greenery. On steps and in stony courtyards, housewives with brushes and buckets scrubbed the stone and brick. In surrounding alleys were small stores, buzzing with activity.

With shock, Noah suddenly realized that here was the ghetto, that he was standing before a vestige of the past which thus far in his life had been only an ugly word to him. It was the presence of the wall that provided the

shock, he knew. It had no gate, there was no one to prevent you from departing through it, but if it were up to him he would have had it torn down on the spot.

A strange place, Rome. Wherever you turned were the remainders of the cruel past. Memorials to man the persecuted. This wall, the catacombs, the churches built to martyrs, the Colosseum. There was no escaping their insistent presence.

Carlo's destination turned out to be a butcher shop—the shop of Vito Levi, according to the sign over it. The butcher, a burly, gray-haired man, stood behind his chest-high marble counter hacking at a piece of meat, exchanging loud repartee with a shriveled old woman, a shawl over her head, a string bag in her hand, waiting for her order. While Carlo was addressing him he continued to chop away with the cleaver, then suddenly placed it on the counter and came around to meet Noah in the street, wiping his hands on his apron as he came. The old woman followed, peering at Noah with beady-eyed interest, and in another minute others from the street were gathering around, getting the news from her. Ezechiele Coen may have been dead twenty years, Noah thought, but his name was still very much alive in these quarters.

He was not sorry that the matter was going to be discussed in public this way. As a young patrolman on the beat, he had learned not to be too quick to break up a crowd around an accident or crime; there might be someone in the crowd who had something to say worth hearing. Now he gathered from the heat of discussion around him that everyone here had something to say about Ezechiele Coen.

With Carlo serving as interpreter, he put his questions first to Levi the butcher, and then to anyone else who volunteered information. Slowly, piece by piece, the picture of Ezechiele Coen and his crime took shape. It was Levi who supplied most of the information—the time, the place, the event.

The butcher had known Ezechiele Coen well. Like all others, he had trusted him, because no man had a greater reputation for honesty than the doctor. He was a great doctor, a man of science; yet he was a man of God too, devout, each morning binding on his phylacteries and saying his prayers, each Sabbath attending the synagogue. Not that there was any gentleness in him. He was a proud man, an arrogant man, a man who would insult you to your face for the least offense. After all, it was one thing to be honest, but it was something else again to behave as if you were the only honest man in the world. The only one on earth who would never compromise with truth. That was Ezechiele Coen. You might trust him, but you could not like him. He was too good for that.

Then the trust was betrayed. Over the years one had learned to live with Il Duce, but when the Germans came to Rome the Resistance of a generation ago awoke. Sabotage, spying, a hidden press turning out leaflets which told the truth about Il Duce and his ally. Many said it was useless, but Vito Levi, the butcher, and a few others continued their secret efforts, knowing they had nothing to lose. Jews were being deported now, were being shipped to the Nazi slaughter pens in carloads. What else to do then but join some of their Gentile neighbors in the Resistance?

"Ask him," said Noah to Carlo, "if Ezechiele Coen was one of the Resistance," and when Carlo translated this the butcher shook his head.

Only once was the doctor called on to help. Three leaders of the Resistance had managed to get into Rome from the mountains—to help organize the movement here, to give it leadership. They were hidden in a cellar in Trastevere, across the river, one of them badly wounded. The doctor's son, only a boy then, no more than fifteen years of age, was a courier for the partisans. He had brought his father to attend the wounded man, and then, soon after, the three men together were captured in their hiding place by the Germans. They had been betrayed by the honest, the noble, the righteous Ezechiele Coen.

"Ask him how he knows this," Noah demanded of Carlo. "Was there a confession?"

There was no need for one, as it happened. There was no need for any more evidence than the money case of Major von Grubbner.

Noah silently cursed the tedious process of translation. Carlo Piperno was the kind of interpreter who richly enjoys and intends to get the maximum effect from his role. It took him a long time to make clear who and what Major von Grubbner was.

The major was one of the men assigned to the panzer division quartered along the Tiber. But, unlike the German officers around him, Major von Grubbner was cunning as a fox, smooth in his manner, ingratiating in his approach. Others came with a gun in their hands. He came with an attaché case, a black leather case with a handsome gold ornament on it, a doubleheaded eagle which was a reminder of the great name of his family. And in the case was money. Bundles of money. Packages of lire, fresh and crisp, a fortune by any estimate.

Give the devil his due. This von Grubbner was a brave man as well as a cunning one. He walked alone, contemptuous of those who needed guards to attend them, the money case in his hand, a smile on his lips, and he invited confidences.

"After all," he would say, "we are businessmen, you and I. We are practical people who dislike trouble. Remove the troublemakers and all is peaceful, no? Well, here I am to do business. Look at this money. Beautiful, isn't it? And all you have to do is name your own price, expose the troublemakers, and we are all happy. Name your own price, that's all you have to do."

And he would open the case under your nose, showing you the money, fondling it, offering it to you. It was more than money. It was life itself. It could buy the few scraps of food remaining to be bought, it could buy you a refuge for your wife and children, it could buy you safety for another day. Life itself. Everyone wants life, and there it was in that little black leather case with the doubleheaded eagle in gold marking it.

Only one man was tempted. The day after the three partisans were taken, Ezechiele Coen was seen fleeing with that case through the alleys, running like a rabbit before the hounds of vengeance he knew would soon be on him. Only Ezechiele Coen, the devout, the honorable, the arrogant, fell, and died soon for his treachery.

Vito Levi's words needed translation, but not the emotion behind them. And the crowd around Noah, now staring at him in silence, did not need its feelings explained. Yet the story seemed incomplete to him, to Detective Noah Freeman, who had learned at his job not to live by generalities. The evidence, that was what had meaning.

"Ask them," he said to Carlo, "who saw Ezechiele Coen with the case in his possession." And when Carlo translated this, Levi drove a thumb hard into his own chest. Then he looked around the crowd and pointed, and a man on its outskirts raised his hand, a woman nearby raised hers, someone else raised a hand.

Three witnesses, four, five. Enough, Noah thought, to hang any man. With difficulty, prompting Carlo question by question, he drew their story from them. They lived in houses along Via del Portico. It was hot that night, a suffocating heat that made sleep impossible. One and all, they were at their windows. One and all, they saw the doctor running down the street toward the Teatro Marcello, the leather case under his arm. His medical bag? No, no. Not with the golden eagle on it. It was the doctor with his blood money. This they swore on the lives of their children.

During siesta time that afternoon, Noah, with the connivance of Signora Alfiara, drew Rosanna out of doors for a walk to a cafe

in the Piazza Navona. Over glasses of Campari he told her the results of his investigation.

"Witnesses," she said scathingly. "Have you found that witnesses always tell the truth?"

"These people do. But sometimes there can be a difference between what you imagine is the truth, and the truth itself."

"And how do you discover the difference?"

"By asking more questions. For example, did your father live in the ghetto?"

"During the war, yes."

"And according to my street map the Teatro Marcello is outside it. Why would he be running there with the money instead of keeping it safe at home? Even more curious, why would he carry the money in that case, instead of transferring it to something that couldn't be identified? And why would he be given that case, a personal possession, along with the money? You can see how many unanswered questions come up, if you look at all this without prejudice."

"Then you think—"

"I don't think anything yet. First, I want to try to get answers to those questions. I want to establish a rational pattern for what seems to be a whole irrational set of events. And there is one person who can help me do this."

"Who?"

"Major von Grubbner himself."

"But how would you ever find

him? It was so long ago. He may be dead."

"Or he may not be. If he is not, there are ways of finding him."

"But it would be so much trouble. So much time and effort."

The way she was looking at him then, Noah thought, was more than sufficient payment for the time and effort. And the way she flushed when he returned her look told him that she knew his thought.

"I'm used to this kind of effort," he said. "Anyhow, it may be the last chance I'll have to practice my profession."

"Then you're not going back to your work with the police? But you're a very good detective. You are, aren't you?"

"Oh, very good. And," he said, "honest, too, despite the popular opinion."

"Don't say it like that," she flashed out angrily. "You are honest. I know you are."

"Do you? Well, that makes two of us at least. Anyhow, the vital thing is for me to locate von Grubbner if he's still somewhere to be found. After that, we'll see. By the way, do you know the date when all this happened? When your father was seen with that case?"

"Yes. It was the fifth of July in 1943. I couldn't very well forget that date, Mr. Freeman."

"Noah."

"Of course," said Rosanna. "Noah."

After returning her to her desk at the *pensione*, Noah went directly to police headquarters. There he found his credentials an open sesame. In the end he was closeted with Commissioner Ponziani, a handsome urbane man, who listened to the story of Ezechiele Coen with fascination. At its conclusion he raised quizzical eyebrows at Noah.

"And your interest in this affair?"

"Purely unofficial. I don't even know if I have the right to bother you at all." Noah shrugged. "But when I thought of all the red tape to cut if I went to the military or consular authorities. . . ."

The Commissioner made a gesture which dismissed as beneath contempt the clumsy workings of the military and consular authorities. "No, no, you did right to come here. We are partners in our profession, are we not, signore? We are of a brotherhood, you and I. So now if you give me all possible information about this Major von Grubbner, I will communicate with the German police. We shall soon learn if there is anything they can tell us about him."

"Soon" meant days of waiting, and, Noah saw, they were bad days for Rosanna. Each one that passed left her more tense, more dependent on him for reassurance. How could anyone ever find this German, one man in millions, a man who might have his own reasons for not wanting to be found? And if by some miracle they could confront him, what would he have to say? Was it possible that he would say her father had been guilty?

"It is," said Noah. He reached out and took her hand comfortingly. "You have to be prepared for that."

"I will not be! No, I will not be," she said fiercely. Then her assurance crumpled. "He would be lying, wouldn't he? You know he would."

The passage left Noah shaken. Rosanna's intensity, the way she had clutched his hand like a lost child—these left him wondering if he had not dangerously overreached himself in trying to exorcise the ghost of Ezechiele Coen. If he failed, it would leave things worse than ever. Worse for himself too, because now he realized with delight and misery that he was falling hopelessly in love with the girl. And so much seemed to depend on clearing her father's reputation. Could it be, as Rosanna felt, that Ezechiele Coen's spirit really waited here on the banks of the Tiber to be set at rest? And what if there were no way of doing that?

When Signora Alfiara called him to the phone to take a message from the police, Noah picked up the phone almost prayerfully.

"*Pronto,*" he said, and Commissioner Ponziani said without preliminary, "Ah, Signor Freeman.

This affair of Major von Grubbner becomes stranger and stranger. Will you meet with me in my office so that we may discuss it?"

At the office, the Commissioner came directly to the point.

"The date of the unhappy event we are concerned with," he said, "was the fifth of July in 1943. Is that correct?"

"It is," said Noah.

"And here," said the Commissioner, tapping a finger on the sheet of paper before him, "is the report of the German authorities on a Major Alois von Grubbner, attached to the panzer division stationed in Rome at that time. According to the report he deserted the army, absconding with a large amount of military funds, on the sixth of July in 1943. No trace of him has been discovered since."

The Commissioner leaned back in his chair and smiled at Noah. "Interesting, no? Very interesting. What do you make of it?"

"He didn't desert," said Noah. "He didn't abscond. That was the money seen in Ezechiele Coen's possession."

"So I believe too. I strongly suspect that this officer was murdered—'assassinated' may be a more judicious word, considering the circumstances—and the money taken from him."

"But his body," Noah said. "Wouldn't the authorities have allowed for possible murder and made a search for it?"

"A search was made. But Major von Grubbner, it seems, had a somewhat—" the Commissioner twirled a finger in the air, seeking the right word—"a somewhat shady record in his civilian life. A little embezzling here, a little forgery there—enough to make his superiors quickly suspect his integrity when he disappeared. I imagine their search was a brief one. But I say that if they had been able to peer beneath the Tiber. . . ."

"Is that where you think he ended up?"

"There, or beneath some cellar, or in a hole dug in a dark corner. Yes, I know what you are thinking, Signor Freeman. A man like this Dr. Ezechiele Coen hardly seems capable of assassination, robbery, the disposal of a body. Still, that is not much of an argument to present to people violently antagonistic to his memory. It is, at best, a supposition. Fevered emotions are not to be cooled by suppositions. I very much fear that your investigation has come to an abrupt and unhappy ending."

Noah shook his head. "That attaché case and the money in it," he said. "It was never found. I was told that when Ezechiele Coen was found shot by the partisans and left lying in the Teatro Marcello, the case was nowhere to be seen. What happened to it?"

The Commissioner shrugged. "Removed by those who did the shooting, of course."

"If it was there to be removed. But no one ever reported seeing it then or afterward. No one ever made a remark—even after the war when it would be safe to—that money intended to be used against the Resistance was used by it. But don't you think that this is the sort of thing that would be a standing joke—a folk story —among these people?"

"Perhaps. Again it is no more than a supposition."

"And since it's all I have to go on, I'll continue from there."

"You are a stubborn man, Signor Freeman." The Commissioner shook his hand with grudging admiration. "Well, if you need further assistance, come to me directly. Very stubborn. I wish some of my associates had your persistence."

When Rosanna had been told what occurred in the Commissioner's office she was prepared that instant to make the story public.

"It is proof, isn't it?" she demanded. "Whatever did happen, we know my father had no part in it. Isn't that true?"

"You and I know. But remember one thing: your father was seen with that attaché case. Until that can be explained, nothing else will stand as proof of his innocence."

"He may have found the case. That's possible, isn't it?"

"Hardly possible," Noah said.

"And why would he be carrying it toward the Teatro Marcello? What is this Teatro Marcello anyhow?"

"Haven't you see it yet? It's one of the ruins like the Colosseum, but smaller."

"Can you take me there now?"

"Not now. I can't leave the desk until Signora Alfiara returns. But it's not far from here. A little distance past the synagogue on the Via del Portico. Look for number thirty-nine. You'll find it easily."

Outside the *pensione* Noah saw Giorgio Coen unloading a delivery of food from a truck. He was, at a guess, ten years older than his sister, a big, shambling man with good features that had gone slack with dissipation, and a perpetual stubble of beard on his jowls. Despite the flabby look of him, he hoisted a side of meat to his shoulder and bore it into the building with ease. In passing, he looked at Noah with a hangdog, beaten expression, and Noah could feel for him. Rosanna had been cruelly wounded by the hatred vented against her father, but Giorgio had been destroyed by it. However this affair turned out, there was small hope of salvaging anything from those remains.

Noah walked past the synagogue, found the Via del Portico readily enough, and then before the building marked 39 he stood looking around in bewilderment. There was no vestige of any ruin

resembling the Colosseum here— no ruin at all, in fact. Number 39 itself was only an old apartment house, the kind of apartment house so familiar to run-down sections of Manhattan back home.

He studied the names under the doorbells outside as if expecting to find the answer to the mystery there, then peered into its tiled hallway. A buxom girl, a baby over her shoulder, came along the hallway, and Noah smiled at her.

"Teatro Marcello?" he said doubtfully. "*Dove?*"

She smiled back and said something incomprehensible to him, and when he shook his head she made a circling gesture with her hand.

"Oh, in back," Noah said. "Thank you. *Grazie.*"

It was in back. And it was, Noah decided, one of the more incredible spectacles of this whole incredible city. The Theatro Marcello fitted Rosanna's description: it was the grim gray ruin of a lesser Colosseum. But into it had been built the apartment house, so that only the semicircle of ruins visible from the rear remained in their original form.

The tiers of stone blocks, of columns, of arches towering overhead were Roman remains, and the apartment house was a facade for them, concealing them from anyone standing before the house. Even the top tier of this ancient structure had been put to use, Noah saw. It had been bricked and windowed, and behind some of the windows shone electric lights. People lived there. They walked through the tiled hallway leading from the street, climbed flights of stairs and entered kitchens and bedrooms whose walls had been built by imperial slaves two thousand years ago.

Incredible, but there it was before him.

An immense barren field encircled the building, a wasteland of pebbly earth and weeds. Boys were playing football there, deftly booting the ball back and forth. On the trunks of marble columns half sunk into the ground, women sat and tended baby carriages. Nearby, a withered crone spread out scraps of meat on a newspaper, and cats—the tough-looking pampered cats of Rome—circled the paper hungrily, waiting for the signal to begin lunch.

Noah tried to visualize the scene twenty years before when Ezechiele Coen had fled here in the darkness bearing an attaché case marked with a double-headed eagle. He must have had business here, for here was where he lingered until an avenging partisan had searched him out and killed him. But what business? Business with whom? No one in the apartment house; there seemed to be no entrance to it from this side.

At its ground level, the Tea-tro Marcello was a series of archways, the original entrances to the arena within. Noah walked slowly along them. Each archway was barred by a massive iron gate beyond which was a small cavern solidly bricked, impenetrable at any point. Behind each gate could be seen fragments of columns, broken statuary of heads and arms and robed bodies, a litter of filthy paper blown in by the winds of time. Only in one of those musty caverns could be seen signs of life going on. Piled on a slab of marble were schoolbooks, coats, and sweaters, evidently the property of the boys playing football, placed here for safety's sake.

For safety's sake. With a sense of mounting excitement, Noah studied the gate closely. It extended from the floor almost to the top of the archway. Its iron bars were too close together to allow even a boy to slip between them, its lock massive and solidly caked with rust, the chain holding it as heavy as a small anchor chain. Impossible to get under, over, or through it—yet the boys had. Magic. Could someone else have used that magic on a July night twenty years ago?

When Noah called to them, the boys took their time about stopping their game, and then came over to the gate warily. By dint of elaborate gestures, Noah managed to make his questions clear, but it took a package of cigarettes and a handful of coins to get the required demonstration.

One of the boys, grinning, locked his hands around a bar of the gate and, with an effort, raised it clear of its socket in the horizontal rod supporting it near the ground. Now it was held only by the cross rod overhead. The boy drew it aside at an angle, and slipped through the space left. He returned, dropped the bar back into place, and held out a hand for another cigarette.

With the help of the Italian phrase book, Noah questioned the group around him. How long had these locked gates been here? The boys scratched their heads and looked at each other. A long time. Before they could remember. Before their fathers could remember. A very long time.

And how long had that one bar been loose, so that you could go in and out if you knew the secret? The same. All the *ragazzi* around here knew about it as their fathers had before them.

Could any other of these gates be entered this way? No, this was the only one. The good one.

When he had dismissed them by showing empty hands—no more cigarettes, no more coins— Noah sat down on one of the sunken marble columns near the women and their baby carriages, and waited. It took a while for the boys to finish their game and depart, taking their gear with them, but finally they were gone.

Then Noah entered the gate, using his newfound secret, and started a slow, methodical investigation of what lay in the shadowy reaches beyond it.

He gave no thought to the condition of his hands or clothes, but carefully pushed aside the litter of paper, probed under and between the chunks of marble, all the broken statuary around him. At the far end of the cavern he found that once he had swept the litter aside there was a clear space underfoot. Starting at the wall, he inched forward on his knees, sweeping his fingers lightly back and forth over the ground. Then his finger tips hit a slight depression in the flinty earth, an almost imperceptible concavity. Despite the chill in the air, he was sweating now, and had to pull out a handkerchief to mop his brow.

He traced the depression, his finger tips moving along it, following it to its length, turning where it turned, marking a rectangle the length and width of a man's body. Once before, in the course of his official duties, Detective Noah Freeman had marked a rectangle like this in the weed-grown yard of a Bronx shanty, and had found beneath it what he had expected to find. He knew he would not be disappointed in what would be dug up from this hole beneath the Teatro Marcello. He was tempted to get a tool and do the digging himself, but that, of course, must be the job of the police. And before they would be notified, the pieces of the puzzle, all at hand now, must be placed together before a proper witness.

When Noah returned to the Pensione Alfiara, he brought with him as witness the rabbi, bewildered by the unexplained urgency of this mission, out of breath at the quick pace Noah had set through the streets. Rosanna was at her desk. She looked with alarm at Noah's grimy hands, at the streaks of dirt and sweat on his face. For the rabbi she had no greeting. This was the enemy, an unbeliever in the cause of Ezechiele Coen. She had eyes only for Noah.

"What happened?" she said. "What's wrong? Are you hurt?"

"No. Listen, Rosanna, have you told Giorgio anything about von Grubbner? About my meeting the Police Commissioner?"

"No."

"Good! Where is he now?"

"Giorgio? In the kitchen, I think. But why? What—?"

"If you come along, you'll see why. But you're not to say anything. Not a word, do you understand. Let me do all the talking."

Giorgio was in the kitchen listlessly moving a mop back and forth over the floor. He stopped when he saw his visitors, and regarded them with bleary bewilderment. Now is the time, Noah thought. It must be done quickly and surely now, or it will never be done at all.

"Giorgio," he said, "I have news for you. Good news. Your father did not betray anyone."

Resentment flickered in the bleary eyes. "I have always known that, signor. But why is it your concern?"

"He never betrayed anyone, Giorgio. But you did."

Rosanna gasped. Giorgio shook his head pityingly. "Listen to him! *Basta, signor. Basta.* I have work to do."

"You did your work a long time ago," Noah said relentlessly. "And when your father took away the money paid to you for it, you followed him and killed him to get it back."

He was pleased to see that Giorgio did not reel under this wholly false accusation. Instead, he seemed to draw strength from it. This is the way, Noah thought, that the unsuspecting animal is lured closer and closer to the trap. What hurt was that Rosanna, looking back and forth from inquisitor to accused, seemed ready to collapse. The rabbi watched with the same numb horror.

Giorgio turned to them. "Do you hear this?" he demanded, and there was a distinct mockery in his voice. "Now I am a murderer. Now I killed my own father."

"Before a witness," Noah said softly.

"Oh, of course, before a witness, signor?"

"Someone who has just told the police everything. They'll bring him here very soon, so that he can point you out to them. A Major von Grubbner."

"And that is the worst lie of all!" said Giorgio triumphantly. "He's dead, that one! Dead and buried, do you hear? So all your talk—!"

There are animals which, when trapped, will fight to the death for their freedom, will gnaw away one of their own legs to release themselves. There are others which go to pieces the instant the jaws of the trap have snapped on them, becoming quivering lumps of flesh waiting only for the end. Giorgio, Noah saw, was one of the latter breed. His voice choked off, his jaw went slack, his face ashen. The mop, released from his nerveless grip, fell with a clatter. Rosanna took a step toward him, but Noah caught her wrist, holding her back.

"How do you know he's dead, Giorgio?" he demanded. "Yes, he's dead and buried—but how do you know that? No one else knew. How do you happen to be the only one?"

The man swayed, fell back against the wall.

"You killed von Grubbner and took that money," Noah said. "When your father tried to get rid of it, the partisans held him guilty of informing and shot him

while you stood by, refusing to tell them the truth. In a way, you did help kill him, didn't you? That's what you've been carrying around in you since the day he died, isn't it?"

"Giorgio!" Rosanna cried out. "But why didn't you tell them! Why? Why?"

"Because," said Noah, "then they would have known the real informer. That money was a price paid to you for information, wasn't it, Giorgio?"

The word emerged like a groan. "Yes."

"You?" Rosanna said wonderingly, her eyes fixed on her brother. "It was you?"

"But what could I do? What could I do? He came to me, the German. He said he knew I was of the Resistance. He said if I did not tell him where the men were hidden I would be put to death. If I told, I would be saved. I would be rewarded."

The broken hulk lurched toward Rosanna, arms held wide in appeal, but Noah barred the way. "Why did you kill von Grubbner?"

"Because he cheated me. After the men were taken, I went to him for the money, and he laughed at me. He said I must tell him about others, too. I must tell everything, and then he would pay. So I killed him. When he turned away, I picked up a stone and struck him on the head and then again and again until he was dead. And I buried him behind the gate there because only the *ragazzi* knew how to get through it, and no one would find him there."

"But you took that case full of money with you."

"Yes, but only to give to my father. And I told him everything. Everything, I swear it. I wanted him to beat me. I wanted him to kill me if that would make it all right. But he would not. All he knew was that the money must be returned. He had too much honor! Who else on this earth would try to return money to a dead man?"

Giorgio's legs gave way. He fell to his knees and remained there, striking the floor blow after blow with his fist. "Who else?" he moaned. "Who else?"

The rabbi looked helplessly at Noah. "He was a boy then," he said in a voice of anguish. "Only a boy. Can we hold children guilty of the crimes we inflict on them?" And then he said with bewilderment, "But what became of the blood money? What did Ezechiele Coen do with it? What became of it?"

"I think we'll soon find out," said Noah.

They were all there at the gates of the Teatro Marcello when Commissioner Ponziani arrived with his men. All of them and more. The rabbi and Carlo Piperno, the postcard vender, and Vito Levi the butcher, and a host of others whose names were inscribed on the rolls of the synagogue. And tenants of the Teatro Marcello, curious as to what was going on below them, and schoolboys and passersby with time to spare.

The Commissioner knew his job, Noah saw. Not only had he brought a couple of strong young *carabinieri* to perform the exhumation, but other men as well to hold back the excited crowd.

Only Giorgio was not there. Giorgio was in a bed of the hospital on Isola Tiberina, his face turned to the wall. He was willing himself to die, the doctor had said, but he would not die. He would live, and, with help, make use of the years ahead. It was possible that employment in the hospital itself, work which helped the unfortunate, might restore to him a sense of his own worth. The doctor would see to that when the time came.

Noah watched as the police shattered the lock on the gates and drew them apart, their hinges groaning rustily. He put an arm around Rosanna's waist and drew her to him as the crowd pressed close behind them. This was all her doing, he thought. Her faith had moved mountains, and with someone like this at his side, someone whose faith in him would never waver, it would not be hard to return home and face down the cynics there. It didn't take a majority vote of confidence to sustain you; it needed only one person's granite faith.

The police strung up lights in the vaulted area behind the gate. They studied the ground, then carefully plied shovels as the Commissioner hovered around them.

"*Faccia attenzione,*" he said. "*Adagio. Adagio.*"

The mound of dirt against the wall grew larger. The men put aside their shovels. Kneeling, they carefully scooped earth from the hole, handful by handful. Then the form of a body showed, fleshless bones, a grinning shattered skull. A body clad in the moldering tatters of a military uniform.

And, as Noah saw under the glare of droplights, this was not the first time these remains had been uncovered. On the chest of the skeletal form rested a small leather case fallen to rot, marked by the blackened image of a doubleheaded eagle. The case had come apart at all its seams, the money in it seemed to have melted together in lumps, more like clay than money, yet it was clearly recognizable for what it was. Twenty years ago, Ezechiele Coen had scraped aside the earth over the freshly buried Major Alois von Grubbner and returned his money to him. There it was and there he was, together as they had been since that time.

Noah became aware of the rabbi's voice behind them. Then another voice and another, all merging into a litany recited in deep-toned chorus. A litany, Noah thought, older than the oldest ruins of Rome. It was the Kaddish, the Hebrew prayer for the dead, raised to heaven for Ezechiele Coen, now at rest.

Questions for Analysis and Discussion

1. The story follows the pattern of a typical mystery story. What is the mystery Noah Freeman seeks to solve? How does he get himself involved in the case of Ezechiele Coen? What questions are raised in his mind as he pursues his investigation? How does he solve the mystery?

2. A mystery story is usually an exercise in logic. Each discovery fits into a chain of evidence that leads to the solution. List the sequence of Noah's discoveries. Do they fall into a logical order leading to the solution? Are there any errors in the sequence?

3. The basic purpose of a mystery story is to entertain, to help a

reader escape from the realities of his existence. *The Crime of Eze-chiele Coen* attempts more. It deals with a time and with events of tragic import. It seeks to move the reader to make a judgment about the criminal acts of the Nazi forces when they marched into Italy. In judging the quality of the story, the reader needs to determine the extent to which the tragic events move him emotionally and involve him in the happenings of the tale. To what extent has the narrator created an emotional tie between the reader and any of the characters in the story? The character who suffers most in the story is Giorgio. Does the reader sympathize with him? Is the reader deeply moved by the devotion of Rosanna? Does the reader feel admiration, pity or contempt for Ezechiele Coen? Are these three characters made real? Is Noah Freeman real? If the characters are not made real, and if the reader is not drawn into the struggle of the Italian partisans against the Nazi invaders, then the story is a melodrama of some interest but of little depth. Do you agree with this statement?

4. In order to arouse interest, the author has set his story in a unique world and dealt with a unique personality. What is the world of this story? The people in the story lived through a time of crisis. What was the nature of this crisis? What values and what relationships existed in the time of crisis and afterwards? Why did the people of the ghetto continue to ostracize the children of Ezechiele Coen? What was unique about the character of Ezechiele Coen? How would you characterize his heroism? Explain the statement: "Ezechiele Coen was a man whose honorable character in a time of war was obsolete and destructive; but he was not a traitor."

5. Ezechiele's obsession with honor and integrity, his sense of superiority, and his feeling that he was above the weaknesses of the common herd made him in his world a ludicrous and yet a profoundly tragic figure. Still, *The Crime of Ezechiele Coen* is not a tragic story. Why? Similarly, it could have been a tragic story about Giorgio's act of betrayal and his subsequent anguish. But it is not such a story. Why? Is it that the author had another purpose in mind? Should a reader fault an author for not probing the full potentials of his plot and for writing one type of story—in this case a mystery melodrama—rather than another type?

6. Show that Noah Freeman is the protagonist—the central character—of the story. Consider his situation at the beginning of the story and at the end. What has the investigation into the affair of Ezechiele Coen done for him? In what ways has he changed? What can he look

forward to in the future? If Noah is the protagonist of the story, why is it called *The Crime of Ezechiele Coen* and not "The Restoration of Noah Freeman"? Why does the story end with the reciting of the *Kaddish*—the Hebrew prayer for the dead—to ease the soul of the dead Ezechiele, and not with Noah's declaration of love to Rosanna?

7.   The villain of the story is Major von Grubbner. What qualities and what actions make him the villain? What devices does the author use to individualize von Grubbner? Does he succeed in making von Grubbner unique? Do you see von Grubbner as an unusual satanic personality or do you see him as a typical SS officer?

8.   One of the conflicts in the story is between good and evil. What characters represent the good? What characters evil? On which side would you place Giorgio? In what ways does good triumph in this story? Must good always triumph in a melodrama?

9.   In a melodrama one usually finds heroic or noble exploits, characters excessively good or excessively evil, romantic situations, an unusual environment, unexpected coincidences, and a happy ending. Show that *The Crime of Ezechiele Coen* is a melodrama.

10.   *The Crime of Ezechiele* attempts to go beyond the requirements of melodrama or mystery tale. It deals with a tragic experience in Jewish history—the suffering of the Jewish people under Nazi domination during World War II. The anguish of the Jews in the ghetto of Rome during the Nazi occupation is touched upon as is the aid given to Jews by Italian partisans. The reader is aware of the suffering of Rosanna, Giorgio, and Ezechiele during the occupation. Does the tone of the story or the action in any way highlight the Jewish tragedy in Rome under the rule of the Nazis? What in your estimation could the author have done to sharpen this theme of his story? Would this have made the story better or worse?

11.   Study the characterization of the minor figures in the story: Signora Alfiara, Carlo Piperno, the Rabbi, Vito Levi, Major von Grubbner, and Commissioner Ponziani. What attempt does the author make to individualize each one? Does he succeed? Can you visualize these characters from his descriptions? Are they real or romantic figures? Are they types rather than real people?

12.   The author of this story need not have chosen Jewish characters to be the central figures of *The Crime of Ezechiele Coen*. Giorgio could have been the son of a non-Jewish doctor, fighting the hated

Nazis as a Roman partisan. Can you think of any reasons, personal and literary, that persuaded Stanley Ellin to make his protagonists Jewish?

Suggested Activities

1. Set up the classroom as a court to try Giorgio Coen for treason. The characters needed for the "trial" are Giorgio Coen, a judge, a prosecuting attorney, a defense attorney, and the following witnesses: Rosanna, Signora Alfiara, the Rabbi, Vito Levi, Commissioner Ponziani, a man from the ghetto, a woman from the ghetto, a former Italian partisan, an assistant to Major von Grubbner, and Noah Freeman. The rest of the class serves as jury. For it to be effective, the trial scene will need to be carefully worked out and the witnesses thoroughly and carefully prepared to present testimony.

2. Organize a committee of three or four students to undertake the responsibility of getting information concerning the Nazi occupation of Rome. Questions to be answered in the investigation are:

a. How large a force did the Nazis have in Rome?

b. To what extent did the Italian fascist forces and the Italian community cooperate with them?

c. What attempts did the Germans make to round up and deport the Jews?

d. To what extent did they succeed?

e. What populations in Rome organized the partisan groups?

f. How did the partisans function?

g. Did Jews integrate into the partisans group or did they set up their own partisan units?

h. How much assistance did the Jewish community get from the Italian partisans?

i. What part did the Church play in partisan activities?

j. How much help did Allied invading forces get from the Italian partisans?

k.   How were the Nazis driven out of Rome?

l.   What happened to the Jewish community of Rome?

A good source for this information is *Black Sabbath: A Journey Through a Crime Against Humanity* by Robert Katz (New York: Macmillan, 1969).

3.   You may be interested in the history of the Roman Jewish community, especially in what this community is like today; what part it plays in the city's cultural, political, or economic life; what institutions it supports, and so forth. There is an excellent article on this subject in Volume XIV of the *Encyclopedia Judaica*. Check this article and report your findings to your class.

Margaret Bourke-White. *Today's Troops, Tomorrow's Officers, Germany, 1932.* Reprinted by permission of Time-Life Picture Agency.

By Abraham Rothberg

The Animal Trainer

Introduction: **To Forgive or not to Forgive**

When Hitler and the Nazi party became the rulers in Germany, the educational system underwent a radical change. In the new education of the Nazis, fostering intellectual curiosity, a critical attitude, and the desire for knowledge was of minor importance. What was paramount was training for physical strength, for racial pride and awareness, for the fellowship of battle, and for unquestioning loyalty to the Volk *and the* Fuehrer.

The National Socialist educational revolution discarded the aim of producing an educated, cultured man who, moved by intelligence and independence, sought answers to the riddles of man, government, society, and universe. Instead it sought to produce a vigorous, uniquely German personality who shed his individuality, put blinders on his mind, accepted the totality of the dogmas of the Party, joined the hypnotized masses, and learned unquestioning obedience. Young people, even those with sharp, searching minds, were contaminated by the contagion created by the wearing of uniforms, by organized gatherings in tremendous stadiums, by innumerable hikes, marches, and parades, and by constant reminders of the supreme glory of the leader.

Even the parents were caught up by the patriotism and excitement generated by the propagandists. Those among them, whose vision was not fouled by the lies and distortions, discovered that they could not compete with the state for the minds and hearts of their children. Helplessly, they watched their children turning into fanatic robots, saluting every symbol of the new regime and shouting the "Sieg Heils" at every mention of the Fuehrer.

This was the youth that learned to hate the supposed enemies of the Germans, with a particular venom for the Jews. This was the youth that was trained in such total obedience and destructiveness that the sight of a tortured or dead enemy, even a woman or child, brought no sense of compunction. This was the youth that believed that there was no greater glory than to die for one's country and one's Fuehrer.

What would happen if a former Nazi soldier trained from childhood in the Nazi system were to find himself a student in an American college, with a Jewish professor as his teacher of English? Would he be capable of redemption? That is the basic situation in The Animal Trainer.

A fundamental moral issue is raised in The Animal Trainer. *It relates to the question of forgiveness. Is it possible for a Jew, especially one who has suffered the shocks of the Holocaust or who, as a soldier in the Allied armies, has witnessed first hand the afflictions visited upon his people by the Germans, to forgive them? If hatred has been generated, should this hatred extend to all Germans? After all, some Germans were opposed to the Nazis and suffered for such opposition. Ought the new generation, those who were children or not yet born during the period of the Third Reich, be blamed for the sins of their parents?*

Jews turn to the Bible, the Talmud, and to learned rabbis for guidance. Their ethical tradition contains statements about forgiveness such as these:

"If a man can forgive the one who has stirred up his hatred, and not hate in return; if he takes no revenge even when he has the opportunity of doing so and bears no grudge but forgets it all as if it had not happened, he is indeed courageous and heroic."

"Forgiveness is easy only for the angels who possess no evil traits of character not for 'those that dwell in houses of clay, whose foundation is in the dust.'"

"One who pardons can never become cruel."

"If a man asks pardon of his neighbor whom he has offended and if the neighbor refuses to pardon him, he, the neighbor, and not the offender is called a sinner."

Evil is not an abstraction. It cannot be separated from the evildoer. What does one do when a nation turns evil? Should everyone be condemned or ought one still consider each person as a separate entity and judge him as an individual?

These are some of the questions the story invites you to think about and discuss.

THERE WAS always the tense moment of self-consciousness when he entered a class for the first time, and Cohen was aware of it again, the silence sudden, the conversation suspended in mid-sentence.

He walked from the door to the desk, put his briefcase down, and wrote on the blackboard in a big legible scrawl: English Composition IX, MFW, Room 713, Mr. Douglas Cohen. When he turned to look at the class, the faces were blurred and indistinct but he knew that he would soon be able to pick out individual features, and in a few weeks he would be able to connect faces to names. Cohen tried to spend the first lesson the same way each time: read the names from the class cards, ask for corrections of his pronunciation of them, and then, after assigning the short story text and the first half dozen themes, he tried to explain the purpose of the course. It was a course in how to read and write more intelligently, and, he added wryly, because it always brought forth an uncomfortable titter, through those things to learn, perhaps, how to behave more intelligently.

The first assignment was an autobiography, a good choice Cohen had found, because it helped him to get to know them, and at the same time it made them write from their own experience, and, he hoped, got them better acquainted with themselves.

Cohen read the names slowly, taking care with the pronunciation, and the replies were soft, and, as usual, reluctant, almost as if they hesitated about identifying themselves. The last two class cards had strange names, and Cohen read them even more slowly.

"Von Harnisch, Wolfgang."

"Yah, Herr Doktor."

For a moment, Cohen thought it was an attempt at a joke, a freshman playing the clown, but when he followed the voice to the man, sitting tall and erect in the very last row, older and more ravaged than a joking freshman could possibly be, Cohen knew it was not a joke.

"I'm not a doctor . . . yet," Cohen smiled, and the class shuffled uncomfortably, not knowing whether to laugh or look serious. "So just say 'Here.'" Von Harnisch nodded, his head bowing stiffly from the neck as if struck from behind at the collarbone.

The last card read, "Zilanko, Yakov," and the name belonged to a darked-eyed pale boy who sat quietly near a window in the front row, almost without breathing, and whose "Here" was so feathery soft that Cohen almost missed it.

When he dismissed the class, the students rose, suddenly at ease and graceful, and Cohen watched them file out in twos and threes while he took his cigarettes out. "Mr. Cohen?" he turned and saw Von Harnisch moving down the aisle toward him, dragging crippled legs on the floor, the tall spare body jack-knifed over two rubber-tipped yellow canes. Cohen felt the pity sting his eyeballs, and he remembered his own terrible fear of being crippled in the war. For a moment he felt as if he himself was hunched over the canes, feeling the strain in his shoulders and the dragging of his legs; then the match he had lit singed the hair of his fingers and brought him to lighting his cigarette and quickly blowing the match out. When he looked up, he hoped he had pushed the pity and the fear from his face.

"Yes, Mr. Harnisch?" he said.

"—Von Harnisch," the voice corrected gently, the eyes remote and dark, the lips full and curved in what might have been, but for the twisted corners of the mouth, a smile.

"Well, what is it?" Cohen asked, feeling irritation inside mix with and take the place of his fear.

"I am not native born here, and I do not speak English good." He stopped as if he had to reconstruct from the German in his head first. "You think I am successful?"

"Sure, why not?"

"I will maybe need your help."

The lips smiled, but the eyes were distant, almost unseeing, and Cohen wondered what the boy was trying to say.

"Of course," Cohen said, making his voice hearty. "That's my job. It's too bad we don't have foreigners' language classes here, but I'll do what I can to help."

"Good," Von Harnisch said, with the little, stiff-necked bow. "*They* said there was maybe trouble."

"Trouble?" Cohen asked. "What kind of trouble?"

Von Harnisch's eyes looked away from him to his cigarette, his shoes, and then finally to the rubber tips of his own canes. "Because I am . . . was . . . a German soldier," he said, fumbling for the right tense, his eyes suddenly meeting Cohen's, his face stiffening, his body almost snapped erect.

A Nazi, Cohen thought. A Nazi soldier. He fought down the leaping pity and terror inside him. Probably wounded in the legs or spine. Shrapnel. Again he could almost feel himself on the canes, crippled, and then clearly he thought, "Serves the bastard right." He felt his hands shaking and dropped his cigarette. "*They* told you?" he said aloud.

Von Harnisch's eyes wavered, then dropped, and he repeated as if by rote, "*They* told me," but his hands fluttered helplessly toward the empty chairs in the classroom. Then he leaned heavily on the canes and began to pull himself toward the door.

"What else did *they* tell you?" Cohen made himself ask, not wanting to ask or know, his eyes seeing only the hunched shoulders and the long thin legs that buckled under the torso. It was here, again, in his own country, in his own classroom.

Von Harnisch was framed in the doorway when he turned, his fists bulking white-knuckled around the canes. "They said you *are* a Jew," and Cohen could almost feel the change of emphasis in the pronouns like a blow. Then he was gone, the sound of his dragging feet sibilant and threatening in the corridor. At his own feet his cigarette still glowed. Cohen picked it up, put it in his mouth, the dustiness of the floor dry on his lips.

"Even here," he thought again, "as if there are Furies following me from another life." Against his will, fighting back the sight and sound recalled, he remembered Dachau and Buchenwald, and the vivisection room—"for medical experiments," the Germans had said quite calmly—with its hooks in the ceiling for bodies to be hung from. He had picked up a worn mallet there, hefted it in his hand aimlessly, the wood smooth against his palm, until he noticed the flat head stained with brown dried blood. Then his fingers, with a mind of their own, had gone limp and let the mallet fall to the concrete floor.

He didn't often think of it anymore. Sometimes, when he did remember, his memory blurred the outlines so that it seemed like a book he had read, or a nightmare from his childhood, filled with the horror of the slaughterhouse scenes of *The Jungle* and the inscrutable injustice of *The Trial*, or like some of the newsreels he had seen after he had come home from Germany, grayed-out scenes that looked as if they had been sifted through ashes. "Human ashes," he thought, flicking the cigarette ash, "gone through a crematorium chimney."

Cohen picked up his briefcase, walked to the door and absently turned the lights out. In the hall, the dark-eyed boy was leaning against the wall, his eyes narrowed against the smoke that curled up about his face from the cigarette in the hands that moved restless and strange in front of him.

"They never forget, hah?" the boy said.

"*They?* Who?" Cohen asked, remembering the mallet and the smell, the murderous smell of incinerated flesh that still lingered in his head like an ache. As they walked toward the exit, Cohen tried to shake the smell out of his head by thinking about the boy's name, but he couldn't remember it.

"The Nazis," the boy said quietly. "The Germans."

"What do you know about that?" Cohen asked angrily as they came into the faded February sunshine.

They stood facing each other like contestants until the boy forced a laugh. "What do I know about it? Nothing. Nothing, I guess. Just what I read in the papers." The dark eyes darkened and the red mouth, almost fruit-stained looking, pursed. "Sorry I bothered you, Mr. Cohen," he said and walked away toward Bonner Hall, across the campus. Cohen watched him go with a vague feeling of regret, as if he had somehow misunderstood what the boy was trying to say. He tried to shake the feeling off. After all, what did that kid know about it anyway? Then he remembered the boy's name, Zilanko, Yakov. A foreign name. And there was the elusive trace of accent in the speech. Was the boy a refugee? No. That couldn't be. He couldn't possibly have learned English so well and so quickly.

At lunch, when he met John Summers, his best friend in the department, he told Summers about Von Harnisch and Zilanko.

"I'll take the pig-head off your hands, if you want me to," Summers offered, his thin, blue-eyed face detached and comfortable. "I've got a comp section that same hour."

Cohen considered it for a moment and then shook his head.

"You think you're going to re-form a Nazi?" Summers smirked.

"No, it's not that."

"Then what is it? The best you can accomplish is to prove to him that you're a 'white Jew.' Big deal. That won't give him a twinge of remorse about the millions of Jews he and his buddies made into lampshades and burned for incense."

"And used for guinea-pigs," Cohen thought, still feeling the bloodied mallet in his hand, but he did not say the words. He sipped the bitter taste of the usual cafeteria coffee. He wanted to explain, but he didn't know how. The words he thought of were pompous or shopworn, and he didn't know how to make them say what he wanted to, so he let it go with, "Let me try for a while. If it doesn't work out, John, I'll transfer him to your class."

"Okay, Doug, but you're a sap for keeping him. He'll have some kind of respect for me because I'm a blue-eyed *goy*." He grinned at the unusual Yiddish word in his mouth. "And for me, he'll be just another Joe. But for you he's going to be a Judas, or a crown of thorns." He looked up, his shrewd blue eyes narrowed. "Or is that what you want?"

For the first week, Von Harnisch was like all the other students, reserved and unprepared. The second week, when the class handed the autobiographies in,

Cohen was impatient to read Von Harnisch's and, because of his impatience, kept the paper for last. He felt, somehow, that the autobiography would be the second skirmish with Von Harnisch in a battle already joined. But he knew that the battle he had joined was not only with the German; it was with himself. When he had come home from Germany, he had deliberately laid the problem aside. He was not a statesman, he told himself—he was a school teacher. But the problem would not stay put, any more than the Belsens and the Auschwitzes would remain quiet. The corpses cried out, and the mallet memory remained bludgeoned in his brain, and always he wondered what he would have done; kept quiet, gone about his business, and like the vast majority of them made believe there were no camps, no crematoria, no horror? Or would he have *resisted*? And how did one *resist*? Once, when they talked about it, Summers had said: "In any critical time, most people shut their doors and wait until the crisis is over." With tyranny and liberation alike.

Two or three papers before Von Harnisch's, Cohen came on Zilanko's paper, entitled, "Zilanko's Journey."

It was written in restrained sentences, simple and compound, rarely complex, and in good idiomatic English. Zilanko had been born in Poland in Lodz, in 1930. His father was a physician, his mother a concert pianist. Both of them had been educated in England and they had taught the boy English as a child, and continued to use it as the second language in the house after Polish. Zilanko was an only child, lonely because his parents were busy and had to leave him much of the time with Magda, the servant girl. Zilanko wrote how he had tried for their attention one day when he stole six zlotys from his mother's purse and treated all the kids in his gang to candy and a droshky ride around the town. But the principal of the school had seen him and reported the incident to his mother, and Zilanko had gotten the kind of attention he didn't want.

Cohen laughed out loud at the story, picturing the small, dark-eyed boy directing the droshky driver through the main streets of Lodz, where the principal had spotted them. It seemed like another world, a world of innocence and beauty long since gone. And soon the other world arrived, the world of September, 1939, when the Nazis invaded and his father had been called up. Dr. Zilanko had sent the boy and his mother into the country to stay with relatives. Six weeks later the doctor's regiment was wiped out by the panzers.

The boy and his mother had been taken into Germany when

the roundup of Jews was begun, to East Prussia, to Bavaria, to the Ruhr, and finally to Buchenwald where Mrs. Zilanko, weak and sickly, had been cremated. In 1945, Zilanko was liberated by the Americans—why the Nazis hadn't cremated him he wasn't sure, but he suspected it was because he could still work. Then his father's only brother, in America, had found him through the Joint Distribution Committee, and brought him to the United States. Zilanko wanted to go to Israel, but his Uncle Max prevailed on him to remain until he finished work at the University and became a doctor like his father.

When he put the paper down, the sheets going white and blank before his eyes, Cohen fumbled blindly for a cigarette. When he lit it, he didn't smell the comforting odor of tobacco. The gray burnt-flesh odor seemed to fill his head instead. And he had been short with the boy when Zilanko had tried to talk to him! The boy hadn't spoken to him since, except when called on in class, and then replying as briefly as possible, he had avoided Cohen's eyes. Cohen felt sick. He went to the cupboard for a drink, but the bourbon didn't wash the smell or the taste away.

And suddenly, as he picked up Von Harnisch's paper, the hatred was black and bilious in him, and his fingers trembled with the urge to tear the paper once across, and then again, and again, until the bits fluttered white to the floor. But instead he put it down on his desk and began to read.

It was briefer than the others and titled, "The Life and Work of Wolfgang Von Harnisch."

For a moment, thinking of the usual Germanic scholarship of the graduate schools, and their lives and works of, Cohen smiled. They were so thorough, so efficient, that even his American teachers had felt themselves distinguished when they were referred to in the footnote of a German scholarly work.

Von Harnisch had been born in Hamburg in 1924, where his father, an experimental physicist, worked for one of the big industrial firms. In 1934, after his father joined the National Socialist Party, Wolfgang and his brother Hans had entered the Jugend. Theirs had been a pleasant childhood, with skiing trips to the Tyrol and Norway, and bicycle trips to Italy and through the Rhine Valley. After his brother was killed in 1942—Hans was in the Afrika Korps—Von Harnisch had volunteered first for the Luftwaffe, and then, changing his mind, had gone into the Elite Guards instead. When he left for the Russian front in 1943, his parents could not see him off because they were at Peenemunde where his father was working on experimental rockets.

Von Harnisch had fought on

the Russian front until well in 1944, when, having been twice wounded and decorated, he was transferred to the Western front to, as he put it, fight the Americans. There he was wounded and decorated again. In 1946, his father had been brought to the United States to help the United States Navy to develop guided missiles, and the boy and his mother had gone along. In California, Von Harnisch had found work as an animal trainer, work he loved, but when his father had been sent East to work with one of the larger aircraft firms, Von Harnisch, at his parents' urging, had accompanied them and returned to the university.

Cohen put the paper down and went for another bourbon. The hatred inside him was knotted in his throat and chest so that his breathing came hard, and swallowing was painful. But what good is it? he almost cried out to the empty room, as he paced up and down. Still, he knew that hatred was healthy and had an astringency and meaning of its own if well directed. And besides, was there any alternative to hatred?

It wasn't until the third week in March that Cohen was able to make appointments with Von Harnisch and Zilanko. Appointments were for fifteen-minute conferences in which Cohen went over the students' papers—more valuable by far, he had found,

than all the red pencil marks about structure, diction, spelling and puntuation he made in the margins of their papers. He tried to see every student in his classes at least twice a term in conference and, if possible, three or four times. Von Harnisch came in first, his dragging feet sounding in the corridor outside of Cohen's office, announcing his presence beforehand, and giving Cohen time to compose his face and fight down the hatred he felt rising. He turned his chair to the window, lit a cigarette, and called, "Come in."

The door opened slowly and Von Harnisch stood uncertainly on the threshold. "Come in," Cohen made himself repeat. "Sit down." Von Harnisch moved to the chair next to the desk, placed his yellow canes together against Cohen's desk, and then folded himself into the chair. "Smoke?" Cohen offered, swiveling to face Von Harnisch, but the boy shook his head and spread his papers on the desk. Cohen went over them line by line, explaining errors, making corrections, and occasionally and reluctantly giving explanations in German when Von Harnisch didn't seem to understand. Von Harnisch was inattentive and several times Cohen, bent over the papers, was aware that the boy was looking out of the window over his shoulder. Finally, angry, Cohen said: "Look here, Harnisch, this is for you, not me. I know all this stuff. If you're not interested, we can both save ourselves this time and trouble."

Von Harnisch was brought up short for a moment, and then, slowly and very distinctly, he said, "I have not wanted to go to school. I like on the outside to be."

"Then why did you come to the university?"

Von Harnisch looked his contempt plainly. "What else could I do . . . with these," he pointed to his sprawled legs, ". . . dance?"

Cohen turned to look out of the window, noticing the peculiar diamond whiteness of the March afternoon lightening the blueness of the spruces outside, hoping to give the boy time to recover himself. Recover himself? The laughter inside was shrill. Recover? No one could be recovered, and why of all people should he care about a Nazi's recovery? Could Zilanko recover his father, or his mother, gone up in smoke from a crematorium chimney, without the dignity of burial, the grace of restoration to earth? Could the boy recover the beauty and innocence of those stolen zlotys and that droshky ride? After the silence, Cohen turned back and asked if Von Harnisch could still train animals.

"You see ever how animals train?" Von Harnisch inquired.

Cohen shook his head.

Leaning on one cane with his left arm, Von Harnisch lurched to his feet, brandishing the second cane in his right hand. "You pick up two by four, go into cage, with only two by four. When lion jumps, or panther or leopard, you hit with two by four." He swung the yellow cane viciously whoosh-whiiish, whiiish-whoosh. "Best on nose. He jump again, you hit again, until he knocked down. Then you hit more so he know you are boss. After, he is good trained lion." Von Harnisch stopped, his eyes white and alive, and looked down at Cohen. "Outside people think animals trained with soft hand, but impossible. Must use two by four, or you dead and animal wild."

Von Harnisch bowed into the chair, as if he had completed a performance, and Cohen felt the surges of nausea and pity together. He remembered the mallet and the dried blood on it, and the picture of it seemed to swim between him and Von Harnisch, and change to a two by four, and then back again into a mallet. To keep the dizziness down, he asked, "If you did it before, why can't you do it again?"

"Before?" Von Harnisch rasped. "Before I have legs." He slapped his thigh with an open palm, making a loud flat sound. "I get these sticks like this," and, as Von Harnisch explained, Cohen realized for the first time that the

German hadn't been wounded in the war. He used to feed snakes and take out their venom until one day he'd been bitten. He didn't remember when, but suddenly he was paralyzed from the neck down. They took him to a hospital and told him it was a snake bite, or maybe another animal's bite. They weren't sure which. He would never get out of bed again, they said, but Von Harnisch did not believe them.

He had begun to try moving immediately, starting with the right thumb, and after a year had accomplished what the doctors said was utterly impossible: he had recovered his entire right arm. After that, with the doctors' help, he had recovered the use of the top half of his body in the second year, but the legs would not respond to treatment. The doctors said he would spend his life in a wheelchair—better than being in bed, they reassured him. But Von Harnisch would not accept that either. Ten and twelve hours a day he had practiced with the canes until he had passed out on the floor, but always the next day, he was up and trying the yellow canes once more. But, he explained, sweat drops standing out on his forehead as if he was reliving the whole thing as he told it, that was the best he'd been able to do.

"There's been no further improvements." He was convinced of the hopelessness of his being able to walk again, ever. He was tired of trying, too. "So," the German concluded, looking out at the blue spruces to avoid Cohen's eyes, "I come to the university. Here, maybe, I learn to make living—something when I am sitting, where I need no legs."

He had courage, Cohen was forced to admit, and he knew his pity and grudging admiration compromised his judgment. Still, what could such a man do? If he wanted to make a living he had to do something at a desk, anything that would require . . . "Listen," he heard himself say, "whatever you do, you've got to know the language. Without English, you can do nothing."

Von Harnisch nodded, and Cohen suggested tutoring. The German said he would be able to pay, and Cohen promised to find someone to help him. Then Von Harnisch stood up, irresolutely put his hand out, and said, in German, "You are very good to me. Thanks." But there was a question in the statement, and Cohen felt it in the handshake too. It said, Why are you doing this for me? I am a German, a Nazi. You are a Jew. And worst of all, Cohen didn't know the answer.

When Zilanko knocked, Cohen was still staring out of the window at the spruces, wondering why he wanted to help Von Harnisch. Zilanko came in and sat down, putting his papers on the desk. When Cohen swiveled to face him, he noticed how the dark blue turtleneck sweater accented Zilanko's pallor and dark eyes. The boy always wore clothing that was a little out of date, too, a little strange and shabby—as if it had been rescued from trunks hidden away in old, musty attics.

"There isn't much to say to you, Mr. Zilanko," Cohen began. "Your work is good—surprisingly good for someone here so short a time."

"I spoke English in Poland, Mr. Cohen."

"That's right," Cohen said, "I remember now. Your mother taught you, didn't she?" As soon as he said it he was sorry, for a shadow stole through the pallor of the boy's face and was lost behind the dark eyes.

"Both my parents spoke English," Zilanko said quietly.

"I'm sorry," Cohen mumured.

"Sorry?" the boy said, as if the word was somehow beyond his vocabulary.

Cohen went through Zilanko's papers, but the boy's silent tenseness unnerved him, until almost against his will, he blurted, "Would you like to do some tutoring?"

"I could use the money," Zilanko said, looking directly into his face and then waited.

"We have students, some of them with foreign language problems," Cohen blundered on, already sorry he had begun and finding no way to stop, "like Von Harnisch—"

"—Von Harnisch!" Zilanko's body writhed like a whip. "If he was dying before my eyes, I would not help his kind."

"It was only a suggestion," Cohen apologized lamely. "Don't get so excited."

"Don't get excited! You Americans are all alike. Don't get excited, you say. Why shouldn't I? I hate Nazis. My memory is good and they gave me something personal to remind me." He ripped up the left sleeve of the blue sweater, exposing a slender, hairless forearm. "You see that!" On the forearm was stencilled the number 30707. "That's their number. Whenever I forget it, I look at it—and I remember." He stopped, swallowed hard, and put his face in his hands. "It's easy for you Americans who didn't see, who don't know."

"You're wrong," Cohen said wearily. "I saw. I know. And I didn't forget. But sometimes here, we forgive."

Zilanko's face came out of his hands, belief and disbelief quivering together on his face. "Then how can you—and you're a Jew, too—how can you treat them—him —so nice? An SS man. He even carries the Iron Cross Hitler gave him."

"Look, Zilanko," Cohen said, "you can't blame Von Harnisch for what happened in Germany.

You can't personalize a world war. The whole world failed, and you can't put all the blame on him. He's just one man." But even as he spoke, Cohen was not convinced himself. He knew about Versailles and the Weimar Republic. Maybe the world and not the man had failed. But, if it was that way, hadn't the man failed too? He was willing to admit that the whole was greater than its parts, but the sum of the parts made up the whole too. It was . . .

". . . that's very nice . . . in theory," Zilanko interrupted his train of thought. "Love thy neighbor as thyself. Turn the other cheek, or maybe," he pulled the sweater sleeve down over the number on his arm, 'in my case, the other arm. No, Mr. Cohen, you are wrong. *A man is his brother's keeper.* They were all responsible, every damned one of them." He picked up his papers, paused awkwardly as if he had something more he wanted to say, and then, without saying it, went out.

At lunch, when he told Summers about the conference, his friend painfully swallowed the dry sandwich he was chewing. Carefully, he followed it with two measured sips of coffee, and then said, "Doug, you're a fool. What'd you want to do that for?"

"I thought it might bring them together like civilized men, like human beings."

"The lion and the lamb lying down together in Cohen's Comp I, huh? Look, Doug, it's no academic experiment for them—"

"—or for me," Cohen said fiercely. "Should I hate Von Harnisch because he was brought up a Nazi, and love Zilanko because he happens to be a Jew who suffered through Buchenwald?"

"I didn't say that, now, did I?" Summers said patiently. "Maybe you could educate their kids—and I'm not saying you can—but not them. They've lived with their hate so long it's like pernicious anemia."

"There are cures for anemia."

"Not this kind," Summers said. "The Nazis were right about one thing. You can effectively kill something off for all practical purposes if you wipe out all its exponents. What was it Hitler wrote in *Mein Kampf*—If Christ came to earth again we could beat him to death with a rubber truncheon? And both of those boys know it from experience. Maybe if we'd done that to the Nazis, knocked off about six million of their leadership from Krupp down to the SS boys, we might really have defeated them."

"—and become just like them ourselves," Cohen said. "How do you judge? Who'd do the shooting? You? Me? Zilanko would, and he'd become a Von Harnisch, or worse. Besides, how would we have acted if we'd been Germans?"

"Or European Jews?" Summers

said.

His own reply hadn't satisfied him, and Cohen felt the logic and horror of what Summers had said, but he didn't know what to make of it. Would he have hated like Zilanko, or killed like Von Harnisch? Walking home after his last class, mulling it over in his mind, Cohen met with what was almost gratitude the gray sheet of rain that curtained the streets. The rain, the grayness, and the leafless trees black with rain matched his feeling better than the morning's sunshine had, and they made him more bitterly aware of Summers' comments.

At midterm, Von Harnisch was failing the course and Zilanko was getting an A minus. Zilanko's papers were impersonal and intelligent, and deliberately withdrawn. Von Harnisch's themes were intense and personal, and his English was abominable. He had no command of grammar, usage, or vocabulary and since he had discovered that Cohen knew German, he had taken to writing in German what he couldn't express in English. In the class discussions, Von Harnisch's comments on the short stories were straightforward, frequently incorrect, and often so arrogantly asserted that they cut off all further comment by the class. Zilanko's remarks were hesitant, delivered tentatively, and were usually perceptive enough to open up discussion.

Although Cohen was several times forced to caution Von Harnisch about classroom etiquette, the German boy continued to interrupt others, to speak without waiting for acknowledgement, and to make hoarse asides during others' recitations, while the class sat back in astonished politeness and watched. The three-cornered tension was obvious to the class, and it waited with an almost sadistic delight for the discussions to flow. Cohen knew but could not control. The arguments usually began with his own, "Don't you think?" followed by Von Harnisch's "No, Mr. Cohen, it is—the *is* always emphatic—and finally, cool but persistent, Zilanko's "Perhaps, but also . . ."

No one of them seemed to convince the other, or, for that matter, the class either, but none ever abandoned a position in the face of the others, and the class looked on the contest like Romans watching gladiators performing in the Colisseum, their thumbs always down. Cohen knew he had lost control of his class for the first time in his teaching career, and he did not see how he could regain it and still maintain the democratic way in which he conducted his classes.

When he mentioned Von Harnisch's classroom behavior to Summers at a faculty meeting, Summers said, "If you're looking for a metamorphosis in the pig-headed Nazi by treating him with decency and consideration, Doug, you're a bigger jackass than I thought. He's gonna think you're afraid to shut him up, a yellow Yid, and what's more, the class'll agree with him. Neither he nor they will know you're presenting the . . ." he laughed ". . . Christian ideal in action. They'll just imagine you're scared."

It was only a week before the end of April that the class discussion was on Thomas Mann's *Mario and the Magician*. The students had found the story very difficult to understand, and Cohen tried to clarify its meaning for them by explaining it as an allegory of the rise of Fascism, with Cipolla, the magician, mesmerizing his audience as dictators mesmerized the mass of the people. Carefully, Cohen showed how the whip and the drinking and the testy nationalism were all part of the picture. Almost as an afterthought, he pointed up the obvious irony of Mann's picture of it in Italy, since only a few years after the story was written, the same disease was to come to his own country, Germany, where its brutality and horror were to be carried far beyond anything accomplished in Italy.

Zilanko raised his hand to point out that the story showed further the degradation which Fascism inflicted on its devotees, making them, symbolically, stick out their tongues at others, cater to class prejudices, ignore scientific judg-

ments, and fall into states of what Mann called "military somnambulism."

Von Harnisch's roar came like the cry of anguish from a wounded animal, and he staggered to his feet, hunched over his canes and bellowing, "It was not like that! It was . . . *wundershön* . . . beautiful . . . I do not listen more to this . . ." He began to drag himself out of the row.

"Sit down!" Cohen's command was stentorian thunder in the class, and Von Harnisch stopped in his tracks. "Sit down!" Cohen repeated, and for a moment they stood staring at each other, tense and rigid, until slowly, slowly, Von Harnisch sank back into a chair.

"We've had enough of your arrogance," Cohen said, feeling the blood pounding in his trembling hands and shaking throat. "I've let you talk, interrupt others, and make a general damned fool of yourself, because we believe in giving even fools the privilege of shooting off their faces. But now, by God, you're going to listen, because we also believe that democracy imposes on its citizens the obligations of being informed. And you're going to be informed right here and now."

He paused, wet his lips, and swept the class with his eyes, noting Von Harnisch's stony expression and frightened, angry eyes, and Zilanko's shining face in almost the same glance. But he didn't care about either of them now. He felt a sudden freedom and power, a calm certainty. "Nazism was a cesspool," Cohen began, "an utter abomination." He told them about the Nazi horror, from Lidice to Rotterdam, from Warsaw to Dachau. He told them about the hostages, the wholesale slaughter, the slave labor, the assignments to brothels, the systematic starvations and "medical experiments," the gas chambers and crematoria, and the twenty million dead they were responsible for, not to mention the wounded, the maimed, and the havoc wrought all through Europe.

"They were wild animals," Cohen concluded, "and wild animals sometimes have to be beaten to train them. We beat them back to their lairs with their tails between their legs, but that doesn't mean that they're domesticated yet. And I don't dare use the word civilized. It takes a lot longer, it seems, to beat the jungle out of a man than out of an animal. And if we can ever beat it out of many men in a country, or a society, I don't know."

When he came in to lunch, Cohen found Summers waiting for him with a big grin on his face, his blue eyes lit with sardonic laughter. "Well, Douglas, I hear you bombed Berlin today, with blockbusters."

"Maybe, but that only destroys

houses. It doesn't replace them with new ones," Cohen said quietly. "Who told you, anyway?"

"Oh, things get around. In fact, it spread around the school like wildfire, and the kids will probably elect you the favorite professor of the freshman class."

"Shows how little they know."

"I wouldn't say that. They all think you're *dedicated.*"

"Your word, John, or theirs?"

"Theirs. Honest injun. And there are half a dozen other faculty members who have Von Harnish in their class who're going to vote you a bonus."

Dedicated, Cohen thought. To what? To anger, or hatred, or bombing the Wilhelmstrasse? But there was a point to it, he was forced to admit. He now had control of his class again, and perhaps some sort of control of Von Harnisch, too.

In early May, Cohen made an appointment for Von Harnisch's second conference. When the German came into the office, Cohen noted with a remote sadness that the boy looked older and more ravaged still. His sallow skin was waxen yellow, and the hollows were deep and dark under his eyes. He did not look up at Cohen as he slipped almost helplessly into the chair next to the desk, and dropped his papers down before Cohen.

"Is something wrong, Harnisch?" Cohen asked. He had to tell the boy that unless he passed the final exam, he would fail the course, and he was finding it difficult to find the right words.

Von Harnisch nodded, his head limp and unstrung as a marionette's. His Adam's apple leaped faintly in his throat, and when he tried to speak, no words came out. Faintly, syllables began to come, then words and phrases, in a stream. He had really tried, he said. He had worked. He was failing all his courses and all because of the language. His father had even hired a private tutor for him, but he just couldn't learn English.

Cohen said, "Be patient. You don't learn a language overnight."

But Von Harnisch said there was no more time. If he couldn't learn the language, he might as well quit the university.

"What will you do?" Cohen asked, touched in spite of himself, and half wishing the German would quit so he himself would be relieved of the problem of grading him. "What will you do to make a living?" and, he wanted to add, to make a life?

Von Harnisch shrugged feebly. He didn't know what he would do, he said, or what he could do. He didn't care.

"It's not the end of the world if you fail," Cohen said. "You can take the course over, and the others too."

Von Harnish stared and shook his head slowly to and fro, so finally, so worn out, that Cohen really believed that such an alternative was impossible for him.

"But look what you did after that snake bite," he said, astonished to find himself encouraging the boy, fighting to make him hold on. "Look at what patience and hard work did then."

The head shook again. "For that it is too late," Von Harnisch said in German. "I am too tired to struggle like that again."

Von Harnisch shook his head once more, and wavered to his feet, leaning heavily on the yellow canes.

"You know," Cohen said, getting up with him, "everything depends on the final examination."

"Everything?" Cohen thought. Was it more than merely the course and the German's career at the university? Unexpectedly, it seemed like a reckoning: it was almost life itself. "Whoa," he said to himself, "you're overdramatizing. He'll come back even if he fails," but even while he thought it, he knew he did not believe Von Harnisch would come back.

As the German was about to go out, he turned and Cohen called to him, "If there's anything I can do—"

Von Harnisch smiled. It was the first time Cohen had seen him really smile, and for a moment the face flashed blooming and youthful in the doorway. Cohen could see him in his *wanderjahre* on the Rhine and in the Tyrol and in Norway. As if on the instant English were impossible for him, the German said, in his own language, "You are a man, a fair man, Mister Cohen." And then, with the effort stark and painful on his face, he said in English, "A . . . fair . . . man."

During the last weeks of the term, Von Harnisch was subdued. He said almost nothing in class, and when he was called on he spoke with new tentativeness and mildness. It was obvious from his theme papers that he was making a renewed effort. He wrote only in English even when he came to the most difficult passages, but Cohen knew his English was still far below passing. Zilanko's face had darkened into quiet jubilation that showed in his unobtrusive certitude in class, in a new warmth in his papers. Cohen avoided prolonged talks with either of them, feeling only a quiet numbing sense of futility and despair that the springtime yellowing of forsythia seemed to mock. He even avoided John Summers because he didn't want to talk about whether or not he would have to pass Von Harnisch.

The English composition classes all took their final exam in the auditorium on the last day in May, and after seeing his class settled and started, Summers walked over to where Cohen was proctoring his class.

"Well, Doug," Summers said, "glad it's all over?"

Cohen nodded. "Damn glad."

"How's the pig-head making out?"

"He's still got an F average."

"You gonna fail him?"

"I don't know. Haven't made up my mind yet." He didn't tell Summers about his last conference with Von Harnisch.

"Well, if he's doing F work, that makes it easy. What's there to make up your mind about?"

"About what the F really means," Cohen said.

"You want it to mean something?" Summers asked, smiling. "To him or to you?"

"Wouldn't you, John," Cohen said, "want it to mean something to both of us? Seriously?"

Summers shrugged, saw an upraised arm, and walked down the aisle to give a student another examination booklet.

Late that night, marking the papers, Cohen left Von Harnisch's paper for last. Zilanko's blue book was an A, and Cohen gave him a final grade of A. Then Cohen read Von Harnisch's blue book twice, slowly and deliberately. The examination was a failure. On re-reading it, Cohen discovered a little note on the very last page, a note he had missed in the first reading. It was not addressed to him, nor was it signed by Von Harnisch, although it was in the German's oddly formal handwriting. It read:

"What matter? I fail."

Cohen stared at the line until it expanded and contracted in his vision, appearing and disappearing like a mirage. Was it an appeal for pity? the desolate awareness of failure? the questioning of a whole world order? Cohen read it again and still again, but the meaning of the four words were sealed off from him. Finally, he put the examination booklet away without grading it and went to bed. He couldn't fall asleep. "What matter? I fail." The words kept flashing through his mind like a neon sign on a dark street, casting shadows of confusion in his mind and filming everything with red neon glow. Asleep, he dreamed of Zilanko holding a blood-stained mallet and of Von Harnisch in a droshky. When he awoke, he felt confused and almost sleep-drunk.

At breakfast, he read Von Harnisch's paper all the way through again, right to the little four-word note. Then, in red pencil, he marked a firm passing grade on it. He entered the passing final grade—just passing—in his roll book and then on the registrar's grade sheet. He put the grade sheet into an envelope, addressed it to the registrar, and, after he had shaved and dressed, walked through the sallow June sunshine to mail it. For a moment, the khaki color of the mailbox put him off, but then he smiled, dropped the envelope in, and clanged the lid shut. It was done, over with.

At commencement exercises,

Cohen was putting his hood on and trying to adjust it properly when John Summers came up. "Hello, Doug," he said, setting the hood in place. "I hear you passed the Dutchman." Cohen put his mortarboard on and adjusted the tassel. "Did he pass the final?" Summers asked, stepping back to admire Cohen's handiwork with the tassel.

"Yes. . . . Well, no, not really," Cohen said.

"Then why'd you pass him?" John asked, the blue eyes appraising, but not surprised.

"If you don't know by now, John, I can't explain it to you."

"Well, try. Make believe I'm a freshman. I'll be patient. Is it because he's crippled?"

"Which crippling?" Cohen asked, almost of himself. And then, "That's part of it, I suppose, but not all of it. It's . . . it's . . ." but the words about Von Harnisch not being Germany, about individual and collective guilt, about the necessity for judging but not for punishing, and about a job sitting down, wouldn't come out. Nor could he explain that Von Harnisch still understood force at least, and could be taught, could grow. But Zilanko, his victim, no longer felt anything but hate, no longer believed in anything but the comradeship of hate and suffering.

Summers laughed at his struggle for words. "Forget it," he admonished. "I think I'm glad you passed him." He put his arm through Cohen's and together they walked across the campus toward the football field where summer graduation exercises were held. As they passed Bonner Hall, Cohen saw Zilanko leaning against one of the doric columns, smoking, and for an instant, their eyes met. Zilanko flicked his cigarette to the pavement, crushed it beneath his heel, and then, as Cohen waved to him, the boy turned his back and walked into the building.

"Well," Summers said, "I guess he told you, huh?"

Cohen nodded sadly. He didn't blame the boy. He could understand Zilanko's hatred. But hatred was not enough, nor ever would be.

"Come on," Summers said, tugging at his robe, "let's go graduate another batch."

"Sure," Cohen said, "might just as well," and together they walked toward the football field.

Questions for Analysis and Discussion

1. How does the author introduce his main character? Is there anything in the first two paragraphs that reveals the author's attitude toward his protagonist? Is it clear that the author is sympathetic, that Cohen will be the author's spokesman? Look to see whether the author moves into the minds of any of the characters other than Cohen.

2. Why is Cohen's first assignment to his class the writing of an autobiography? What responses are evoked in the mind of Cohen when at the end of class he sees the crippled Von Harnisch coming down the aisle to speak to him? The omniscient author tells the reader Cohen's thoughts. Why doesn't he tell the reader Von Harnisch's thoughts? The major focus is on Cohen. The story will deal with the growth of a new attitude, a new view, in Cohen. Study the story to see how this is developed.

3. What fears does the sight of the crippled Von Harnisch raise in Cohen's mind? Why is Von Harnisch troubled about being in Cohen's class? What are Cohen's reactions when he learns that Von Harnisch has been a Nazi soldier? When Von Harnisch leaves, the author takes the reader into Cohen's mind. What thoughts and memories are evoked in Cohen's mind by the confrontation with Von Harnisch? How is the worn mallet used symbolically?

4. When he leaves his classroom, Cohen meets Zilanko. How does

the author create in the reader curiosity about Zilanko? Why is Cohen irritated with Zilanko? Is Zilanko in this scene reflecting the turmoil in Cohen's mind?

5. Summers, Cohen's best friend in the English department, offers to take Von Harnisch into his class. Why does Cohen refuse to have Von Harnisch transferred? What inferences concerning Cohen's reasons for wanting to keep Von Harnisch in his class does the author wish the reader to draw? Is it true, as Summers suggests, that Cohen wanted to be a "white Jew"?

6. Cohen is the author's protagonist. The story is concerned with the mind and actions of Cohen. The author never tells the reader the thoughts of either Von Harnisch or Zilanko. The reader is expected to accept without a glimpse into their minds Cohen's belief at the end of the story that Von Harnisch has been moved by Cohen's impassioned indictment in class of Nazi atrocities and that Zilanko remains stubbornly inflexible in his hatred of Germans. Would you consider this to be a flaw in the story?

7. Cohen had been an American soldier who had liberated the inmates of concentration camps. With Von Harnisch and Zilanko as his students a battle rages in his mind. Cohen reads both Zilanko's and Von Harnisch's autobiographies. What responses does each account evoke in him? What experience of Zilanko's is ironic in the reader's view even though the experience is amusing and causes Cohen to laugh aloud as he reads about it? In a conversation early in their friendship, Summers had said to Cohen that "in any critical time, most people shut their doors and wait until the crisis is over." Is his view true? What do you think? If Summer's view about human nature is true, will you accept a belief of Cohen's that one should forgive individual Germans and not punish the ordinary person for the crimes committed by the German nation?

8. Cohen calls Von Harnisch in for a conference on his composition. At this meeting, Von Harnisch reveals to Cohen his experiences in America, the accident that caused his paralysis, his valiant efforts to conquer his handicap, and his unhappiness at his inability to learn English. What conflicting emotions does Cohen experience during this interview with Von Harnisch? What does Cohen learn about the trick of training animals? Who is the animal trainer? What relationship is there between the title and the theme of the story? In training animals, Von Harnisch says he used a two-by-four. How is the image of the two-by-four related to the earlier image of the mallet with dried

blood on its flat head? Von Harnisch appreciates Cohen's kindness. What is the question in both their minds?

9. Zilanko follows Von Harnisch in meeting Cohen for a review of his composition. With Zilanko, Cohen finds himself engaged in an argument. What is Zilanko's response when Cohen suggests that Zilanko tutor Von Harnisch? Cohen argues that one man—Von Harnisch—cannot be blamed and should not be punished for what happened in Germany. What is Zilanko's response? With whom is the author's sympathy in this exchange? How do you know? With whom is your sympathy?

10. Cohen discusses Von Harnisch and Zilanko with his friend Summers. What is Summer's view concerning the possibility of establishing a civilized relationship between the Von Harnisches and the Zilankos? What are his views concerning the effects of mass killing, the belief that no people is immune from the danger of committing genocide? What are your responses to Summers' views?

11. What new problem with Von Harnisch does Cohen face after the interview? How is Zilanko involved in this situation? The class discussion of Thomas Mann's *Mario and the Magician* brings the conflict between Cohen and Von Harnisch to a head. What were Cohen's and Zilanko's interpretations of Mann's story? Why do these interpretations arouse intense emotional protest in Von Harnisch? How does Cohen respond to Von Harnisch's outburst? In this response to Von Harnisch, Cohen becomes the animal trainer. How? What weapons does Cohen use in seeking to "educate" or "train" Von Harnisch? From Summers, Cohen learns that his "performance" had made an impact. On whom was this impact made?

12. At their second conference on his work in English, Cohen tries to encourage Von Harnisch. Why? Can you define Cohen's ambivalence in his total relationship with Von Harnisch? Is it believable? How does Von Harnisch react to Cohen's kindness? Is there the suggestion in this scene that once the animal is tamed and subdued with harshness, it is possible to deal with him with kindness? In what ways does Van Harnisch show the effects of Cohen's angry harangue on the vicious cruelties of the Nazis?

13. What is Cohen's dilemma about passing or failing Von Harnisch? At the end of his final examination paper, Von Harnisch writes four words: "What matter? I fail." How does Cohen interpret these

words? What, in Cohen's view, was Von Harnisch's question in these four words?

14. What were Cohen's real reasons for passing Von Harnisch? How do you, as the reader, explain this gesture? Is it sentimental; noble; foolish; dishonest; or unethical? Is it rational or irrational? Does the author approve of Cohen's action? Why did Cohen find it difficult to explain his reasons to Summers? Zilanko knew that Cohen had passed Von Harnisch. How did he react? In your view who was right —Zilanko or Cohen?

15. The world of this story is a peaceful college campus. What are the qualities of this world as revealed by the author? No world, no matter how peaceful, is immune to the diseases that infect the total universe. What sick and harsh worlds impinge on this campus world? What is the effect of this trespass? Does the college world regain its equilibrium at the end of the story, or is it in some way distorted? According to the author, is humanitarianism the cure for human baseness? Is cruelty the cure? Or is it a combination of both? If it is a combination, what is the formula, according to the author, for the mixture of the two curative elements?

Suggested Activities

1. Three works of literature are mentioned in this story: Upton Sinclair's *The Jungle*, Franz Kafka's *The Trial*, and Thomas Mann's *Mario and the Magician*. Plan a series of reports on the three works emphasizing their relationships to the themes of the story.

2. Organize a series of debates or discussions on the topics listed below. These subjects are highlighted by the action of the story.
   a. Neither the people of Germany nor the soldiers who fought in the war can be blamed or punished for the crimes of their Nazi leaders.
   b. The Western world was as guilty as was Germany for the Holocaust resulting from the anti-Semitic policies of the Nazis.
   c. The Jewish people must forget and forgive Nazi atrocities in the hope of building a better world in the future.

3. Two students playing the roles of Cohen and Summers improvise a conversation conducted a year after the events of the story.

The two friends discuss what has happened during the year to Von Harnisch and Zilanko. The two students playing the roles will need to decide whether Von Harnisch has really been chastened by Cohen's sympathy and kindness and whether Zilanko has remained inflexible. Remember that Von Harnisch had failed all his subjects except English.

4. The story raises a moral issue. Von Harnisch did fail the course. Yet for reasons unrelated to his performance as a student in the English class, Cohen passsed him. Discuss whether Cohen was morally justified in passing Von Harnisch.

5. Attempt the following exercises in creative writing:

a. Write a scene between Von Harnisch and his father, after Von Harnisch has received his marks, in which the two talk about the young German's problems at school and about his feelings toward his English professor.

b. Write a scene between Zilanko and his uncle in which Zilanko talks about his English class, Von Harnisch and his English professor.

c. The author does not tell us what goes on in the minds of Von Harnisch and Zilanko. Write a monologue revealing Von Harnisch's thoughts after he receives his marks. Write a monologue revealing Zilanko's thoughts after he ignores Cohen's greeting at the end of the story and walks away.

Jacob Rubin and M. Barkai; Joseph Yoseloff, 1968. *Pictorial History of Israel*. Reprinted by permission of A.S. Barnes & Co.

By Hugh Nissenson

The Throne of Good

Introduction: **The East European Ghetto Fighter in Israel**

The Jewish people who lived in the towns of Poland and Russia that were overrun and captured by the Nazis could not at first believe that they were destined for annihilation. They sought to cooperate with their captors. But when they were crowded into ghettos, when numbers of them were regularly marched out of the ghettos to disappear, and when rumors of the death camps reached them, the young men and women among them began to form resistance groups. In the face of German might, their efforts were doomed to failure, but they fought with a courage and heroism born of desperation and faith.

The very young among them especially were motivated by two passions: to survive as long as possible and to kill as many of the enemy as possible. They acquired unique skills. They could move through sewers, cellars, and underground passageways with speed and with a sixth sense that kept them away from the enemy. They could smell danger far away and know just where to turn. Above all, they not only found and smuggled weapons into the ghetto but they were adept in turning objects of various kinds and liquids like kerosene and gasoline into destructive weapons. They learned to use dynamite and whatever other explosives they could lay their hands on. And when the cause in the ghetto was lost, many of them were able to escape into the forests to continue the fight against the Nazi enemy. They became cold, angry machines, oblivious to pain and hunger, dedicated solely to destruction.

Many of those ghetto fighters escaped to Palestine after the war. They joined either the Haganah, the moderate military force opposing British mandate policy to limit immigration to Israel or the extreme terrorist groups—the Irgun Tzvai Leumi or the Stern gang. Haganah

167

officers and soldiers believed that the terrorist activities of the Irgun and the Stern organization hampered their efforts to smuggle Holocaust survivors into Israel and interfered with their attempts to achieve an understanding with the British rulers. They tried to control the bombings and the assassinations that in their view made accommodation with the British mandatary difficult and delayed the hope of an independent Israel.

This is the stage on which The Throne of Good *is played. It explains the dilemma of the narrator.*

D ECEMBER 12, 1946. Ari Rosenberg, who I now realize is a member of the Stern gang, has made an appeal to my professional conscience. A 16-year-old boy his organization has somehow managed to smuggle into the country from a British detention camp in Cyprus has fallen ill.

"I think it's pneumonia," says Rosenberg.

"What're his symptoms?"

"You'd better have a look at him yourself," he tells me, and lowering his voice even though my office is empty, adds, "He's here in Tel Aviv. I've got him hidden in the cellar of an empty house on Hebron Street, near the Old Cemetery. He hasn't been out of there in three weeks."

"In this weather?"

"That's what worries me. He has a primus stove, but we have had a hard time supplying him with enough fuel. The C.I.D. and the Haganah are on our necks right now, and we've got to be very careful about being followed. Unheated, that place is as cold and damp as a tomb. Will you have a look at him? He's had a bad time of it."

"What about your own doctors?"

"We can't be sure they're not being watched."

Another gust of wind off the sea rattles the window above the leather chair. The glass is blurred by rain. And yet I can make out a woman huddled in the doorway across the street. She has gray hair. Is it possible that I'm under surveillance? Does the British Criminal Investigation Department employ middle-aged Jewish women as spies? It doesn't surprise me.

In any case, Rosenberg, who followed my glance, has seen her too, but says nothing. Only his expression has changed, the look in his eyes, which gleam maliciously. He has already implicated me in his activities and knows that I know it.

"What's the boy's name?" I ask.

"What's the difference?"

"Suit yourself."

He repeats, "Will you come

and see him?"

"All right."

"Good. Meet me exactly at midnight tonight on the corner of Tchernichovsky and Gan Meir."

"I'll be there."

"I appreciate it." And he adds, without any irony I can detect, "For old times' sake."

But at the door, he alters his tone. "During the Vilna ghetto uprising, in the war, he took the name *Zemsta*."

"*Zemsta?*"

"Polish for 'revenge,' " Rosenberg explains.

It's taken two hours—we doubled back twice on Rothschild Boulevard—for Rosenberg to lead me to the boy's hide-out: the cellar of a small abandoned house on Hebron Street. And now I wait alone for almost ten minutes in the back yard. It's a shame, the garden has gone to hell: a single pomegranate tree, above my head, sways in the wind. All its round, reddish fruits, bursting with juicy scarlet seeds, have long since dropped in the mud and rotted away.

The outside cellar door opens a crack, and Rosenberg whispers, "Come ahead."

He has a flashlight. We carefully climb down the wooden steps into the darkness. The beam of light, flitting here and there, illuminates a small room: in one corner, an iron cot, a small table, and a Primus stove at the head of the bed, on the concrete floor.

Here, the air is stifling. The bed clothes and the boy's hair reek of naptha fumes.

The boy is suffering from bronchorrhea, characterized by a slight fever at night—now a little over 38.° C.—diffuse râles, and a persistent cough which brings up a thin, purulent, yellow phlegm. As I have no antibiotics—there are none as yet available for civilians in the country—I prescribe aspirin, rest, and calcreose, 5 gr., in chocolate-coated tablets to be taken three times a day.

He asks me in excellent Hebrew, "When will I be well enough to get out of here?"

"A couple of weeks."

"You can do better than that." Racked by coughing, he is unable to continue.

"Do you want the truth?" I whispered to Rosenberg at the head of the stairs. "That boy is going to get a lot worse unless you move him out of there immediately."

"It can't be done."

"Why not?"

"Our plans are set, and we can't take a chance of having him captured. Anyway, he's a volunteer. He accepts the risk."

He hands me the flashlight and draws a British service revolver from his side pocket.

"A Webley-Fosbery," he explains. "Unreliable. A speck of dust and it jams. Still, we use whatever we can get our hands on. We have our orders, you know."

"What kind of orders?"

"Turn off the light."

He opens the door, looks out, and says, "This way."

Stuffing the revolver back into the pocket of his mackintosh, he leads me across the yard, under the pomegranate tree. The mud sucks at our shoes. Hebron Street is deserted. Huge, inert pools of water have gathered in the drainless street.

Rosenberg accompanies me home. Across Allenby Road, under a street lamp, a patrol of British paratroopers, whom our children have nicknamed "poppies" because of their red berets. Blue eyes, sandy hair, mottled, beardless cheeks: they are little more than children themselves, but they are all armed. Each one has a finger on the trigger of the Sten gun slung across his chest.

Rosenberg leads me around the corner. He is grinding his teeth together with such force that his jaw muscles bulge on the right side of his face, beside his ear. It's a habit he has retained from childhood. We grew up on the same block in Haifa, but in that dark mackintosh, with one hand thrust in a pocket gripping a gun, he has become unrecognizable to me. The bulging jaw belongs to someone else; none of our common childhood memories which might bind us together again is evoked: the smell of boiling *kebab*, mingled in the salty air with

crude oil from the refineries; the one-legged Arab beggar, in black rags, sprawled on the sidewalk near the Town Hall, whom we passed every afternoon on our way home from school. Rosenberg, who was already proficient in idiomatic Arabic, would stop and chat with him. The beggar invariably refused our proffered coins.

"Why?" I once asked Rosenberg.

"Because I listen to what he has to say," he explained.

We were even in the same class at the Hebrew University, where he took a degree in Hebrew literature. I thought I knew everything about him, but realize I know nothing.

He has deliberately placed his Webley on the table between us. It has recently been oiled. Has he actually killed anyone with it? Detonated an electric mine? It's inexplicable.

He drinks off his third brandy; his eyelids droop.

"Tell me about the boy," I ask.

He yawns. "There's not much to tell. He was born in Molodechno, where his father was a grain merchant, and his mother the only daughter of a cantor in Vilna. The father did pretty well. He started the kid in *cheder* at three and wanted him to go to a yeshiva and become a rabbi. The kid was bright enough, but restless. He skipped classes and roamed the fields with the local peasants. His father begged him to study, but it wasn't any use. The old man took a strap to him more than once.

"Anyway, the whole family was deported to the Vilna ghetto in May 1941. A month later, the parents were murdered in the pogrom in the Nowograd marketplace. The kid was saved because he was studying Talmud with his grandfather at the time.

"He ran away the next day, taking a bread knife and, of all things, his father's prayer book, and joined the United Partisan Organization. The F.P.O. First he served as a courier, and then, the next spring, at the age of thirteen, he stabbed to death a Lithuanian policeman, a 'man-hunter' they used to call them, who helped the Germans round up Jews in the ghetto for extermination in Treblinka. As a result, the kid was posted to Itzik Beinisch's command on Staszuma Street, the building that was the first line of defense in the uprising against the Germans. They fought like hell but didn't stand a chance. Most of them were wiped out, except for a few hundred who somehow managed to escape to the forests outside the city or, like the kid, were able to hide in the sewers and underground bunkers until they were liberated by the Red Army in July of 1944."

"In the sewers?"

"In the sewers," Rosenberg repeats. "He spent almost eleven months in those sewers." He picks up his revolver and asks, "Do you know any songs of the Vilna partisans?"

"No."

"I'm translating some of them from Yiddish into Hebrew. We want to bring out a Hebrew edition. But it's hard to preserve the idiom. Do you remember any Yiddish?"

"Some."

His bleary eyes have suddenly cleared; he recites in an animated voice:

Sligt ergetz fartayet,
Der feint veea chayeh
Der Mauser, er vacht in mine
*   hant . . .*

"It's a problem," he goes on. "A literal translation is easy: 'the enemy' . . . what? . . . 'harkens; a beast in the darkness; the Mauser, it wakes in my hand . . .'"

Absorbed in thought, he slips on his mackintosh, returns his revolver to his pocket, and absent-mindedly pats it. Is it possible that his literary imagination—or aspirations—compels him to assume this role? Is such a thing likely?

December 15, 1946. For the last two days, I've been under surveillance; there's no doubt of it. First, by that middle-aged woman lurking in the doorway across the street, and then, as I make my daily rounds, by a tall young man who wears a leather jacket. Today, making no effort to conceal himself, he followed me to the clinic on Etzion Gever, sponsored by the Zionist Federation of Labor.

A few Arab women from Jaffa still bring their children to be treated here for trachoma, boils, ringworm, and chronic dysentery. The boys, particularly, amaze me. They lie naked and motionless on the sheet, under the overhead light, never uttering a sound, while I incise and then drain the boils that usually cover their buttocks and the backs of their thighs. Only the women, whom I hear through a thin partition, moan aloud. This afternoon one of them fainted dead away. Observing the Arab custom, I had Miss Guinzburg, my nurse, remove her veil and bring her around with spirits of ammonia.

Finished at five, I walked, in the rain, to the café on Dizengoff, where I usually have a cup of Arab coffee and a brandy. Leather Jacket remains just outside. The rain has plastered his hair to his forehead and hangs in shining drops from the tip of his nose and his earlobes. As I am about to leave, a roving patrol of Royal Marines stops and carefully examines his papers. Apparently satisfied, the sergeant, who has a bristling mustache, shoos him away.

"Go on," the sergeant yells, "'op it!" and waits until Leather Jacket has boarded a bus on the corner.

Rosenberg, in his black mackintosh, is waiting for me outside the door of my flat.

"The kid's getting worse," he says. "Much worse. Will you come and have a look at him again?"

He's clearly worried but insists on taking the usual precaution. We wander around the city for an hour and a half, until we reach the Old Cemetery and the cellar on Hebron Street. No one follows us. Apart from a solitary Arab policeman, armed with a British rifle, on Allenby Road, the flooded streets are empty. The Arab wears a *kulpack*, obligatory for native police. It's a kind of fez made from black lamb's wool. But it's much too big for him, and as he turns his head to watch us pass, it slips down to the bridge of his nose.

On the table in the cellar a flickering candle, stuck in its own grease, on an overturned glass, throws our enormous, leaping shadows on the peeling whitewashed wall.

"It's freezing down here," I tell the boy. "Do you want to catch pneumonia? Why don't you use that Primus?"

"I ran out of fuel yesterday."

"I'll try and send him some tomorrow morning," Rosenberg says.

"Then bundle up, for God's sake."

"The cold doesn't bother me,"

the boy says.

He is suddenly convulsed by a cough and he spits into a filthy handkerchief. The sputum now is grayish white and separated into an upper layer capped with frothy mucus and a thick sediment in which there are dirty yellow masses. He has developed putrid bronchitis.

"Well?" Rosenberg asks.

"You'd better get him to a hospital tonight."

"I can't."

"There's nothing I can do for him here."

"Don't you understand? He has forged ID papers, but the C.I.D. has a complete dossier on him. They know he's in the country. If they catch him, they'll cure him all right, but then what do you think will happen? He knows too much, but he won't talk. At least not under physical torture. But they're smart. They'll keep him in some cell in Acre."

The boy repeats, "In Acre? Undeground?" He shakes his head. "No, I don't think I could take that. I've already been down here almost a month. To tell you the truth, I'm beginning to hear things."

"What kind of things?" I ask.

"A rattling chain and a growling dog. Isn't that odd? A huge, savage dog at the end of a long chain tied to the doorknob, at the head of the stairs, outside."

"It's only your fever. It'll pass."

He says, "You think so? I'm not so sure. The SS in Vilna sometimes chained vicious dogs to the gratings on the streets to prevent us from coming up at night to scrounge around the city for a bite to eat."

"Did you ever try to escape through the sewers to the forests and join the partisans?"

"I couldn't," he says. "It was *beshaert,*" he adds in Yiddish. "Fated. I know that now. I was fated for other things. For a long time, I had a whatchamacallit— I don't know the word in Hebrew. You know, from a bad knock on the head."

"A concussion."

"Yes. I was on the second floor of our headquarters on Stazvuma Street, stuffing a rag into a bottle of gasoline. The Germans were attacking. There was a bright flash, dust and plaster flying through the air, and I suppose the ceiling fell down. I can't remember. The next thing I know was that Shmuel Epstein, one of Itzik's lieutenants, was carrying me on his back through the sewers. That's very vivid. My head ached something terrible, but I hung on, my arms wrapped around his neck, with all my strength. He had a pillowcase, a linen pillowcase stuffed with something, between his teeth. Once he forgot himself and opened his mouth to speak to me, and it dropped into the filth.

"'What's in it?' I asked him, and he said, 'Three candles, a box of matches, two loaves of bread, and your *siddur*.' 'Mine?' I asked him, and he told me he found it in my jacket pocket. Can you imagine? It was the prayer book that belonged to Papa. I always carried it around with me, after his death, and Shmuel took the trouble to bring it along. That's the kind of man he was. Of course, the pillowcase was soaked through, oozing black, stinking drops. Anyway, he held it between his teeth and kept going. The sewer pipe was about seventy or eighty centimeters high, and he crawled on his elbows in order not to bang my head again. It kept aching something terrible. He went very slowly. It was like a dream in slow motion. First his right arm and his right leg together, then his left . . . I don't know how long. My feet, up to the ankles, trailed behind in the slime. I remember passing the waterfall under Stephen Street. The water dropped six or eight meters there and made a terrific roar in those pipes. But gradually it faded away.

"Then Shmuel stopped. I realized he was exhausted and slipped off his back. I followed him for as long as I could, but there was a sudden rush of water, and I lost him. He was swept away before my eyes. I managed to brace my arms and legs against the pipe, or I would have drowned too. A day or so later . . . I can't be sure . . . it must have rained.

The current in the sewers was very strong. I barely managed to keep my head above water.

"After that, I'm not sure what happened. I went off my head. I began seeing things. I must have been thinking about the forest, because I saw flowers growing down there, in that muck. But they were black. Can you imagine that? Spiny black stems and black petals. And then, for a time, I heard Mama calling me. It was her voice, all right. I'd know it anywhere. I'd know it right now. And it echoed, as though it were real. She'd come down to try and find me. Lead me back up. She kept calling out my name and moaning. I wanted to answer her, but I was afraid to open my mouth. I was lying back on my elbows, against the pipe, up to my chin in that slime, and I was terrified that if I opened my mouth, and a sudden current caught me, I'd drown."

He closes his eyes. "Malka Kravitz eventually found me and took me to her bunker under the cellar at 19 Deitshishe Street, where I spent the rest of the war. We even had a radio and an electric light. We used to sleep during the day, and roam around the sewers at night. Visit other bunkers. We dug a cemetery in the bunker under 9 Gelzer Street and even had a synagogue, where I used to pray. I knew I had been saved for a purpose and tried to prepare myself."

"What purpose?"

He stares at the ceiling and moistens his dry lips with the tip of his tongue.

December 16, 1946. Noon. In my office. Leather Jacket, who tells me his name is Nahum, turns out to be an agent of the Haganah. He says, "Your friend Rosenberg, you know, planned the murder of Major Henry in September."

"Henry?"

"The British area security officer."

As I doodle on my prescription pad, it all comes back to me: the shots in the night, the explosion, according to the newspapers, of two hundred kilograms of dynamite, and the smoldering debris of the villa on Levinsky Street, which I saw the next morning, where the dying major and the bodies of two Arab policemen were found.

"Was Rosenberg really responsible for that?"

"There's no question of it," he says, resting one arm on top of the locked glass cabinet where I keep my toxic drugs. Wearing rubber boots in which he's tucked the ends of his khaki pants, he gives the impression of a cavalryman; all he needs is a braided riding crop. Or at least he tries to give that impression. He stands without grace, his huge feet too wide apart, and he has the hands of a farmer: red knuckles and dirty fingernails.

He goes on. "Henry was married, you know."

"I had no idea."

"Oh, yes. To a pretty little French girl. She was caught in the blast, of course. From what we've heard, no one knows whether she'll make it or not."

"I'm very sorry to hear it."

"I believe you. We know the kind of man you are."

"What kind is that?"

He smiles. "If you told us where the boy is hiding, we'd pick him up and put him on ice for a while, on a kibbutz in the Galilee."

"He's got a bad infection."

"Has he? Well, we've got a well-equipped infirmary, a good nurse, and a doctor who drops by from Tiberias three times a week. He'll be in good hands. I promise you."

"Is the kibbutz near Tiberias?"

"Close enough."

"Are you a member?" I asked him.

He hesitates, and then, with the air of sharing a confidence, replies, "Yes." He sniffs at his right palm. "I'm in charge of the sheep. Lord, what a stink! You can never get rid of it."

"Rosenberg is armed, you know," I tell him. "He won't be taken alive."

"We have no intention of tangling with him, or any other Jew, unless we have to. Is the boy armed?"

"No, I don't think so."

"Good." He goes to the window and peers down. "God only knows what they're cooking up this time."

I rise and follow him. The middle-aged woman across the street is smoking a cigarette. Nahum says, "Don't worry about Rosenberg. We'll keep an eye on him. When you make up your mind to tell us where the boy is hiding, tell Guela down there."

It's begun to drizzle. The gray-haired woman steps back into the doorway and turns up the collar of her blue coat.

December 18, 1946. I've returned to the cellar alone. The door is unlocked, and my wet shoes squeak as I carefully make my way down the stairs. It suddenly occurs to me that the boy may now have a gun. I pause and strike a match. A brown rat scurries between my feet. The match goes out.

"It's Doctor Spitzer," I call out. "Remember? Rosenberg's friend. I'm all alone. I came by to see how you're coming along."

The boy answers in a hoarse voice, "Of course. Come on down."

"I can't see a damn thing."

"Wait a minute, I'll light my candle," he says. "Come over here and warm up."

Wrapped in his blanket, he is hunched over the edge of his cot, rubbing his hands over the hissing Primus.

"How's this for service?" he asks, thumping his shoe against a jerrican on the floor. "British Army-issue gasoline for the stove. Two of our girls stole it last night from an army lorry waiting for a green light on Ben Yehuda."

"Lie down and let me have a look at you."

He shakes his head. "No, what's the sense? I'll be leaving here in a day or two anyway, maybe less."

"Leaving?"

"Orders," he says, and asks, "Have you ever killed a man face to face with your bare hands?"

"No."

He coughs into his handkerchief. "I stabbed a Lithuanian man-hunter, you know, when I was thirteen. With a bread knife I always carried on me, under my shirt, stuck in my belt . . ."

Pale, sweaty, completely enervated, he lies back with his hands behind his head. His chest is distended. But then he resumes talking with the same passion as before, as if his memory alone remains inexhaustible.

"I stabbed him in the stomach, face to face, in an alley just off Rudnitzer Street, at night. A beautiful spring night, with a full moon. I could see everything. There I was, turning the corner, with a message for Itzik in my pocket, and he was standing there, lighting a cigarette. He had very bushy blond eyebrows, I remember.

"It was all over in a second. I didn't give him a chance. I threw myself at him and stuck the bread knife into his guts, right up to the hilt. He didn't make a sound. Then I pulled it out, very slowly, and let him have it again. He was already on his knees, holding on to the hilt with both hands. The blood seeped between his fingers. It looked black. Then he fell on his face. His peaked cap rolled off his head. He was wearing a white arm band, by the way, all the man-hunters did. I don't know why."

He coughs again and spits on the floor. "Then I started running. It was a stupid thing to do. I should have taken his pistol. We had almost no weapons. But I got scared, I suppose, and ran like hell until I got back to Itzik and gave him the message. 'You're all covered with blood,' he said. 'Yes,' I told him, 'I stabbed a man-hunter to death in an alley off Rudnitzer Street.'

"He put his arm around me. 'Never mind,' he said. 'You'll get used to it after a while.' 'Used to it?' I said, and I looked at the sadness on his face; on all the other faces, too. The same grief.

" 'Give me something to drink,' I told them. 'Haven't we got a drop of schnapps left around here?' Itzik passed me a bottle of Polish vodka, the best, with the blade of grass in it. I took three solid swigs, and it went right to my head. The real stuff.

" 'Come on,' I said. 'For God's sake, this is a celebration. Drinks all around. Who knows a song?'

"But what did they do? Stared at me, open-mouthed. 'Well, I do,' I told them." And raising himself up on his elbows, he sings a verse in Yiddish, clapping his hands.

"Do you understand it?" he asks me and, without waiting for an answer, translates it into Hebrew in his hoarse voice:

Heavy sheaves full of wheat,
Full of cheerful songs.
And the sun, it burns like fire.
Every hour is precious to us.
The field has given us bread
For the beautiful new life.

Then he lies back again, gasping for breath. "I took another couple of healthy swigs from that bottle. Wonderful stuff. I swear it smelled of that grass. The next thing I remember was waking up, in a corner, in Yankele's arms. We called him 'The Rebbe.' He was a yeshiva bocher, about seventeen, who'd joined us about a week before. When he wasn't running messages like me, he was praying.

" 'Do you feel better?" he asked me.

" 'Me? I never felt better in my life,' I told him. 'I stabbed him twice, you know. And when I pulled the knife out the first time, he grabbed the blade and cut his fingers.'

" 'Is that so?' Yankele said. He

scratched the back of his neck—
we were all crawling with lice—
and asked me, 'Do you know
what the Besht, may his memory
protect us, once said?' And he
leaned forward and whispered in
my ear, 'Evil is only the throne
of good.'"

"And is that what you believe?"
I asked the boy.

"It's true," he says. "How can
you deny it?"

December 19, 1946. It's done.
I've betrayed the boy's hide-out.
This morning I had a few words
with poor Guela, who's caught a
bad head cold from lurking in
that doorway.

"You'd better move tonight," I
tell her. "They're up to something."

She sneezes and, with her nose
in a handkerchief, turns on her
heel toward Allenby, but I stop
her. "Do you have the address
of my flat?"

"Of course."

"Then ask Nahum to drop by
when it's all over, will you?"

She nods, and it's the café on
Dizengoff for me where I order
a pint of Johnnie Walker Red,
which I can't afford. Two agents
of the C.I.D. are seated at the
next table, to my right, wearing
identical clothes: gray flannel
trousers and single-breasted blue
tweed jackets that bulge from the
revolvers they carry in shoulder
holsters against their hearts. One
of them orders two glasses of

whisky, with a siphon of soda, in
a Hebrew which his thick Man-
chester accent renders almost un-
intelligible. The waiter, who is a
survivor of Sachsenhausen, pre-
tends not to understand and
shrugs.

"The bloody Yid," the agent
says in English.

"Forget it," the other one says.
"Needn't make a moan of it." He's
older, wearier, with a drawn sallow face. "To hell with him. Let's
pack it in. It's been a long day."

At the door, they put on their
trench coats. It's raining again, as
if to console them with a memory
of home.

Maybe it's the Scotch; I've already had three stiff drinks, but
I can't help feeling a twinge of
pity for them. A working knowledge of Hebrew entitles them to
a bonus of five pounds sterling a
month, and from the look of their
frayed collars and cuffs, they can
use it.

1 p.m. In my flat. Nahum is
seated on the chair under the
bookshelf with his head in his
hands. He's soaked to the skin,
and his rubber boots are covered
with mud, which he has tracked
on my Persian carpet.

"The boy's gone," he says. "Vanished." He looks up. "Do you have
something for a headache? My
head's splitting."

"What happened?"

"Just one of those things. We'd
posted a lookout on Hebron

Street, opposite the house, to keep an eye out for Rosenberg. Just a kid, but a damn police mobile force, cruising around, picked him up for routine questioning. They took him to the police station on Jaffa Street, checked his papers, which were all in order, of course, asked him a few questions, and then let him go. But by that time, it was too late. Eli and I . . . you don't know Eli, do you? No, of course not. He served in the night squads with Wingate in '37 . . . Anyway, we arrived at Hebron Street at exactly 10 p.m., as we'd planned. The lookout, of course, wasn't there, but we decided to take a chance. We went into the back yard, but I knew something was wrong. The cellar door was wide open, banging in the wind. Eli shined his flashlight down there, but the place was empty. A cot, a table, a Primus, and a jerrican of gasoline. There was a rat on the table gnawing on a candle. The boy was gone.

"Rosenberg's no fool. My guess is that he must have hidden himself in the cemetery and, when he saw our lookout picked up, ran back to the cellar, wrapped the boy up in a blanket—there was no blanket on the cot—and took him away. And now he's on the loose."

"He needs medical attention. He won't get far without it.'"

"Rosenberg'll manage it somehow. You can bet on it. He's got special plans for that boy."

He shuts his eyes and rubs his forehead. "I hate to bother you, but my head is splitting wide open."

He drinks the bromide I mix for him in the kitchen and then repeats, "He's loose."

December 21, 1946. 7:30 p.m. Clear weather since early morning, but now it's clouding up. I've decided to return to Hebron Street, and for the first time by the shortest route: up Allenby Road.

The street is jammed; the crowd in an ugly mood. In a café on the corner of Brenner Street, behind a streaked window, a ranting middle-aged man bangs his fist on a table. The whole town seems possessed by an unsubstantiated rumor that a French freighter, chartered by the Haganah and crammed with over six hundred "illegal" Jewish refugees, has been intercepted in the Aegean and escorted to Cyprus.

In any case, the C.I.D. is making a show of force, along with the British and Arab constabulary. They range up and down the street, with drawn revolvers, demanding ID papers from screaming Jews who are made to stand with their hands raised while being frisked.

For some reason, the British have gotten it into their heads that members of the Stern gang have taken to disguising themselves as religious Jews. In the middle of the next block, in front of a pharmacy, a ruddy-faced British policeman wearing a soft peaked cap is carefully examining, page by page, a thick tractate of the Talmud for concealed copies of *The Front*, the propaganda pamphlet of the Stern gang that is generally distributed by fifteen- or sixteen-year-old kids. The bearded old man to whom the book belongs wrings his hands.

Hebron Street is dark and quiet. I stand in the muddy back yard. The cellar door creaks on its rusty hinges and is abruptly thrown open by a gust of wind. All that comes to mind is Nahum's repeated whisper, filled with horror, as he wiped the bromide from his lips, "He's loose . . ."

And then I imagine the boy, wrapped in that blanket reeking of naphtha, emerging from underground and disappearing into the darkness above. Where is he, I wonder? Has Rosenberg managed to smuggle him out of town?

I start back home, past the Old Cemetery, down Ben Yehuda and Allenby. The streets are littered with sodden scraps of paper. In front of The Lord Nelson, a bar particularly popular with British N.C.O.'s, the owner—a fat South African Jew—has dragged a case of imported Guinness stout out on the sidewalk, and bending over, he solemnly smashes the full bottles, one by one, against the curb. The crowd, which has grown considerably, watches in silence.

A British armored car is now parked at the intersection of Allenby and Hess. It swivels its turret, from which the barrel of a machine gun protrudes, toward a young girl with disheveled blond hair shaking her furled umbrella in the air.

"He's loose . . ."

Is it conceivable that any good can come of it?

Questions for Analysis and Discussion

1.   The story is told in the present tense. What might the author's purpose be in having his narrator tell the story this way?

2.   Who is the narrator? What do you learn about him as the story unfolds?

3.   In what time and in what milieu does the story take place? In what way has Ari Rosenberg implicated his friend the doctor, in his (Ari's) activities?

4. Why does Ari seek the doctor's help? How did the sick sixteen-year-old boy come to get the name Zemsta? What does the narrator notice about the back yard in the abandoned house on Hebron Street where the boy is hiding? What is the nature of the boy's illness? Why can't the doctor prescribe antibiotics? Why is it impossible to move the boy to a hospital?

5. Why does Ari show the doctor the British service revolver he is carrying? What significance in the story does the revolver have?

6. How does the narrator describe the British soldiers patrolling the streets of Tel Aviv? Does his description indicate sympathy or hatred for the soldiers? In what way does this scene prepare the reader for the later actions of the doctor?

7. Why does the doctor do what Ari asks of him? What experiences tie them in friendship? Why does the doctor find Ari unrecognizable? What kind of activities is Ari engaged in?

8. The doctor wants to know the background of the sick boy. What does Ari tell him? What kind of activities did the boy engage in? How did he escape the Nazis? What song of the Vilno partisans does Ari recite for the doctor? What is the boy doing in Israel?

9. Why does the author have the narrator describe the doctor's treatment of Arab children in the clinic on Etzion Gever and his sensitive care of the Arab mother who fainted? Can you prove that the purpose of this scene, like the narrator's attitude toward the British soldiers, is to prepare the reader for the decision the narrator will make concerning the boy?

10. Ari calls a second time for the doctor's help. On their round-about way to the cellar on Hebron Street, they see only a solitary Arab police officer. What purpose in the story does this incident serve? Is it unnecessary?

11. The boy fears being caught by the British because they will place him in a cell in Acre. Why is he fearful of Acre? What do you learn about the Jewish partisans from the boy's story? How is the boy's life saved? In the boy's view why was his life spared?

12. Who is the young man in the leather jacket who has been following the narrator? What does he tell the doctor about Ari Rosenberg? Is there any suggestion in the story that the boy, as well as Ari, was responsible for the attack in which Major Henry, the British security

officer, and two Arab policemen were killed? What does Nahum ask
of the doctor? Why does the Haganah wish to put the boy "on ice"?

13.   Why does the doctor visit the boy alone? What moral dilemma
is he facing? What experiences does the boy recount this time? How
was he affected by his killing of the Lithuanian man-hunter? Yankele,
one of the partisans, in seeking to console the boy quotes from the
founder of Hasidism. What is Hasidism? What does Yankele mean by
the statement, "Evil is only the throne of good"? Is his meaning the
same as that of the author?

14.   Why does the doctor reveal the boy's hideout to the Haganah?
What are his motives? In your view is his action justified? Is there a
relationship between the narrator's account of the difficulty two British agents of the C.I.D. have in trying to order whisky and soda and
the decision of the narrator to reveal the boy's hideout?

15.   The Haganah, acting on the doctor's information, planned to
pick the boy up. Why did their plan fail? How, according to Nahum,
did the boy get away? Why was Nahum so troubled that the boy was
"loose"?

16.   The doctor decides to return to Hebron Street. Why? He finds
a crowd on Allenby Road in an ugly mood. Why are the people
angry? How are the British dealing with the unrest? The narrator finds
Hebron Street quiet. He is troubled by Nahum's repeated whisper,
"He's loose." Why?

17.   What relationship does the author wish the reader to establish
between the boy's escape, the unrest on Allenby Road, the smashing
of the bottles of Guinness stout, and the British armored car pointing
the barrel of its machine guns at the young girl?

18.   Who was right? The doctor and Nahum or Ari and the boy?
From a careful reading of the story, can you discern where the sym-
pathies of the author lie? Does he support the views and actions of
Dr. Spitzer or those of Ari Rosenberg? Or is he dispassionate, presenting both sides objectively?

19.   How do you interpret the saying of the founder of Hasidism
that Yankele quotes to the boy to console him: "Evil is only the throne
of good"? What is the relationship between this saying and the theme
of the story?

20.   The story focuses on a number of symbols and symbolic actions: the pomegranate tree outside the building in the cellar of which

Ari is hiding Zemsta, the name Zemsta, the unreliable service revolver that Ari carries, Ari's placing the revolver on the table between him and the doctor as they talk about the sick boy, the prayerbook that Zemsta carried with him constantly while serving in the Vilno underground, the delirious dream of Zemsta in which he finds himself in a forest in which all the flowers are black, the breaking of the bottles of Guinness stout by the South African bar owner, the use of the word "loose" to describe Zemsta's escape from the Haganah. How do you explain each of these symbols or actions? How are they related to the events of the story? Are they effectively integrated in the story and effectively used?

Suggested Activities

1. In order better to understand this story, it is necessary to get information about certain events in the history of the Jewish people: a) the resistance of Jews in the Warsaw ghetto, the Vilno ghetto and other ghettos and concentration camps during the Nazi occupation of Poland and parts of Russia and b) the conflict between the Haganah and the Stern group in the attempt of Israeli Jews during the period of the British mandate of Palestine to smuggle Jews into Palestine. The best sources for information concerning the Vilno partisans are *The Jewish Catastrophe in Europe* edited by Judah Pilch (New York: American Association for Jewish Education, 1968) and *They Fought Back* edited by Yuri Suhl (New York: Schocken, 1974). For information concerning the Haganah-Stern group conflict, see *The Course of Modern Jewish History* by Howard Morley Sachar (New York: Dell, 1958); *Palestine Under the Mandate* by A. M. Hyamson (London, 1950); *The Struggle for Palestine* by J. C. Hurewitz (New York, 1950). Organize two committees, one to do research on Jewish resistance against the Nazis and the other to do research on Jewish opposition to British rule in Palestine. Arrange for the committees to report their findings to the class before discussion and analysis of the story.

2. Get a map of Tel Aviv. Maps of Tel Aviv are obtainable from the World Zionist Organization (515 Park Avenue, New York, N. Y. 10022). Mark on the map the places mentioned in the story. Draw lines indicating a direct route from a place on Allenby Road to Hebron Street and a circuitous route that you might take in the event that you suspect you are being followed and you wish to confuse your trackers.

3. After you have consulted a history of the period and are aware of the attitudes of different Israeli groups toward the British and British rule of Palestine, plan a debate between Nahum and Ari in which each defends the action he takes in the story.

4. Dr. Spitzer finds himself facing a moral dilemma. He makes the decision to reveal Zemsta's hiding place to the Haganah. Put yourself in Dr. Spitzer's place. Write a letter to a friend telling what you have done and justifying your action.

5. Write an editorial for a Haganah newspaper criticizing the assassination of Major Henry as an act harmful to Jewish aspirations in Palestine.

6. Put yourself in Ari Rosenberg's place. Write a letter to an Israeli newspaper defending your views and your actions.

7. Organize a committee to prepare a short anthology and, if possible, a short program of partisan songs that heartened the oppressed people of the occupied countries in their struggle against the Nazi conquerors.

8. Write a scene in fictional or play form in which, after the establishment of the state of Israel, Dr. Spitzer meets Zemsta on a street in Tel Aviv. How will they greet one another? What will they say to one another? Will there be any accusations or recriminations? Will they be friendly or polite to one another, or angry and insulting? How will they have been changed by Israeli victory and independence? What parts will both have played in the Israeli-Arab war that followed independence?

9. Plan a debate in an American Zionist organization between advocates and opponents of the Irgun tactics.

10. Hugh Nissenson is an American Jewish writer. The setting for many of his stories is Palestine. Find out what you can about Hugh Nissenson's life and activities, perhaps by writing to his publishers, to determine how he came to write such a story as *The Throne of Good* and other stories about Jews in the Yishuv (the Jewish community and government in Palestine under the British Mandate).

The Bilu School. Zionist Archives and Library, New York.

By Michael Rosenak

Behold the Dreamer

Introduction: **Israel and the American Jew**

The Jew came to America from countries where Jews were considered aliens, where they were at best tolerated, and where, therefore, life was hard. Jews were generally relegated to a ghetto and had almost no opportunities to advance economically and politically. Social aspirations were stifled and scorned; yearnings and reachings remained unfulfilled. Only in the study of the holy books, in the belief in God, in the rituals of faith and in the solace found in the synagogue as well as in family life could one have the emotional and intellectual experiences that made existence tolerable.

Here and there in Europe during the nineteenth century opportunities were offered to break out of the shell, to move into the larger community, and to taste its life and culture. But almost always, except in the relatively democratic states like England and Holland, the doors remained open only for short periods. The worst of the experiences occurred in Germany during World War II.

In democratic America, under a constitution created by people who recognized and honored the right of each person to be free and equal within the limits of personal and national security, the Jew encountered a world where it was possible to live without fear. Except for occasional economic and social discrimination, happiness could be found in study, work, and recreation. Only the normal vicissitudes of every day experiences and the human errors that led the country into unwise adventures marred the even tenor of life. Jews became totally identified with Americans who suffered the traumas of wars, the unrest of student uprisings, the bane of drug culture, the turmoils of desegregation conflicts, and the other upheavals of the twentieth century.

The establishment of Israel and the victories won by the Israelis against the Arab forces seeking to drive them into the sea raised the spirits of Jews all over the world. The American Jew was emotionally concerned with the fate of Israel, contributed financially to its growth, and visited the country, whenever possible, to delight in its growth, and to be revitalized spiritually. One would come home uplifted by the progress Israelis had made in building their new society. Cities seemed to have sprung up overnight; forests were beginning to cover arid land; deserts were being converted into farms; industries of many kinds were coming into existence and thriving.

The American Jews' primary loyalty has been to America, the land that provided freedom and security and the opportunity for self-fulfillment. But their feelings toward Israel have been different from their feelings toward America. Israel is tied up with history. It is a spiritual center that brings one closer to God.

Many American Jews are ready to offer some of their talent and time as teacher, scholar, artist, engineer, scientist, and so forth to help Israel. It is a kind of spiritual offering and takes on the mystic quality of sacrifice and prayer. This is the subject of Behold the Dreamer *by Michael Rosenak.*

Y OU MEET the strangest people at Ratner's Dairy Restaurant. The summer when Jerry Oppenheimer was sixteen and working for a printer on the East Side, he used to go to Ratner's a lot for lunch (potato pancakes and apple sauce). And that's where he met, across from him at the table of solitary eaters, Mr. Zeigelboim, a Yiddish journalist of sorts. Mr. Zeigelboim was a thin and worn-looking six-footer with flaxen white hair turning yellowish, with the complexion of the cheese blintzes he loved. And one day, after about a week of silent lunches, the old man shyly revealed that he was a student of the mystics, a devotee of the *kabbala.* In almost conspiratorial tones, he told Jerry that the world, including his room on Second Avenue, was actually over-flowing with Divine energy, a white radiance. The trouble was, this light of God was imprisoned within a thick husk, a kind of shell. And that explained the dreariness of things.

Zeigelboim, biting into his third blintz of the meal, explained that the whole trick was to realize that even the thickest shell was so completely permeated with the Light that even it, the husk, was holy; actually, if you only struggled hard enough, a kind of passageway to the Divine. The journalist bit thoughtfully, penetratingly, on the last bite of blintz. Then he lit a cigarette and greeted it with a hard cough. "Once in a while that spark of Divine Light glows through the shell, you can sense the white flame searing the crust till it becomes a lucid screen. Some people see it on mountain tops, others while facing the peeling pillars of old synagogues, but everyone glimpses it some time or another. *They* sometimes see it in the lines of Gothic spires. It's a feeling that if you only strain hard enough, you can push through the shell and grab hold of redemption." The yellowish man sighed.

Jerry stirred the sugar in his coffee. "Then why . . ."

"Ah, that's the big question. If things are so good, then why so bad, eh?" Zeigelboim raised his cup with an unsteady hand and then, embarrassed by the shaking, replaced it in the saucer. "The thing is, no matter how intensely we reach up the roots, to the Light, we remain creatures of the unredeemed world, held in the trance of Exile. The shell may appear paper-thin at some moments, but we are still sealed in its membrane. So, even at the moment when the encasing shell seems to be no more than a corridor to the radiance, an integral part of it even, a voice intrudes and asks, 'Why do you, vile creature spawned in darkness, pollute Redemption with your uncleanliness?' Then we retreat, shamed, and the Light recedes once again, a flickering dance of shadows."

Jerry blushed at the Redemption and the uncleanliness. Zeigelboim laughed and risked lifting the coffee cup again. "That voice is very somber, you know. It

sounds as though it must surely be the voice of God. But it isn't, Oppenheimer, that's the thing you have to know. It isn't. It's just the Evil Impulse, guardian of the shell. You see, Oppenheimer, the Evil Impulse, crouching on the dark exterior of the shell, doesn't know that the husk was created by God only to contain the Light." He leaned across the table, like a man confiding in his beloved. "The Evil Impulse doesn't know because it's only a fragment of God's design." He was whispering now, whispering and coughing. "But *we* know. That's the thing to remember, no matter how bad it gets. *We* know."

Somehow, Jerry didn't get around to eating at Ratner's after that day. The sultry Manhattan summer gave way to September gusts followed by icy rains and sleet storms on Second Avenue and the Concourse. Zeigelboim, coughing in his drafty room, was locked in one shell; Jerry, struggling with Regents exams and worried about college admission and the army, was confined to another. To say that in our language, they forgot each other.

Then one day right after his twenty-fourth birthday, when things had got to be very bad indeed for Jerry, he left the Bronx for Israel. It was an impulsive step. When he bought his plane ticket with the bulk of his savings, he was suddenly thinking of Zeigelboim and the shell that had to be shattered to dispel the darkness. Jerry, who had long flirted with Zionism, had the idea that perhaps the shell was simply the thick crust of Exile, with the Light just six thousand miles away.

Zeigelboim might not have seen it that way, of course. The Light, he would have said with one of those patient Jewish smiles, is much nearer and yet far more remote than that. It might have saddened him to hear the shell of ideology mistaken for the light of truth. But who can judge? The Light is the same everywhere, for God is one. But each of us has a shell all to himself.

And yet, there were times when Jerry wasn't sure there *was* a Light, though the shell was real enough. Sitting at a window of the Tel Aviv-Tiberias bus, it all seemed too familiar for comfort. He was still Jerry, and Jerry remained a fleshy husk, extending all the way to the tight circle at the pit of his stomach. His legs, somewhere below, were still his legs, maneuvering endlessly for comfort. The omnipresent sensation of his flabby body, sticking in moist heat to the leathery seat, was still there. So were the horny yellowed glasses, slipping on the narrow bridge of an incongruously thin nose and having to be pushed up again and again. What difference is there between all that in the Bronx and in Israel, or between the "D" train and a two-tone bus in Galilee? Below the white light of an Asiatic summer sun, the dull Philistine plain outside the window gave way to jagged hills and primly verdant valleys, and though Jerry had never been here before, had left New York only a week ago, that sight was familiar as well.

Jerry, whose Hebrew name was Gershon, had for years gazed inwardly at these trim fields and significantly jutting cliffs and the red roofs shimmering through thick orange groves that made up this Land of Promise. Now that he was here, he found himself wondering which was the real thing—the countryside all about him (beautiful but cramped landscapes, swarthy faces, tired mountains) or the colored slides, the visions of the Holy Land that had sustained him with a pinkish glow amidst the dreary brickishness of his native street. Now, on this bus, far from the cauliflower smells and Sunday beeriness of his Bronx apartment house, he had trouble deciding where the picture ended and the real thing began.

Looking out of a streaked window through slipping glasses, he concluded that it wasn't an easy question to answer. Take, for example, the moments before his plane landed. As the aircraft droned low over Tel Aviv, after hours of cloud-flecked ocean, he had thought. Finally . . . Home! But then, right before the ridiculous gulp of self-realization that happens only in stories, he had had the sense to check himself. This view from the airplane was, after all, only a picture. You thought you saw the totality of it, the glistening postcard whiteness of Tel Aviv, but that was an illusion of course. What kind of concrete wholeness could there be at the height of a mile, what kind of reality was that? And later, standing at the bustling corner where the Central Post Office was, the word "bustle," so descriptive of the scene, had come to warn him, to restore his sense. "Bustle" was picturesque. Which meant that it happened only in pictures. The place was still sweeping around him in images. It was the old problem of words, of concepts, and their relationship to things. The old medieval, eternal problem, the juggling of words and things that had made God such a sure and solid thing before His essence had become a word game.

There, at the Central Post Office on Allenby Street, he had had a heretical thought. Maybe, he reflected, those pictures of the Holy Land—those fine phrases about a past and a future too distant to be defiled by sweating Jews—maybe *that* was the only reality. And the noise and dirt and thready Nazi numbers tatooed on hairy arms were only a fragment, hence a dream. It was a soothing thought, comforting as only genuine heresies can be. It made it possible now to think even of New York, immense miles, six thousand concept-units away, as a vibrant place where eight million people lived in peace and harmony and enjoyed the benefits of democracy. To the chimes of historic City Hall. Seen from an airplane. Heard over the airwaves.

Jerry was traveling to the Galilee, but he felt as he had on those countless mornings when the subway had taken him to City College, where he had studied Literature, hoping to understand Life through stories. When all the best minds there, refugees from Hitler, from experience, had assured him that Literature was only a substitute for Life, albeit much nicer, he had left the Bronx for Brooklyn, there to study a while at the Talmudic Academy of Rabbi Haim Grunzberg, his paternal grand-uncle.

It had not been comforting there. Rabbi Haim and his disciples, their thin arms gesticulating frantically out of dark jackets, had proclaimed that Life *was* Literature. And of course that couldn't be true either. He'd seen it in their white hands, the liquid pools of their eyes. Those hands pulled gently at their cheeks as the dark eyes peered myopically towards God, but human faces made them shrink back in polite revulsion. The hands and the eyes gave them away, despite the agility of their tongues. Their vision was lofty, but it had a musty smell to it; it reached up to avoid the uncleanliness of swarming reality, the fearful challenge of human intimacy.

And the Bronx people in the family, the beefy uncles and aging brothers-in-law, with their Pepsi-Cola and their school teaching, casual agnostics whose lives were red markings in composition books—they were even worse. If Jerry asked them questions about how they made *sense* of it all, they laughed. The laughter was good-natured, but there was an edge of warning in it. Be careful, they laughed, we shall soon lose patience with you. Why don't you learn to *apply* yourself, find your place? Do not provoke us. How many pushups did you do this morning, what you need is a couple of years in the army, buster. Please, they laughed, please do not provoke us.

Through all this, Zionism had been a tentative refuge, a carefully packed suitcase locked against three boroughs, replenished at each stage of adolescent wandering, sometimes half-forgotten in a clutter corner. For Israel, as he understood the concept, was the marriage of significance and pushups; the union of the vision, the eternal vision, with the real day that is today and that is made up of things, trivial things bearing the imprint of truth. The day whose prosaic

deeds must be acted out in love if the vision was not to be exposed as an artful construction of the mind. A word game.

Wrapped in his thoughts, Jerry had all but forgotten the real landscape outside the window, when he suddenly heard the command: "Get thee up, unto the land that I shall show thee." But it was only the driver, saying, "You get off here, at the next stop." The driver spoke a Levantine sort of English and he was pointing with an airy wave of his free hand at the grocery store just coming into view on the curving country road. It must have been the tee-shirt under his open collar that had given Gershon away as Jerry. Israelis always wore regular undershirts. "The school is up on the hill there. You can already see the tiled roofs. It is a lovely structure. Beautiful." The driver spoke with amazing gentleness.

The fact is that Jerry had recognized the school too. He had known that his bus stop would be a grocery like this. But he hadn't considered how hot it would be and how the smell of his sweat would be there to remind him how frightened he was. The driver had noticed it, of course. That explained the gentleness, the unexpected kindness of that stocky bull-necked man.

He would have known those red-tiled roofs anywhere. There had been brochures of this school, or others just like it, arriving for years at the Oppenheimer mail-slot, in large illustrated envelopes. Near the lower margins of the wordy pamphlets there were glossy appeals for funds. But above them one saw pictures of schools with red-tiled roofs, schools where the Torah and worldly wisdom grew together, fused at the roots and growing lush. Brochures of this kind were always falling, like prayers that had lost their sense of direction, into the mail-boxes of dispersed Jewry. Within those large illustrated envelopes, faces from Heaven pleaded soundlessly with the beneficent on earth. The faces bent expressively over Talmud folios or looked with candid interest at chemical formulas spread out chain-like on bright blackboards. The youthful scholars of Israel placed their trust in Martin Oppenheimer (Certified Public Accountant), and Martin Oppenheimer's son, fingering the brochures in the mail tray where such stuff was dumped, fell in love with the concept of the thing —the Torah and the world, sewed together with flesh-colored thread. In Israel, if Zionism was not a hoax, the concept met the world unabashed. God and men found each other there in heavy folios or in a world ordered through chemical formulas or in candid eyes. A well-lighted vision, a song of songs reduced to a brittle plaint in the shell of concepts.

Now Gershon stood at the grocery where the bus stop was. In his back pocket there was a newspaper ad, offering a teaching position at a dormitory school in Galilee, an offer to teach English in a place of Torah. The ad, having clung moistly to his body together with the leather-smudged pants, was limp as he took it out to read again.

He stood for a moment to think it over. The grey and green bus was already moving down the road, a rumbling noise, till it became a mere picture in the distance, and he was left to look at the hill where the school stood, like a painting. Yes, it was still a painting, wasn't it? The roofs and, below them, the distant figures of pupils, walking as on stilts across a remote stage—that wasn't the school itself, was it? Gershon would have to go up there! Talk to the principal and walk into a real classroom. That thought frightened him and he felt himself being drawn into the whirlpool of agnosticism—where words mean nothing—and reality consists of jagged fragments, strewn senselessly about.

God forbid!

Gershon began walking up the hill. The heat shimmered over the fields in miniature valleys all around, and a neat farming village appeared somewhere below as he climbed. When he reached the campus, the expressive, intent faces of the brochure, bedecked with colorfully knit skull-caps, became human faces, etched in ugly curiosity. "Where's the principal's office?" he asked one of the boys who was lying on the lawn, propped up on his elbows.

"He wants the principal's office." The youngster gave a mockingly sharp shake of his head in the direction of his buddy.

"So don't be such a lout," laughed the boy next to him, a pimply red-head whose voice was still changing. He turned towards Gershon with a kind of laughing apology. "You mean the Rosh Yeshiva. He's in the Teachers' Room drinking tea. Here, I'll show you."

"Thank you," Gershon said, feeling like an imposter, exposed as Jerry Oppenheimer from the Concourse. He was flustered. Already a mistake. They didn't call him principal here. They called him Rosh Yeshiva.

"So tell me, Mr. Oppenheimer, what's the solution to my riddle, eh? How do you get *sabras*, Israeli boys, to understand that past perfect tense of yours?"

The Rosh Yeshiva was showing off, of course, but it did Gershon good to see it. The first moments with Rabbi Jacobi had been shocking, a Brooklyn sensation. The man seemed to be all beard and stomach and tired eyes. True, he was wearing an open shirt, with sleeves rolled halfway up, just to the elbow, but the eyes and the beard didn't go with the

citrus smell and the water-towers, the colored slides of orange-and-blue Israel. And then, happily, that bit about the past perfect, making Rabbi Jacobi a man who understood many things.

He discovered himself relaxing, stretching out his legs. "Is that the main problem? The past perfect?"

Rabbi Jacobi laughed, a riotous kind of laugh, uncomfortably familiar. The eyes of the older man dropped their weariness and became immense above the creased cheeks. "Not the main problem, Oppenheimer. English is the problem. The witches of *Macbeth* and Huxley's essays and all of it. Our Yeshiva boys find it hard to swallow."

"I understood from the newspaper that this was a Talmudic Academy and a regular high school. Both in one."

Rabbi Jacobi waved a pudgy hand with a show of briskness. "Yes, yes, of course. A Yeshiva high school. Still, it's difficult to swallow."

"I was hoping you would give me the chance to teach the pupils here how to chew. That makes swallowing easier."

The rabbi laughed again. "Chew, eh? That's good. Very clever. Tell me, did you really come here to live? From America?"

"Yes."

"Wonderful, wonderful. Very good. What made you think of our school?"

"You had an ad in the newspaper yesterday."

"Advertisement? Was there an advertisement? Well, maybe. Anyway, you come from Heaven. It's a fact, there is a position open here, it's true. Wonderful. From America. Why do you want to teach English?"

"English Literature is all I know," Gershon said. "I like the idea of teaching young Israeli Jews something . . . opening some windows to the larger civilization to which they belong. While I learn more of the Torah myself," he added quickly. "I was hoping that someone here could teach me the Torah in my free time."

"Wonderful!" the rabbi proclaimed jubilantly. "You want to learn the Torah." The man looked at Jerry with genuine affection. Then his eyes darkened as a qualifying thought crossed his mind. He rubbed his head and almost dislodged his black skullcap. "About the civilization . . . I don't know about the civilization . . ." The rabbi turned away to look at the hills on the horizon. He came back from the view to face Jerry again. "Far away there, Oppenheimer, there's a Polish village. You can't see it from here but I can see it everywhere. Where I was born. You know something? Jews lived in that village for three hundred years. Three hundred years is a long time, isn't that so, Oppenheimer?"

"Yes." Jerry pulled in his legs and crossed them.

"That's right. A long time. You know what happened there during the war, Oppenheimer? No, of course not, so I'll tell you. The Poles of the village, may their names and remembrance be blotted out, handed over all the Jews to the Nazis—in exchange for potatoes. The peasants had plenty of potatoes that winter, plenty. You understand, a kilo of potatoes for every kilo of Jew, may God avenge their spilled blood." He rumpled his hair. "So I don't know about the civilization . . . What *they* call civilization . . . just a way of talking. . . . Words!"

Gershon hugged his knees. "I've heard of many who helped Jews . . . under the eyes of the Nazis, taking all kinds of risks . . ."

"Could be. I have also heard such things. One hears many things."

The rabbi stopped suddenly and stared. Gershon was uncomfortable. This was an irritating man. Evidently didn't remember his own ad in the newspaper. Irritating, but wasn't it understandable? He thought about the Nazis a lot, that would explain it. Rabbi Jacobi was all right, though. He knew about Huxley. Broad shoulders. An earthy smell, with no trace, almost, of mustiness. "When can we talk about the job? Details, I mean? I can stay overnight. I told my relatives not to expect me."

"*Talk?*" The rabbi returned to

the world of the living with a shout. He slapped the American on the shoulder. Strong hand. A Polish peasant hand, despite what had happened. A warm electric current moved down from Jerry's shoulder. "Talk?" The rabbi chuckled. "Let's see you do some teaching. Why talk?" (Why did he laugh so much. There was a limit to that. It was beginning to sound ludicrous.) "I'll tell you what. Mr. Ben-Yaakov in the Junior class has an English lesson scheduled for one hour from now. He'll be glad to relax." The rabbi jumped to the book case, stomach and all. "Here. Take their textbook. Give a lesson on the short story. They've learned three stories so far. Take any one you like and analyze it. Let's see what you can do."

"How . . ."

"Any story you want. Any way you feel like doing it. You know what our Sages in the Talmud say. The Red River didn't split for our fathers till the first Jew jumped into the water. So jump, Oppenheimer. Here. Sit down. Help yourself to tea. Hot tea for hot weather. Nothing better. Settles the stomach. You need it. Take any story you want."

Gershon thought he was still talking. But when he looked up, the rabbi had left the room.

For twenty minutes Gershon scanned the stories Mr. Ben-Yaakov's class had read. The pages were much fingered, heavy with marginal notes, words and phrases encased in cumbersome explanations that somehow fell short of explaining. Gershon chose "The Devil and Daniel Webster" for his lesson. He bent over his notepaper to jot things down. Character analyses. What is the theme? The climax . . .

The hell with that. He scratched it all out. What could he explain to the class about that story, or any of the others, till he had taught it, coaxed the light out of the husk of words? These kids couldn't possibly understand about the Devil in New England, couldn't fathom that Christian myth, the reality of that Puritan place. To make them see it as it really was, he would have to sit patiently with his pupils, *his* pupils, for weeks, get them to feel the quality of Jabez Stone's fear of failure and damnation, make them wince at the reality of the Devil to that poor devil of a Yankee, Jabez Stone. From where Jerry sat he looked out at the Sea of Galilee, its waters tranquil in their distant tear-shaped crevice. He took a sip of tea.

And then, maybe with an assist from that postcard landscape, he had a good idea. He was sure it was good. A story from the Bible. After all, he and the pupils spoke the same language on that. That was what had brought them to this place, out of the reach of potato-hungry savages, away from the sundry horrors of Exile. And the Torah—what was the Torah if not the place where Exile ended, where all distortions were erased, where all truths met?

He would teach them the story of Joseph? Why not? It was a human tale and the Word of God, an encounter of Literature with Life, a kabbalistic shell permeated with Light. In short, a meeting place for men and God, both preoccupied with redeeming the world.

Gershon returned to his notepaper with forceful strokes. After ten minutes, he closed his notebook, adjusted his glasses, and sat back to look out at the Sea of Galilee in the afternoon sunlight. Here he was, actually here, and the reality of it was beautiful. Like a painting.

The class stood up when he entered. "Please sit down." They sat. Having met the requirements of formal respect, some of the boys settled back to scoff softly. It must be the tee-shirt again. And anyway, they were expecting "The Devil and Daniel Webster." Quite right to scoff then.

"I'm going to try to show you . . ." He caught himself and smiled apologetically at Mr. Ben-Yaakov in the last row, "to review with you, I should say, what it is that makes a narrative . . . er . . . a telling of something, a story." The Rosh Yeshiva sat quietly in a seat near the door. Ben-Yaakov seemed to be fretting, but his restless eyes revealed that this

was his nature. Gershon put his hands into his pockets. The pockets, factory-fresh and stiff, enfolded him slowly and then held him in a firm clasp. He became aware of the khaki newness of the pants, bought yesterday, in Tel Aviv. He was a part of Israel now. "What makes a story . . . a story? Anyone? Yes, please."

It was the pimply redhead. A friend. "Ven you vant to tell somesing."

"Well, eh ("Yossi"), well Yossi, if I were to tell you that I got up this morning and ate breakfast and took a bus from Tel Aviv to your school (From Tel Aviv! To this red-roofed school! And it wasn't a film now or a brochure!) and taught you this lesson . . . Is that a story?"

Yossi laughed. "No, zat is only telling somesing, but it is not at all a story."

"A story hass an idea, hass it not?" The rabbi smiled happily at the second volunteer. Rabbi Jacobi bore his pupils a sentimental love because, though they were Jews who had surely heard that there had been a Hitler in the world, they could still be kind and innocent and curious. The rabbi found himself completely immersed in the lesson. Oppenheimer looked good.

Gershon smiled. "Ah, but a great many books have ideas and yet are not stories. Take the Talmud, for example." The rabbi looked puzzled. Gershon felt suddenly clumsy, though the class was completely attentive now. "A story has a conflict, doesn't it?"

There were no comments from the class; their interest seemed almost sly now. "Look, if I told you that I got up this morning and prayed . . ."

Someone snickered. Had he said the wrong thing? He forced himself not to stop. It probably had nothing to do with him. Some private joke between two boys. ". . . and came to teach you because I am applying . . . er . . . interested in getting a position. . . . that is not a story. But if, unknown to me, someone else is on the same bus, going to the same place, for the same reason . . . and only one of us can get the job . . ."

Here and there, faces reflected in the light of recognition and Gershon was warmly grateful. "Let's take a story we all know. The story of Joseph in the Bible . . ." He swallowed hard without knowing exactly why. "You know, that story in the Torah is considered to be one of the greatest short stories in the world." The rabbi shuffled in his seat. "Now, who can tell me why that is a true short story?"

No hands were raised. The class, mutely expectant, seemed less friendly. "There is a conflict . . . a fight . . . here, right?"

"Who will Father Yaakov give the blessing." It was the boy next to Yossi.

"Yes, exactly. Judah or Joseph? Who is the son of the blessing? So we have a conflict. We want to know who will be the leader, the father of David, of the Messiah."

The boys looked skeptical. We have a conflict between Judah and Joseph, our righteous fathers? Do we? Do we really? Mr. Ben-Yaakov began drumming his fingers against his temple. "Not only a conflict, but we are interested, anxious. At first Joseph seems to be the chosen one. How do we know? His father gives him a coat of many colors, the symbols of the birthright, of the blessing. And let's not forget that he is the first-born of Rachael, the beloved wife. And then, a terrible thing happens. He is sold into slavery by his brothers, to Egypt. It seems tragic to us. What, we wonder, what will happen to his dreams?"

He retold the story for them, bringing them to the climax of blessing through a meandering road of terrible hatreds, of dark pits, of murky dreams and empty grain sacks in years of drought. An occasional nod showed that they were following him.

Outside, the panorama of Israel and the Sea of Galilee waited in the softening hues of afternoon to see how it would all turn out with these brothers, these warlike and godly brothers bound by passion and envy and blessing and guilt, waiting as these hills and rocks had always waited wherever the brothers or their descendants were concerned. Within the classroom, perched high on a hill in Palestine, were Gershon and Joseph and the principle of the short story and the drama of God's designs for a family of destiny, all in place, all incredibly intact somehow, even though there had been a Hitler in the world.

The pupils listened, with the afternoon purple playing on their faces, until Judah was enthroned on the seat of blessing and mankind had set its face toward the End of Days when a redeemer would spring from Judah's loins. And so the lesson ended.

"Come into the Teachers' Room, Mr. Oppenheimer. We can talk there." The rabbi sounded gentle and very tired.

"It's difficult to get teachers to come here, Mr. Oppenheimer. People don't want to live in small Galilee villages anymore." The tone was confiding but there was something too sad for comfort in it. "I don't know what to tell you, Mr. Oppenheimer."

"Please call me Gershon."

The rabbi nodded, smiling faintly, and Jerry knew that this was all wrong. A sour bile rose in his throat. "I don't know what to tell you," the rabbi repeated and looked out of the window.

Gershon thought that a man must live by his faith. To prove it, he swallowed the bile and brought out words. "How did you like the lesson? They got the idea, I think. I wanted to illustrate with a story they know, really know, something that is part of their lives.'"

"Joseph isn't a short story for them, Mr. Oppenheimer. It is Torah."

"I feel that it is both—Torah and a short story. That's what makes it . . ." The rabbi wasn't listening. He looked infinitely sympathetic, but he wasn't listening, so Jerry's lecture fell between them, a game of catch with only one player. The sentence hung in the air, squirming, dying. The Rosh Yeshiva nodded again and smiled again. "The boys don't see it as a story. For them, it is Torah." The purple outside was becoming a deep blue now. "I'll be in touch with you, Mr. Oppenheimer. Leave your address with the secretary, will you?"

"I'd appreciate it."

The rabbi shook hands. He was a good man despite the villagers, those damn potato eaters. So he took Jerry to the door and laid a broad hand on the American's shoulder. "I'll be in touch with you . . . Gershon."

"Thank you." Jerry, walking down the corridor to the secretary's office, wished that the rabbi had remained seated.

On the way back to Tel Aviv, Jerry noticed that the weather had turned chilly. He was sorry that he had taken a window seat, a drafty one, and he rolled down his sleeves and hugged at his chest for warmth.

A woman sat down next to him. She was a heavy person, a peasant woman from Turkey or Bulgaria. For her trip to the city she had lipstick on, but it was artlessly done and she smelled of cows. Her massiveness pushed him closer to the drafty window. He could see her with the cows. He felt imprisoned in his seat. It was so narrow, with that hulking woman and the black window . . . Imprisoned . . .

He had been in prison for over two years now. Brought to this place through Potiphar's wife, through his own passion struggling with his dream of greatness, of God's plan for him. The passion had been conquered, for the sake of God, and now he was here, surrounded by sorrowful eunuchs while he himself burned with manly passion . . . and that was for the sake of God too, who had promised seed to his father, Jacob . . .

Suddenly, a messenger from Pharaoh himself, summoning him to interpret a dream. Pharaoh had seen cows rising out of the Nile, fat cows and no one could relate to Pharaoh the meaning of these slimy beasts. The hope burned hotly, the impertinent flame. Now they would all bow down to the son of Rachael, the man of blessing, a virile man of pleasing form. His brothers had sold him in vain,

in fact that was part of the whole scheme. (Right, God?) He was too important, the beloved son, blessed of God. And besides . . . too handsome . . .

Here was the barber, come to shave him for the royal interview. A smooth fat man, shaving the doomed and the dreamers. Looking at the barber's cruel eyes (or were they only sad eyes, the eyes of Mr. Sarbelli, the Concourse barber?) he realized the absurdity of it. What was his dream of twelve sheaves of grain, with eleven bowing to his, but a fantasy of adolescence, a vain and foolish thing? And what would Freud say? He would smile and lean back in his chair to interpret . . . But it was the plan of God, wasn't it? To feed the world, to rescue the famished from starvation . . . Yes, of course, the Torah said . . . But what could God want with a vain dreamer, what had He to do with boys clawing through the caverns of puberty? Narcissism had brought him to the pit, and the stinking cows in the mind of an overwrought idolator would now release him. With the help of God. . . . No! How banal!

No, no, he shouted at the barber, something is wrong here, there are too many jagged edges in this picture . . . all fragments . . . but if it is Torah, it can't be fragments . . . must make *sense* . . . His uncle poured the Pepsi-Cola and laughed. How many push-ups did you do this morning, buster?

The barber shaved impassively and his uncle burped. In the distance, Potiphar's wife was laughing too. This is the Word of God, Joseph shouted at the barber, the Torah . . . a holy book . . . Potiphar's wife laughed louder. From every corner of the royal dungeon, prisoners began to laugh. It sounded hollow, horrible, but good - natured. Potiphar's wife laughed at the echoes. As she laughed, the thick paint on her carefully composed face came apart, the cosmetics crusted and foul. Joseph jerked his head away and the barber's knife almost drew blood. Looking back at Potiphar's wife, her face washed clean of paint now, she seemed almost beautiful. He thought, she's crying, her laughing is actually tears because she loves the man of blessing . . . As this thought entered his mind, she stopped laughing . . .

The woman had stopped laughing, embarrassed. She was looking at Jerry with sympathy, as though she knew everything. Shyly Jerry lifted his head, fallen in sleep upon her shoulder, and apologized. She said that it was all right, it had been a hot day and that made people tired.

"Tell me what happened to make such a young man so sad." She looked reverent.

He told her.

"You'll get the job, I know. They can't find people to come up here, people who have studied, scholars." She seemed almost carried away by awe.

He felt that he should explain that he wasn't a scholar at all, just a boy from City College, but he realized how pretentious that would sound to this woman. So he fell back into petulant childhood. "I don't think I would want it . . . now . . . I imagined it quite differently. A place of Torah and . . ." Again he caught himself. Nominalism and Realism, shell and light, what had this to do with such a woman?

She patted him familiarly, maternal. "Don't be silly, child. One has to live." Her smile was smudged with a certain condescension. "I don't *know* what you imagined, but let me tell you. A man has to live first. That rabbi, I know him. He won't find anyone else so quick, such a scholar. And it will give you a place, a livelihood. You'll see."

The two of them reached Tel Aviv in the late evening. By then, the hills of Galilee seemed lovely again.

Ten days later, there was a letter, almost illegibly scribbled, from Rabbi Jacobi. Gershon could begin teaching in the fall. Rabbi Jacobi wrote that he had been impressed with Gershon's desire to study Torah. He himself hoped to assist Gershon towards this sacred goal.

The rabbi's letter made Gershon feel illogically vindicated, happy, drunkenfully hopeful. But again, something checked him; something somber inside, from within the tight circle where his integrity was, told him that this bliss was childish. It showed how immature Jerry was, how spineless and naive. (Jacobi wants to teach *you*, to influence you. He doesn't care about *your* dreams . . . Do you really think he can *understand* you? Can *anybody*?)

But there was also another voice, less somber, less chummy, that simply said, "Don't be silly, my child." Jerry remembered, the woman on the bus said something like that, but this was different. The condescension had been filtered out of it. "A man has to live," she'd said, but now he heard it without the weary scorn and only the last word remained, lifted above bitterness, a strong hand on his shoulder, despite what had happened.

That fall, be became an Eng-lish teacher in the Galilee. The pupils took to him and, for some reason, the Rosh Yeshiva never interfered with his lessons. After a few months, on a fragrant evening right after the first rains, Gershon, under the careful tutelage of Rabbi Jacobi, became a student of the Torah. And he met Rachael, who brought in tea at her father's signal.

When she came in, Rabbi Jacobi closed the sacred book with familiar reverence. Then, his arms folded on the richly ornamented cover of his Talmud, he leaned forward heavily. "So tell me," he said in a Talmudic semi-chant, "what is one to make of this Hamlet, eh? Why can't the fellow make up his mind?" Gershon noticed the firm Polish muscle rippling under the tatooed number on the rabbi's arm. He looked up, embarrassed by the Nazi stigma, and saw Rachael smiling as she poured the steaming tea.

Questions for Analysis and Discussion

1. The title *Behold the Dreamer* comes from Genesis 37:19. Joseph is sent by his father Jacob to see "whether all is well" with his brothers and "well with the flock." When his brothers see Joseph coming toward them from afar they remark to one another "Behold this dreamer cometh." What is the relationship between the Joseph story and the dreams of Jerry Oppenheimer? Is this relationship fully established in the story? In what ways are the dreams of Jerry like those of the biblical Joseph? In what ways are they different?

2. Mr. Zeigelboim is an important influence in Jerry's life. What was Zeigelboim's occupation? How did his study of the *kabbalah* influence his thinking? What is Zeigelboim's view of the universe and of good and evil? Which of Zeigelboim's statements are the ones which will influence Jerry later to seek a job in Israel? Explain the statement: ". . . no matter how intensely we reach up the roots, to the Light, we remain creatures of the unredeemed world, held in the trance of Exile." What in Zeigelboim's view will redeem the world? What is the Light?

3. Why does Jerry decide to go to Israel? He wonders whether the light of his dreams is the light of truth. Why? What are his doubts? Jerry realizes how man is confused by the contrast between illusion and reality. What are his illusions? What are the realities? How are illusions and realities related to Zeigelboim's mystic view of life?

4. Jerry is a student of literature. What conclusions about literature does he arrive at from his studies at City College, where some of his instructors are refugees from Germany? Which of the following views about literature do you agree with: a) literature is a substitute for life; b) literature is life? Why was Jerry critical of the rabbis? Why was he critical of his relatives, "the beefy uncles and aging brothers-in-law"? What did he mean when he thought that their "lives were red markings in composition books"? Is this an effective metaphor?

5. How did Zionism come to be a refuge for Jerry? What did he mean when he said it "was the marriage of significance and pushups," the union of vision with the real day? The mystic vision of God in the *kabbalah* often deteriorated into a word game. How? Why did Jerry fear that his vision of mission and *aliyah* might be a word game? How

do we delude ourselves into believing that our actions are motivated by idealism and nobility and not by self-interest?

6. The bus driver stops in front of a grocery store in the Galilee to let Jerry off. What was Jerry's destination? What did he hope to find in a Talmudic Academy in Israel concerning the relationship between God and man?

7. Jerry meets Rabbi Jacobi, the Rosh Yeshiva (principal) of the Academy. What characteristics of the principal strike him as unusual? Jerry's remark about "opening some windows to the larger civilization" in his Israel classroom evokes some memories in Rabbi Jacobi. What are these memories? How does Rabbi Jacobi feel about the larger civilization? If he thinks the larger civilization destructive of the Jews, why does he feel that his pupils should study the works of Shakespeare, Huxley, and other writers?

8. The principal asked Jerry to teach a class a lesson in the appreciation of a short story. Why does Jerry decide *not* to teach "The Devil and Daniel Webster"? Why does he choose the Biblical story of Joseph as the subject of his lesson? What elements and themes in the story of Joseph does he teach? Jerry—in Israel he calls himself Gershon —sees himself as bearing a resemblance to Joseph. What aspects of Joseph's life does he view as similar to his own? How does Jerry's conception of God's design enter into this comparison? What does he believe is God's design for him?

9. Rabbi Jacobi is apparently not impressed with Jerry's trial performance. What had Jerry done wrong? On the way back to Tel Aviv, he dreams of Joseph, reviews some of Joseph's experiences in his mind. In what ways does he see himself as a dreamer akin to Joseph? Why is Jerry discouraged? How does the lady on the bus reassure him?

10. Jerry gets the job. What element of reality has entered his daydreams? Comment on the way the author ends the story? Why is Rachael brought into the story at this point? Why is the tatooed number on Rabbi Jacobi's arm brought in? What does the future hold for Jerry? Is the ending sentimental and unreal? What do you think?

Suggested Activities

1.   We are living in a time when there is great interest in mystic experiences. A committee of the class might be selected to investigate and report on a number of mystic beliefs of various young people's religious groups in America such as: the Jesus movement, Buddhism, Krishna Consciousness, Folk-Rock Hasidism, others. (See whether tapes of the Public Television series on Religious America are available.)

2.   Since the biblical Joseph plays so great a role in the story, one or two members of the class might read the biblical account and compare their interpretation with that of Jerry, the central character in the story.

3.   As a composition exercise, students might be asked to put themselves in Jerry's place as a teacher of English in an Israeli academy and write a letter home to a relative in the U.S. describing their experiences.

4.   Have a number of students take an imaginary trip from Tel Aviv to the Galilee and describe in writing or orally the scenery and people seen from the bus window. An oral account can be illustrated with pictures on slides borrowed from relatives and friends who have visited Israel, or from such organizations as the Israel Government Tourist office, the Israeli Consulate, and so forth.

5.   In the story Jerry decides not to teach "The Devil and Daniel Webster" by Stephen Vincent Benet because it would be difficult to explain to Israeli students the beliefs, superstitions, and values of the Puritans. Have one or two students read the Benet story and describe to the class the Puritan view of life it presents.

6.   Have one or two students read *The Dybbuk* by S. Ansky and *The Tenth Man* by Paddy Chayevsky and report to the class what the two plays are about. Both plays have mystic elements.

Interior of the synagogue on Arkhipova Street, Moscow. Courtesy of the National Conference on Soviet Jewry.

By Bernard Malamud

Man in the Drawer

Introduction: **The Russian Jewish Writer in Chains**

The story of the trials and tribulations of the Russian writer, Aleksandr Solzhenitsyn, is well known. Anxious to publish his exposure of the evils of the Russian prison system (in a book called The Gulag Archipelago*) he managed to smuggle his manuscript out of the country and thereby incurred the further wrath of Soviet authorities. The support he received from the cultural community outside the Soviet Union probably saved his life. Soviet officials finally solved their quarrel with Solzhenitsyn by exiling him from his native land.*

In order to maintain the supremacy of its political and social philosophy, the totalitarian government of the Soviet Union has demanded that its scientists, scholars, and artists conform to established rules and patterns in pursuing and publicizing their works. During the early years, and especially during the regime of Stalin, divergence from regulation and precept was severely punished—sometimes by death, more frequently by incarceration in the far-flung prison camps. For awhile, during the primacy of Khrushchev, there were minor easings of the restrictions. With the advent to power of Kosygin and Brezhnev, however, there was a return to the more repressive measures of the Stalinist era. Though the dissidents are no longer summarily tried and executed—the Soviet Union is seeking to improve its image in the Western world—they are subjected to various types of punishments and indignities. Some are sent to mental hospitals for "treatment," others, to the prison camps; many lose their jobs; most are subjected to various forms of petty harassment.

Dissident writers, especially those who carry identification cards on which their identity as Jews is recorded, find themselves in serious trouble if the themes of their work are contrary to the current official interpretation of Communist ideology. Specifically proscribed are writings that deal with religious conflicts, with dissatisfactions arising from the inability to maintain one's ethnic identity, or with any criticisms of the policies and programs of the government vis-à-vis its conglomerate population or its foreign policy.

In the past, independent writers, especially Jewish writers, fared poorly in Soviet Russia. Isaac Babel, brilliant short story writer, died in a prison camp; Itzik Feffer and Peretz Markish, poets, were executed in the dreaded Lubyanka prison on the night of August 12, 1952; Yuri Galanskov, poet and samizdat publicist, died in a prison camp at the age of 33; Andrei Amalrik, essayist and historian, was imprisoned in a Siberian labor camp; Natalya E. Gorbanevskaya, a poet who demonstrated in Red Square against the Soviet invasion of Czechoslovakia, was forcibly interned in a psychiatric hospital for three years.

The Russian Jewish writers are in a dilemma. Their talent urges them to write. The most vital themes arise from their experiences and the impact of their world. Their identity card labels them Jewish. Even as a dedicated communist and a professed atheist, one cannot divest oneself of one's curiosity about the Jewish people, especially since the newspapers are filled with anti-Israel and anti-Zionist tirades. Almost unconsciously, the ethnic conflicts, the discriminations against Jews, the frequent reversions to ancient rituals, the psychological unrest caused by pointless repression creep into one's work. The writers want to be published; they feel their work is true and honest. But no publisher or editor will touch it. In fact, writers are warned that they will be in serious trouble if what they are about the write becomes known. Such a writer becomes a secret author, a "man in a drawer," yearning to escape. Such a writer is the protagonist of Bernard Malamud's story.

A soft SHALOM I thought I heard, but considering the Slavic cast of the driver's face, it seemed unlikely. He had been eyeing me in his rear-view mirror since I had stepped into the taxi and, to tell the truth, I had momentary apprehensions. I'm forty-seven and have recently lost weight but not, I confess, nervousness. It's my American clothes, I thought at first. One is a recognizable stranger. Unless he had been tailing me to begin with, but how could that be if it was a passing cab I had hailed myself?

He had picked me up in his noisy Volga of ancient vintage on the Lenin Hills, where I had been wandering all afternoon in and around Moscow University. Finally I'd had enough of sightseeing, and when I saw the cab, hallooed and waved both arms. The driver, cruising in a hurry, had stopped, you might say, on a kopek, as though I were someone he was dying to give a ride to; maybe somebody he had mistaken for a friend. Considering my recent experiences in Kiev, a friend was someone I wouldn't mind being mistaken for.

From the moment we met, our eyes were caught in a developing recognition although we were complete strangers. I knew nobody in Moscow except an Intourist girl or two. In the mottled mirror his face seemed mildly distorted—badly reflected; but not his eyes, small, canny, curious—they probed, tugged, doubted, seemed to beg to know: give him a word and he'd be grateful, though why and for what cause he didn't say. Then, as if the whole thing wearied him insufferably, he pretended no further interest.

Serves him right, I thought, but it wouldn't hurt if he paid a little attention to the road now and then or we'll never get where we're going, wherever that is. I realized I hadn't said because I wasn't sure myself—anywhere but back to the Metropole just yet. It was one of those days I couldn't stand a hotel room.

"Shalom!" he said finally out loud.

"Shalom to you." So it was what I had heard, who would have thought so? We both relaxed, looking at opposite sides of the street.

The taxi driver sat in his shirt sleeves on a cool June day, not more than 55° Fahrenheit. He was a man in his thirties who looked as if what he ate didn't fully feed him—in afterthought a discontented type, his face on the tired side; not bad-looking—now that I'd studied him a little, even though the head seemed pressed a bit flat by somebody's heavy hand although protected by a mat of healthy hair. His face, as I said, veered to Slavic: round; broad cheekbones, small firm chin; but he sported also a longish nose and a distinctive larynx on a slender hairy neck; a mixed type, it appeared. At any rate, the shalom had seemed to alter his appearance, even of the probing eyes. He was dissatisfied for certain this fine June day—his job, fate, appearance—what? And a sort of indigenous sadness hung on him, coming God knows from where; nor did he seem to mind if who he was was immediately visible; not everybody could do that or wanted to. This one showed himself. Not too prosperous, I would say, yet no underground man. He sat firm in his seat, all of him driving, a touch frantically. I have an experienced eye for such details.

"Israeli?" he asked in a whisper.

"Americansky." I know no Russian, just a few polite words.

He dug into his shirt pocket for a thin pack of cigarettes and swung his arm over the seat, the Volga swerving to avoid a truck making a turn.

"Take care!"

I was thrown sideways—no apologies. Extracting a Bulgarian cigarette I wasn't eager to smoke —too strong—I handed him his pack. I was considering offering my prosperous American cigarettes in return but didn't want to affront him.

"Feliks Levitansky," he said. "How do you do? I am the taxi driver." His accent was strong, verging on fruity, but redeemed by fluency of tongue.

"Ah, you speak English? I sort of thought so."

"My profession is translator— English, French." He shrugged sideways.

"Howard Harvitz is my name. I'm here for a short vacation, about three weeks. My wife died not so long ago, and I'm traveling partly to relieve my mind."

My voice caught, but then I went on to say that if I could manage to dig up some material for a magazine article or two, so much the better.

In sympathy Levitansky raised both hands from the wheel.

"Watch out, for God's sake!"

"Horovitz?" he asked.

I spelled it for him. "Frankly, it was Harris after I entered college but I changed it back recently. My father had it legally changed after I graduated from high school. He was a doctor, a practical sort."

"You don't look to me Jewish."

"If so why did you say shalom?"

"Sometimes you say." After a minute he asked, "For which reason?"

"For which reason what?"

"Why you changed back your name?"

"I had a crisis in my life."

"Existential? Economic?"

"To tell the truth I changed it back after my wife died."

"What is the significance?"

"The significance is I am closer to my true self."

The driver popped a match with his thumbnail and lit the cigarette.

"I am marginal Jew," he said, "although my father—Avrahm Isaakovich Levitansky—was Jewish. Because my mother was gentile woman I was given choice, but she insisted me to register for internal passport with notation of Jewish nationality in respect for my father. I did so."

"You don't say."

"My father died in my childhood. I was rised—raised?—to respect Jewish people and religion but I went my own way. I am atheist. This is almost inevitable."

"You mean Soviet life?"

Levitansky smoked without replying as I grew embarrassed by my question. I looked around to see if I knew where we were. In afterthought he asked, "to which destination?"

I said, still on the former subject, that I had been not much of a Jew myself. "My mother and father were totally assimilated."

"By their choice?"

"Of course by their choice."

"Do you wish," he then asked, "to visit Central Synagogue on Arkhipova Street? Very interesting experience."

"Not just now," I said, "but take me to the Chekhov Museum on Sadovaya Kudrinskaya."

At that the driver, sighing, seemed to take heart.

Rose, I said to myself.

I blew my nose. After her death I had planned to visit the Soviet Union but couldn't get myself to move. I'm a slow man after a blow, though I confess I've never been one for making his mind up in a hurry about important things. Eight months later, when I was more or less packing, I felt that some of the relief I was looking for derived, in addition to what was still on my mind, from the necessity of making an unexpected serious personal decision. Out of loneliess I had begun to see my former wife, Lillian, in the spring; and before long, since she had remained unmarried and still attractive, to my surprise there was some hesitant talk of remarriage; these things slip from one sentence to another before you know it. If we did get married we could turn the Russian trip into a sort of honeymoon—I won't say second because we hadn't had much of a first. In the end, since our lives had been so frankly complicated—hard on each other —I found it impossible to make up my mind, though Lillian, I give her credit, seemed to be willing to take the chance. My feelings were so difficult to define to myself I decided to decide nothing for sure. Lillian, who is a forthright type with a mind like a lawyer's, asked me if I was cooling off to the idea, and I told her that since the death of my wife I had been examining my life and needed more time to see where I stood. "Still?" she said, meaning the self-searching, and implying, I thought, forever. All I could answer was "Still," and then in anger, "Forever." I warned myself afterward: Beware of any more complicated entanglements.

Well, that almost killed it. It wasn't a particularly happy evening, though it had its moments. I had once been very much in love with Lillian. I figured then that a change of scene for me, maybe a month abroad, might be helpful. I had for a long time wanted to visit the U.S.S.R., and taking the time to be alone and, I hoped, at ease to think things through, might give the trip additional value.

So I was surprised, once my visa was granted—though not too surprised—that my anticipation was by now blunted and I was experiencing some uneasiness. I blamed it on a dread of traveling that sometimes hits me before long trips, that I have to make my peace with before I can move. Will I get there? Will the plane be hijacked? Maybe a war breaks out and I'm surrounded by artillery. To be frank, though I've resisted the idea, I consider myself an anxious man, which, when I try to explain it to myself, means being this minute halfway into the next. I sit still in a hurry, worry uselessly about the future, and carry the burden of an overripe conscience.

I realized that what troubled me mostly about going into Soviet Russia were those stories in the papers of some tourist or casual traveler in this or that Soviet city, who is, without warning, grabbed by the secret police on charges of "spying," "illegal economic activity," "hooliganism," or whatnot. This poor guy, like somebody from Sudbury, Mass., is held incommunicado until he confesses, and is then sentenced to a prison camp in the wilds of Siberia. After I got my visa I sometimes had fantasies of a stranger shoving a fat envelope of papers into my hand, and then arresting me as I was stupidly reading them of course for spying. What would I do in that case? I think I would pitch the envelope into the street, shouting, "Don't pull that one on me, I can't read Russian," and walk away with whatever dignity I had, hoping that would freeze them in their tracks. A man in danger, if he's walking away from it, seems indifferent, innocent. At least to himself; then in my mind I hear the sound of footsteps coming after me, and since my reveries tend to the rational, two husky KGB men grab me, shove my arms up my back and make the arrest. Not for littering the streets, as I hope might be the case, but for "attempting to dispose of certain incriminating documents," a fact it's hard to deny.

I see H. Harvitz yelling, squirming, kicking right and left, till his mouth is shut by somebody's stinking palm and he is dragged by superior force—not to mention a blackjack whack on the skull —into the inevitable black Zis I've read about and see on movie screens.

The cold war is a frightening business, though I suppose for some more than others. I've sometimes wished spying had reached such a pitch of perfection that both the U.S.S.R. and the U.S.A. knew everything there is to know about the other, and having sensibly exchanged this information by trading computers that keep facts up to date, let each other alone thereafter. That ruins the spying business; there's that much more sanity in the world, and for a man like me the thought of a trip to the Soviet Union is pure pleasure.

Right away at the Kiev airport I had a sort of fright, after flying in from Paris on a mid-June afternoon. A customs official confiscated from my suitcase five copies of *Visible Secrets*, a poetry anthology for high school students I had edited some years ago, which I had brought along to give away to Russians I met who might be interested in American poetry. I was asked to sign a document the official had carefully written out in Cyrillic, except that *Visible Secrets* was printed in English, "secrets" underlined. The uniformed customs officer, a heavy-set man with a layer of limp hair on a smallish head, red stars on his shoulders, said that the papers I was required to sign stated I understood it was not permitted to bring five copies of a foreign book into the Soviet Union; but I would get my property back anyway at the Moscow airport when I left the country. I worried that I oughtn't to sign but was urged to by my lady Intourist guide, a bleached blonde with wobbly heels whose looks and good humor kept me more or less calm, though my clothes were frankly steaming. She said it was a matter of no great consequence and advised me to write my signature quickly because it was delaying our departure to the Dniepro Hotel.

At that point I asked what would happen if I willingly parted with the books, no longer claimed them as my property. The Intouristka inquired of the customs man, who answered calmly, earnestly, and at great length.

"He says," she said, "that the Soviet Union will not take away from a foreign visitor his legal property."

Since I had only four days in the city and time was going fast, faster than usual, I reluctantly signed the paper plus four carbons—one for each book—or five mysterious government departments?—and was given a copy, which I filed in my billfold.

Despite this incident—it had its comic quality—my stay in Kiev, in spite of the loneliness I usually experience my first few days in a strange city, went quickly and interestingly. In the mornings I was driven around in a private car on guided tours of the hilly, broad-avenued, green-leaved city, whose colors were reminiscent of a subdued Rome. But in the afternoons I wandered around alone. I would start by taking a bus or streetcar, riding a few kilometers, then getting off to walk in this or that neighborhood. Once I strayed into a peasants' market where collective farmers and country folk in beards and boots out of a nineteenth-century Russian novel sold their produce to city people. I thought I must write about this to Rose—I meant of course Lillian. Another time, in a deserted street when I happened to think of the customs receipt in my billfold, I turned in my tracks to see if I were being followed. I wasn't but enjoyed the adventure.

An experience I enjoyed less was getting lost one late afternoon several kilometers above a boathouse on the Dnieper. I was walking along the riverbank liking the boats and island beaches, and before I knew it, had come a good distance from the hotel and was eager to get back because I was hungry. I didn't feel like retracing my route on foot—much too much tourism in three days—so I thought of a cab, and since none was around, maybe an autobus that might be going in the general direction I had come from. I tried approaching a few passers-by whom I addressed in English or pidgin-German, and occasionally trying "Pardonnez-moi"; but the effect was apparently to embarrass them. One young woman ran a few awkward steps from me before she began to walk again. I stepped into an oculist's shop to ask advice of a professional-looking lady in her fifties, wearing pince-nez, a hairnet and white smock. When I addressed her in English, after five seconds of amazement her face froze and she turned her back on me. Hastily thumbing through my guidebook to the phonetic expressions in Russian, I asked, "Gdye hotel?" adding "Dniepro?" To that she gave me an overwrought "Nyet." "Taxi?" I asked. "Nyet," again, this time clapping a hand to her heaving bosom. I figured we'd both had enough ?nd left.

Though frustrated, irritated, I spoke to two men passing by, one of whom, the minute he heard my first few words, walked on quickly, his eyes aimed straight ahead, the other indicating by gestures he was deaf and dumb. On impulse I tried him in halting Yiddish that my grandfather had taught me when I was a child, and was then directed, in an undertone in the same language, to a nearby bus stop.

As I was unlocking the door to my room, thinking this was a story I would be telling friends all winter, my phone was ringing. It was a woman's voice. I understood "Gospodin Garvitz" and one or two other words as she spoke at length in musical Russian. Her voice had the lilt of a singer's. Though I couldn't get the gist of her remarks, I had this sudden vivid reverie, you might call it, of me walking with a pretty Russian girl in a white birchwood near Yasnaya Polyana and coming out of the trees, sincerely talking, into a meadow that sloped to the water; then rowing her around, both of us quiet, in a small lovely lake. It was a peaceful business. I even had thoughts: Wouldn't it be something if I got myself engaged to a Russian girl? That was the general picture, but when the caller was done talking, whatever I had to say I said in English and she slowly hung up.

After breakfast the next morning, she, or somebody who sounded like her—I was aware of a contralto quality—called again.

"If you understood English," I said, "or maybe a little German or French—even Yiddish if you happen to know it—we'd get along fine. But not in Russian, I'm sorry to say. Nyet Russki. I'd be glad to meet you for lunch or whatever you like; so if you get the drift of my remarks why don't you say da? Then dial the English interpreter on extension 37. She could explain to me what's what and we can meet at your convenience."

I had the impression she was listening with both ears, but after a while the phone hung silent in my hand. I wondered where she had got my name, and was someone testing me to find out whether I did or didn't speak Russian. I honestly did not.

Afterward I wrote a short letter to Lillian, telling her I would be leaving for Moscow via Aeroflot tomorrow at 4 p.m., and I intended to stay there for two weeks, with a break of maybe three or four days in Leningrad, at the Astoria Hotel. I wrote down the exact dates and later airmailed the letter in a street box some distance from the hotel, whatever good that did. I hoped Lillian would get it in time to reach me by return mail before I left the Soviet Union. To tell the truth I was uneasy all day.

By the next morning my mood had shifted, and as I was standing at the railing in a park above the Dnieper, looking at the buildings going up across the river in what had once been steppeland, I experienced a curious sense of relief. The vast construction I beheld—it was as though two or three scattered small cities were rising out of the earth—astonished me. This sort of thing was going on all over Russia—halfway around the world—and when I considered what it meant in terms of sheer labor, capital goods, plain morale, I was then and there convinced that the Soviet Union would never willingly provoke a war, nuclear or otherwise, with the United States. Neither would America, in its right mind, with the Soviet Union.

For the first time since I had come to Russia I felt secure and safe, and I enjoyed there, at the breezy railing above the Dnieper, a rare few minutes of euphoria.

Why is it that the most interesting architecture is from Czarist times? I asked myself, and if I'm not mistaken Levitansky quivered, no doubt coincidental. Unless I had spoken aloud to myself, which I sometimes do; I decided I hadn't. We were on our way to the museum, hitting a fast eighty kilometers, which translated to fifty miles an hour was not too bad because traffic was sparse.

"What do you think of my country, the Union of Soviet Socialist Republics?" the driver inquired, turning his head a half circle to see where I was.

"I would appreciate it if you kept your eyes on the road."

"Don't be nervous, I drive now for years."

"I don't like needless risks."

Then I answered. I was impressed by much I had seen. Obviously it was a great country.

Levitansky's round face appeared in the mirror smiling pleasantly, his teeth eroded. The smile seemed to have appeared from within the mouth. Now that he had revealed his half-Jewish antecedents I had the impression he looked more Jewish than Slavic, and possibly more dissatisfied than I had previously thought. That I got from the eyes.

"Also our system—Communism?"

I answered carefully, not wanting to give offense. "I'll be honest with you. I've seen some unusual things—even inspiring—but my personal taste is for a lot more individual freedom than people seem to have here. America has its serious faults, God knows, but at least we're privileged to criticize, if you know what I mean. My father used to say, 'You can't beat the Bill of Rights.' It's an open society, which means freedom of choice, at least in theory."

"Communism is altogether better political system," Levitansky replied calmly, "although it is not in present stage totally realized.

In present stage"—he swallowed, reflected, did not finish the thought. Instead he said, "Our revolution was magnificent and holy event. I love early Soviet history, excitement of Communist idealism, and magnificent victory over bourgeois and imperialist forces. Overnight was lifted up—uplifted—the whole suffering masses. It was born a new life of possibilities for all in society. Pasternak called this 'splendid surgery.' Evgeny Zamyatin—maybe you know his books?—spoke thus: 'The revolution consumes the earth with fire, but then is born a new life.' Many of our poets said similar things."

I didn't argue, each to his revolution.

"You told before," said Levitansky, glancing at me again in the mirror, "that you wish to write articles about your visit. Political or not political?"

"I don't write on politics although interested in it. What I have in mind is something on the literary museums of Moscow for an American travel magazine. That's the sort of thing I do. I'm a free-lance writer." I laughed a little apologetically. It's strange how stresses shift when you're in another country.

Levitansky politely joined in the laugh, stopping in midcourse. "I wish to be certain, what is free-lance writer?"

"Well, an editor might propose an article and I either accept the idea or I don't, or I can write about something that happens to interest me and take my chances I will sell it. Sometimes I don't and that's so much down the drain financially. What I like about it is I am my own boss. I also edit a bit. I've done anthologies of poetry and essays, both for high school kids."

"We have here free-lance. I am a writer also," Levitansky said solemnly.

"You don't say? You mean as translator?"

"Translation is my profession but I am also original writer."

"Then you do three things to earn a living—write, translate, and drive this cab?"

"The taxi is not my true work."

"Are you translating anything in particular now?"

The driver cleared his throat. "In present time I have no translation project."

"What sort of thing do you write?"

"I write stories."

"Is that so? What kind, if I might ask?"

"I will tell you what kind—little ones—short stories, imagined from life."

"Have you published any?"

He seemed about to turn around to look me in the eye but reached instead into his shirt pocket. I offered my American pack. He shook out a cigarette and lit it, exhaling smoke slowly. "A few pieces although not re-cently. To tell the truth"—he sighed—"I write presently for the drawer. You know this expression? Like Isaac Babel, 'I am master of the genre of silence.' "

"I've heard it," I said, not knowing what else to say.

"The mice should read and criticize," Levitansky said bitterly. "This what they don't eat they make their drops—droppings—on. It is perfect criticism."

"I'm sorry about that."

"We arrive now to Chekhov Museum."

I leaned forward to pay him and made the impulsive mistake of adding a one-ruble tip. His face flared. "I am Soviet citizen." He forcibly returned the ruble.

"Call it a thoughtless error," I apologized. "No harm meant."

"Hiroshima! Nagasaki!" he taunted as the Volga took off in a burst of smoke. "Aggressor against the suffering poor people of Vietnam!"

"That's none of my doing," I called after him.

An hour and a half later, after I had signed the guest book and was leaving the museum, I saw a man standing, smoking, under a linden tree across the street. Nearby was a parked taxi. We stared at each other—I wasn't certain at first who it was, but Levitansky nodded amiably to me, calling "Welcome! Welcome!" He waved an arm, smiling open-mouthed. He had combed his thick hair and was wearing a loose dark suit coat over a tieless white shirt, and yards of baggy pants. His socks, striped red-white-and-blue, you could see under his sandals.

I am forgiven, I thought. "Welcome to you," I said, crossing the street.

"How did you enjoy Chekhov Museum?"

"I did indeed. I've made a lot of notes. You know what they have there? They have one of his black fedoras, also his pince-nez that you see in pictures of him. Awfully moving."

Levitansky wiped an eye—to my surprise. He seemed not quite the same man, at any rate modified. It's funny, you hear a few personal facts from a stranger and he changes as he speaks. The taxi driver is now a writer, even if part-time. Anyway, that's my dominant impression.

"Excuse me my former anger," Levitansky explained. "Now is not for me the best of times. 'It was the best of times, it was the worst of times,' " he quoted, smiling sadly.

"So long as you pardon my unintentional blunder. Are you perhaps free to drive me to the Metropole or are you here by coincidence?"

I looked around to see if anyone was coming out of the museum.

"If you wish to engage me I will drive you, but at first I wish to show you something—how do

you say?—of interest."

He reached through the open front window of the taxi and brought forth a flat package wrapped in brown paper tied with red string.

"Stories which I wrote."

"I don't read Russian," I said.

"My wife has translated them, four. She is not by her profession a translator, although her English is advanced and sensitive. She had been for two years in England for Soviet Purchasing Commission. We became acquainted in university. I prefer not to translate my own stories because I do not translate so well Russian into English, although I do it beautifully the opposite. Also I will not force myself—it is like self-imitation. Perhaps the stories appear a little awkward in English—also my wife admits this—but you can read and form opinion."

Though he offered the package hesitantly, he offered it as if it were a bouquet of spring flowers. Can it be some sort of trick? I asked myself. Are they testing me because I signed that damned document in the Kiev airport, five copies no less?

Levitansky seemed to know my thought. "It is purely stories."

He bit the string in two, and laying the package on the fender of the Volga, unpeeled the wrapping. There were four stories, clipped separately, typed on long sheets of thin blue paper. I took one Levitansky handed me and scanned the top page—it seemed a story—then I flipped through the other pages and handed the manuscript back. "I'm not much of a critic of stories."

"I don't seek critic. I seek for reader of literary experience and taste. If you have redacted books of poems and also essays, you will be able to judge literary quality of my stories. Please, I request that you will read them."

After a long minute I heard myself say, "Well, I might at that." I didn't recognize the voice and wasn't sure why I had said what I had. You could say I spoke apart from myself, with reluctance that either he wasn't aware of or chose to ignore.

"If you respect—if you approve my stories, perhaps you will be able to arrange for publication in Paris or either London?" His larynx wobbled.

I stared at the man. "I don't happen to be going to Paris, and I'll be in London only between planes to the U.S.A."

"In this event, perhaps you will show to your publisher, and he will publish my work in America?" Levitansky was now visibly uneasy.

"In America?" I said, raising my voice in disbelief.

For the first time he gazed around cautiously before replying.

"If you will be so kind to show them to publisher of your books —he is reliable publisher?—per-

haps he will wish to put out volume of my stories? I will make contract whatever he will like. Money, if I could get, is not an ideal."

"Whatever volume are you talking about?"

He said that from thirty stories he had written he had chosen eighteen, of which these four were a sample. "Unfortunately more are not now translated. My wife is biochemist assistant and works long hours in laboratory. I am sure your publisher will enjoy to read these. It will depend on your opinion."

Either this man has a fantastic imagination or he's out of his right mind. "I wouldn't want to get myself involved in smuggling a Russian manuscript out of Russia."

"I have informed you that my manuscript is of madeup stories."

"That may be but it's still a chancy enterprise. I'd be taking chances I have no desire to take, to be frank."

"At least if you will read," he sighed.

I took the stories again and thumbed slowly through each. What I was looking at I couldn't say: maybe a booby trap? Should I or shouldn't I? I thought. Why should I?

He handed me the wrapping paper and I rolled up the stories in it. The quicker I read them, the quicker I've read them. I got into the cab.

"As I said, I'm at the Metropole. Come by tonight about nine o'clock and I'll give you my opinion for what it's worth. But I'm afraid I'll have to limit it to that, Mr. Levitansky, without further obligation or expectations, or it's no deal. My room number is 538."

"Tonight?—so soon?" he said, scratching both palms. "You must read with care so you will realize the art."

"Tomorrow night, then, same time. I'd rather not have them in my room longer than that."

Levitansky agreed. Whistling softly through his eroded teeth, he drove me carefully to the Metropole.

That night, sipping vodka from a drinking glass, I read Levitansky's stories. They were simply and strongly written—I had almost expected it—and not badly translated; in fact the translation read much better than I had been led to think although there were of course some gaffes—odd constructions, ill-fitting stiff words, some indicated by question marks, and taken, I suppose, from a thesaurus. And the stories, short tales dealing—somewhat to my surprise—mostly with Moscow Jews, were good, artistically done, really moving. The situations they revealed weren't exactly news to me: I'm a careful reader of *The Times*. But the stories weren't written to complain. What they had to say was achieved as form, no telling the dancer from the dance. I poured myself another glass of the potato potion—I was beginning to feel high, occasionally wondering why I was putting so much away—relaxing, I guess. I then reread the stories with admiration for Levitansky. I had the feeling he was no ordinary man. I felt excited, then depressed, as if I had been let in on a secret I didn't want to know.

It's a hard life here for a fiction writer, I thought.

Afterward, having the stories around made me uneasy. In one of them a Russian writer burns his stories in the kitchen sink. Obviously nobody had burned these. I thought to myself, If I'm caught with them in my possession, considering what they indicate about conditions here, there's no question I'll be up to my hips in trouble. I wished I had insisted that Levitansky come back for them tonight.

There was a solid rap on the door. I felt I had risen a good few inches out of my chair. It was, after a while, Levitansky.

"Out of the question," I said, thrusting the stories at him. "Absolutely out of the question!"

The next night we sat facing each other over glasses of cognac in the writer's small, book-crowded study. He was dignified, at first haughty, wounded, hardly masking his impatience. I wasn't myself exactly comfortable.

I had come out of courtesy and

other considerations, I guess; principally a dissatisfaction I couldn't exactly define, except it tied up with the kind of man I am or want to be, the self that sometimes gets me involved in matters I don't like to get involved in—always a dangerous business.

Levitansky, the taxi driver rattling around in his Volga-Pegasus, amateur trying to palm off a half-ass ms., had faded in my mind, and I saw him now as a serious Soviet writer with publishing problems. There are others. What can I do for him? I thought. Why should I?

"I didn't express what I really felt last night," I apologized. "You caught me by surprise, I'm sorry to say."

Levitansky was scratching each hand with the blunt fingers of the other. "How did you acquire my address?"

I reached into my pocket for a wad of folded brown wrapping paper. "It's on this—Novo Ostapovskaya Street, 488, Flat 59. I took a cab."

"I had forgotten this."

Maybe, I thought.

Still, I had practically had to put my foot in the door to get in. Levitansky's wife had answered my uncertain knock, her eyes worried, an expression I took to be one she lived with. The eyes, astonished to behold a stranger, became outright hostile once I had inquired in English for her hus-

band. I felt, as in Kiev, that my native tongue had become my enemy.

"Have you not the wrong apartment?"

"I hope not. Not if Gospodin Levitansky lives here. I came to see him about his—ah—manuscript."

Her startled eyes darkened as her face paled. Ten seconds later I was in the flat, the door locked behind me.

"Levitansky!" she summoned him. It had a reluctant quality: Come but don't come.

He appeared in apparently the same shirt, pants, tricolor socks. There was at first pretend-boredom in a tense, tired face. He could not, however, conceal excitement, his lit eyes roving, returning, roving.

"Oh ho," Levitansky said, whatever it meant.

My God, I thought, has he been expecting me?

"I came to talk to you for a few minutes, if you don't mind," I said. "I want to say what I really think of the stories you kindly let me read."

He curtly spoke in Russian to his wife and she snapped an answer back. "I wish to introduce my wife, Irina Filipovna Levitansky, biochemist. She is patient although not a saint."

She smiled tentatively, an attractive woman about twenty-eight, a little on the hefty side, in house slippers and plain dress.

The edge of her slip hung below her skirt.

There was a touch of British in her accent. "I am pleased to be acquainted." If so one hardly noticed. She stepped into black pumps and slipped a bracelet on her wrist, a lit cigarette dangling from the corner of her mouth. Her legs and arms were shapely, her brown hair cut short. I had the impression of tight thin lips in a pale face.

"I will go to Kovalevsky, next door," she said.

"Not on my account, I hope? All I have to say—"

"Our neighbors in the next flat," Levitansky grimaced. "Also thin walls." He knocked a knuckle on a hollow wall.

I indicated my dismay.

"Please, not long," Irina said, "because I am afraid."

Surely not of me? Agent Howard Harvitz, C.I.A.—a comical thought.

Their small square living room wasn't unattractive but Levitansky signaled the study inside. He offered sweet cognac in whiskey tumblers, then sat facing me at the edge of his chair, repressed energy all but visible. I had the momentary sense his chair was about to move, fly off.

If it does he goes alone.

"What I came to say," I told him, "is that I like your stories and am sorry I didn't say so last night. I like the primary, close-to-the-bone quality of the writing.

The stories impress me as strong if simply wrought; I appreciate your feeling for people and at the same time the objectivity with which you render them. It's sort of Chekhovian in quality, but more compressed, sinewy, direct, if you know what I mean. For instance, that story about the old father coming to see his son who ducks out on him. I can't comment on your style, having only read the stories in translation."

"Chekhovian," Levitansky admitted, smiling through his worn teeth, "is fine compliment. Mayakovsky, our early Soviet poet, described him 'the strong and gay artist of the word.' I wish it was possible for Levitansky to be so gay in life and art." He seemed to be staring at the drawn shade in the room, though maybe no place in particular, then said, perhaps heartening himself, "In Russian is magnificent my style—precise, economy, including wit. The style is difficult to translate in English because is less rich language."

"I've heard that said. In fairness I should add I have some reservations about the stories, yet who hasn't on any given piece of creative work?"

"I have myself reservations."

The admission made, I skipped the criticism. I had been wondering about a picture on his bookcase and then asked who it was. "It's a face I've seen before. The eyes are poetic, you might say."

"So is the voice. This is picture of Boris Pasternak as young man. On the wall yonder is Mayakovsky. He was also remarkable poet, wild, joyful, neurasthenic, a lover of the Revolution. He spoke: 'This is *my* Revolution.' To him was it 'a holy washerwoman who cleaned off all the filth from the earth.' Unfortunately he was later disillusioned and shot himself."

"I read that."

"He wrote: 'I wish to be understood by my country—but if no, I will fly through Russia like a slanting rainstorm.'"

"Have you by chance read *Dr. Zhivago?*"

"I have read," the writer sighed, and then began to declaim in Russian—I guessed some lines from a poem.

"It is to Marina Tsvetayeva, Soviet poetess, good friend of Pasternak." Levitansky fiddled with the pack of cigarettes on the table. "The end of her life was unfortunate."

"Is there no picture of Osip Mandelstam?" I hesitated as I spoke the name.

He reacted as though he had just met me. "You know Mandelstam?"

"Just a few poems in an anthology."

"Our best poet—he is holy—gone with so many others. My wife does not let me hang his photograph."

"I guess why I really came," I said after a minute, "is I wanted to express my sympathy and respect."

Levitansky popped a match with his thumbnail. His hand trembled, so he shook the flame out before lighting the cigarette.

Embarrassed for him, I pretended to be looking elsewhere. "It's a small room. Does your son sleep here?"

"Don't confuse my story of writer, which you have read, with life of author. My wife and I are married eight years though without children."

"Might I ask whether the experience you describe in that same story—the interview with the editor—was true?"

"Not true although truth," the writer said impatiently. "I write from imagination. I am not interested to repeat contents of diaries or total memory."

"On that I go along."

"Also, which is not in story, I have submitted to Soviet journals sketches and tales many many times but only few have been published, although not my best. Some people, but also few, know my work through *samizdat*, which is passing from one to another the manuscript."

"Did you submit any of the Jewish stories?"

"Please, stories are stories, they have not nationality."

"I mean by that those about Jews."

"Some I have submitted but they were not accepted."

Brave man, I thought. "After reading the four you gave me, I wondered how it is you write so well about Jews? You call yourself a marginal one—I believe that was your word—yet you write with authority about them. Not that one can't, I suppose, but it's surprising when one does."

"Imagination makes authority. When I write about Jews comes out stories, so I write about Jews. I write on subjects that make for me stories. Is not important that I am half-Jew. What is important is observation, feeling, also the art. In the past I have observed my Jewish father. Also I study sometimes Jews in the synagogue. I sit there on the bench for strangers. The gabbai watches me with dark eyes and I watch him. But whatever I write, whether is about Jews, Galicians, or Georgians, must be work of invention or for me it does not live."

"I'm not much of a synagogue-goer myself," I told him, "but I like to drop in once in a while to be refreshed by the language and images of a time and place where God was. That's funny because I have no religious education to speak of."

"I am atheist."

"I understand what you mean by imagination — that praying-shawl story. But am I right"—I lowered my voice—"that you are saying also something about the condition of Jews in this country?"

"I do not make propaganda," Levitansky said sternly. "I am not Israeli spokesman. I am Soviet artist."

"I didn't mean you weren't but there's a strong sympathy for Jews, and after all, ideas are born in life."

"My purpose belongs to me."

"One senses an awareness of injustice."

"Whatever is the injustice, the product must be art."

"Well, I respect your philosophy."

"Please do not respect so much," the writer said irritably. "We have in my country a quotation: 'It is impossible to make out of apology a fur coat.' The idea is similar. I appreciate your respect but need now practical assistance."

Expecting words of the sort I started to say something noncommittal.

"Listen at first to me," Levitansky said, slapping the table with his palm. "I am in desperate condition—situation. I have written for years but little is published. In the past, one—two editors who were friendly told me, private, that my stories are excellent but I violate social realism. This what you call objectivity they call it excessive naturalism and sentiment. It is hard to listen to such nonsense. They advise me swim but not to use my legs. They have warned me; also they have made excuses for me which I do not like them. Even they said I am crazy although I explained them I submit my stories *because* Soviet Union is great country. A great country does not fear what artist writes. A great country breathes into its lungs work of writers, painters, musicians, and becomes more great, more healthy. That I told to them but they replied I am not sufficient realist. This is the reason I am not invited to be member of Writers Union. Without this is impossible to be published." He smiled sourly. "They have warned me to stop submitting to journals my work, so I have stopped."

"I'm sorry about that," I said. "I don't myself believe any good comes from exiling the poets."

"I cannot continue longer any more in this fashion," Levitansky said, laying his hand on his heart. "I feel I am locked in drawer with my poor stories. Now I must get out or I suffocate. It becomes for me each day more difficult to write. I need help. It is not easy to request a stranger for such important personal favor. My wife advised me not. She is angry, also frightened, but it is impossible to go on in this way. I am convinced I am important Soviet writer. I must have audience. I wish to see my books to be read by Soviet people. I wish to have in minds different than my own and my wife acknowledgment of my art. I wish them to know my work is related to

Russian writers of the past as well as modern. I am in tradition of Chekhov, Gorky, Isaac Babel. I know if book of my stories will be published, it will make for me fine reputation. This is reason why you must help me—it is necessary for my interior liberty."

His confession came in an agitated burst. I use the word advisedly because that's partly what upset me. I have never cared for confessions such as are meant to involve unwilling people in others' personal problems. Russians are past masters of the art—you can see it in their novels.

"I appreciate the honor of your request," I said, "but all I am is a passing tourist. That's a pretty tenuous relationship between us."

"I do not ask tourist—I ask human being—man," Levitansky said passionately. "Also you are freelance writer. You know now what I am and what is on my heart. You sit in my house. Who else can I ask? I would prefer to publish in Europe my stories, maybe with Mondadori or Einaudi in Italy, but if this is impossible to you I will publish in America. Someday will my work be read in my own country, maybe after I am dead. This is terrible irony but my generation lives on such ironies. Since I am not now ambitious to die it will be great relief to me to know that at least in one language is alive my art. Mandelstam wrote: 'I will be enclosed in some alien speech.' Better so than nothing."

"You say I know who you are but do you know who *I* am?" I asked him. "I'm a plain person, not very imaginative though I don't write a bad article. My whole life, for some reason, has been without much real adventure, except I was divorced once and remarried happily to a woman whose death I am still mourning. Now I'm here more or less on a vacation, not to jeopardize myself by taking serious chances of an unknown sort. What's more —and this is the main thing I came to tell you—I wouldn't at all be surprised if I am already under suspicion and would do you more harm than good."

I told Levitansky about the airport incident in Kiev. "I signed a document I couldn't even read, which was a foolish thing to do."

"In Kiev this happened?"

"That's right."

He laughed dismally. "It would not happen to you if you entered through Moscow. In the Ukraine —what is your word?—they are rubes, country people."

"That might be—nevertheless I signed the paper."

"Do you have copy?"

"Not with me. In my desk drawer in the hotel."

"I am certain this is receipt for your books which officials will return to you when you depart from Soviet Union."

"That's what I was afraid of."

"Why afraid?" he asked. "Are you afraid to receive back umbrella which you have lost?"

"I'd be afraid one thing might lead to another—more questions, other searches. It would be stupid to have your manuscript in my suitcase, in Russian, no less, that I can't even read. Suppose they accuse me of being some kind of courier transferring stolen documents?"

The thought raised me to my feet. I then realized the tension in the room was thick as steam, mostly mine.

Levitansky rose, embittered. "There is no question of spying. I do not think I have presented myself as traitor to my country."

"I didn't say anything of the sort. All I'm saying is I don't want to get into trouble with the Soviet authorities. Nobody can blame me for that. In other words the enterprise isn't for me."

"I have made inquirings," Levitansky insisted. "You will have nothing to fear for tourist who has been a few weeks in U.S.S.R. under guidance of Intourist and does not speak Russian. My wife said to me your baggage will not be further inspected. They sometimes do so to political people, also to bourgeois journalists who have made bad impression. I would deliver to you the manuscript in the last instance. It is typed on less than one hundred fifty sheets thin paper and will make small package, weightless. If it should look to you like trouble you can leave it in dustbin. My name will not be anywhere and if they find it and track—trace to me the stories, I will answer I have thrown them out myself. They won't believe this but what other can I say? It will make no difference anyway. If I stop my writing I may as well be dead. No harm will come to you."

"I'd rather not if you don't mind."

With what I guess was a curse of despair, Levitansky reached for the portrait on his bookcase and flung it against the wall. Pasternak struck Mayakovsky, splattering him with glass, shattering himself, and both pictures crashed to the floor.

"Free-lance writer," he shouted, "go to hell to America! Tell to Negroes about Bill of Rights! Tell them they are free although you keep them slaves! Talk to sacrificed Vietnamese people that you respect them!"

Irina Filipovna entered the room on the run. "Feliks," she entreated, "Kovalevsky hears every word!"

"Please," she begged me, "please go away. Leave poor Levitansky alone. I beg you from my miserable heart."

I left in a hurry. The next day I left for Leningrad.

Three days later, not exactly at my best after a tense visit to Leningrad, I was sitting loosely in a beat-up taxi with a cheerful Intouristka, a half hour after my arrival at the Moscow airport. We were driving to the Ukraine Hotel, where I was assigned for my remaining days in the Soviet Union. I would have preferred the Metropole again because it is so conveniently located and I was used to it, but on second thought, better some place where a certain party wouldn't know I lived. The Volga we were riding in seemed somehow familiar, but if so it was safely in the hands of a small stranger with a large wool cap, a man wearing sunglasses who paid me no particular attention.

I had had a rather special several minutes in Leningrad on my first day. On a white summer's evening, shortly after I had unpacked in my room at the Astoria, I discovered the Winter Palace and Hermitage after a walk along Nevsky Prospekt. Changing on Palace Square, vast, deserted at the moment, I felt an unexpected intense emotion in thinking of the revolutionary events that had occurred on this spot. My God, I thought, why should I feel myself part of Russian history? It's a contagious business, what happens to men. On the Palace Bridge I gazed at the ice-blue Neva, in the distance the golden steeple of the cathedral built by Peter the Great, gleaming under masses of wind-driven clouds in patches of green sky. It's the Soviet Union but it's still Russia.

The next day I woke up anxious. In the street I was approached twice by strangers speaking English; I think my suede shoes attracted them. The first, tight-eyed and badly dressed, wanted to sell me black-market rubles. "Nyet," I said, tipping my straw hat and hurrying on. The second, a tall, bearded boy of about nineteen, with a left-sided tuft longer than right, wearing a home-knitted green pullover, offered to buy jazz records, "youth clothes," and American cigarettes. "Sorry, nothing for sale." I escaped him too, except that green sweater followed me for a kilometer along one of the canals. I broke into a run. When I looked back he had disappeared. I slept badly—it stayed light too long past midnight; and in the morning inquired about the possibility of an immediate flight to Helsinki. I was informed I couldn't book one for a week. Calming myself, I decided to return to Moscow a day before I had planned to, mostly to see what they had in the Dostoevsky Museum.

I had been thinking a good deal about Levitansky. How much of a writer was he really? I had read four of eighteen stories he wanted to publish. Suppose he had showed me the best and the others were mediocre or thereabouts? Was it worth taking a chance for that kind of book? I thought, the best thing for my peace of mind is to forget the guy. Before checking out of the Astoria I received a chatty letter from Lillian, forwarded from Moscow, apparently not in response to my recent one to her but written earlier. Should I marry her? Did I dare? The phone rang piercingly, but when I picked up the receiver no one answered. On the plane to Moscow I had visions of a crash; there must be many in the Soviet Union nobody ever reads of.

In my room on the twelfth floor of the Ukraine I relaxed in a green plastic-covered armchair. There was also a single low bed and a utilitarian pinewood desk, an apple-green telephone plunked on it for instant use. I'll be home in a week, I thought. Now I'd better shave and see if anything is left in the way of a concert or opera ticket for tonight. I'm in a mood for music.

The electric plug in the bathroom didn't work, so I put away my shaver and was lathering up when I jumped to a single explosive knock on the door. I opened it cautiously and there stood Levitansky with a brown paper packet in his hand.

Is this son-of-a-bitch out to compromise me?

"How did you happen to find out where I was only twenty minutes after I got here, Mr. Levitansky?"

"How I found you?" the writer shrugged. He seemed deathly

tired, the face longer, leaner, resembling a hungry fox on his last unsteady legs but still in business.

"My brother-in-law was chauffeur for you from the airport. He heard the girl inquire your name. We have spoke of you. Dmitri—informed me you have registered at the Ukraine. I inquired downstairs your room number and it was granted to me."

"However it happened," I said firmly, "I want you to know I haven't changed my mind. I don't want to get more involved. I thought it all through while I was in Leningrad and that's my final decision."

"I may come in?"

"Please, but for obvious reasons I'd appreciate a short visit."

Levitansky sat, somewhat shriveled, thin knees pressed together, in the armchair, his parcel awkwardly on his lap. If he was happy he had found me it did nothing for his expression.

I finished shaving, put on a fresh white shirt, and sat down on the bed. "Sorry I have nothing to offer in the way of an aperitif but I could call downstairs?"

Levitansky twiddled his fingers no. He was dressed without change down to his socks. Did his wife wash out the same pair every night or were all his socks red-white-and-blue?

"To speak frankly," I said, "I have to protest this constant tension you've whipped up in and around me. Nobody in his right mind can expect a complete stranger visiting the Soviet Union to pull his chestnuts out of the fire. It's your country that's hindering you as a writer, not me or the United States of America, and since you live here what can you do but live with it?"

"I love my country," Levitansky said.

"Nobody denies that. So do I love mine, though love for country—let's face it—is a mixed bag of marbles. Nationality isn't soul, as I'm sure you agree. But what I'm also saying is there are things about his country one might not like that he has to make his peace with. I'm assuming you're not thinking of counter-revolution. So if you're up against a wall you can't climb or dig under or outflank, at least stop banging your head against it, not to mention mine. Do what you can. It's amazing, for instance, what can be said in a fairy tale."

"I have written already my fairy tales," Levitansky said moodily. "Now is the time for truth without disguises. I will make my peace to this point where it interferes with work of my imagination—my interior liberty; and then I must stop to make my peace. My brother-in-law has also told to me, 'You must write acceptable stories, others can do it, so why cannot you?' And I have answered to him, 'They must be acceptable to *me!*'"

"In that case, aren't you up against the impossible? If you permit me to say it, are those Jews in your stories, if they can't have their matzos and prayer books, any freer in their religious lives than you are as a writer? That's what you're really saying when you write about them. What I mean is, one has to face up to the nature of his society."

"I have faced up. Do you face up to yours?" he asked with a flash of scorn.

"Not as well as I might. My own problem is not that I can't express myself but that I don't. In my own mind Vietnam is a horrifying and demoralizing mistake, yet I've never really opposed it except to sign a couple of petitions and vote for congressmen who say they're against the war. My first wife used to criticize me. She said I wrote the wrong things and was involved in everything but useful action. My second wife knew this but made me think she didn't. In a curious way I'm just waking up to the fact that the United States Government has for years been mucking up my soul."

From the heat of my body I could tell I was blushing.

Levitansky's large larynx moved up like a flag on a pole, then sank wordlessly.

He tried again, saying, "The Soviet Union preservates for us the great victories of our revolution. Because of this I have remained for years at peace with the State. Communism is still to me inspirational ideal although this historical period is spoiled by leaders with impoverished view of humanity. They have pissed on revolution."

"Stalin?"

"Him especially but also others. Even so I have obeyed Party directives, and when I could not longer obey I wrote for drawer. I said to myself, 'Levitansky, history changes every minute and also Communism will change.' I believed if the State restricts two, three generations of artists, what is this against development of socialist society—maybe best society of world history? So what does it mean if some of us are sacrificed to Party purpose? The aesthetic mode is not in necessity greater than politics—than needs of revolution. And what if are suppressed two generations of artists? Therefore will be so much less bad books, poor painting, bad music. Then in fifty years more will be secure the State and all Soviet artists will say whatever they wish. This is what I thought, or tried to think, but do not longer think so. I do not believe more in *partiinost*, which is guided thought, an expression which is to me ridiculous. I do not believe in bolshevization of literature. I do not think revolution is fulfilled in country of unpublished novelists, poets, playwriters, who hide in drawers whole libraries of literature that will never be printed, or if so, it will be printed after they stink in their graves. I think now the State will never be secure—never! It is not in the nature of politics, or human condition, to be finished with revolution. Evgeny Zamyatin told: 'There is no final revolution. Revolutions are infinite!' "

"I guess that's along my own line of thinking," I said, hoping for reasons of personal safety to forestall Levitansky's ultimate confession—one he, with brooding eyes, was already relentlessly making—lest in the end it imprison me in his will and history.

"I have learned from writing my stories," the writer was saying, "that imagination is enemy of the State. I have learned from my writing that I am not free man. This is my conclusion. I ask for your help, not to harm my country, which still has magnificent socialistic possibilities, but to help me escape its worst errors. I do not wish to defame Russia. My purpose in my work is to show its true heart. So have done our writers from Pushkin to Pasternak and also, in his way, Solzhenitsyn. If you believe in democratic humanism you must help artist to be free. Is not true?"

I got up, I think to shake myself free of that question. "What exactly is my responsibility to you, Levitansky?" I tried to contain the exasperation I felt.

"We are members of mankind. If I am drowning you must assist to save me."

"In unknown waters if I can't swim?"

"If not, throw to me rope."

"I'm a visitor here. I've told you I may be suspect. For all I know you yourself might be a Soviet agent out to get me, or the room may be bugged and then where are we? Mr. Levitansky, please, I don't want to hear or argue any more. I'll just plead personal inability and ask you to leave."

"Bugged?"

"Some sort of listening device planted in this room."

Levitansky slowly turned gray. He sat a moment in motionless meditation, then rose wearily from the chair.

"I withdraw now request for your assistance. I accept your word that you are not capable. I do not wish to make criticism of you. All I wish to say, Gospodin Garvitz, is it requires more to change a man's character than to change his name."

Levitansky left the room, leaving in his wake faint fumes of cognac. He had also passed gas.

"Come back!" I called, not too loudly, but if he heard through the door he didn't answer. Good riddance, I thought. Not that I don't sympathize with him but look what he's done to *my* interior liberty. Who has to come thousands of miles to Russia to get caught up in this kind of business? It's a helluva way to spend a vacation.

The writer had gone but not his sneaky manuscript. It was lying on my bed.

"It's his baby, not mine." Angered, I knotted my tie and slipped on my coat, then via the English-language number, called a cab. But I had forgotten his address. A half hour later I was still in the taxi, riding anxiously back and forth along Novo Ostapovskaya Street until I spotted the apartment house I thought it might be. It wasn't; it was another like it. I paid the driver and walked on till once again I thought I had the house. After going up the stairs I was sure it was. When I knocked on Levitansky's door, the writer, looking older, more distant—as if he'd been away on a trip and had just returned; or maybe simply interrupted at his work, his thoughts still in his words on the page on the table, his pen in hand—stared blankly at me. Very blankly.

"Levitansky, my heart breaks for you, I swear, but I can't take the chance. I believe in you but am not, at this time of my life, considering my condition and recent experiences, in much of a mood to embark on a dangerous adventure. Please accept deepest regrets."

I thrust the manuscript into his hand and rushed down the stairs. Hurrying out of the building, I was, to my horror, unable to avoid Irina Levitansky coming in. Her eyes lit in fright as she recog-nized me an instant before I hit her full force and sent her sprawling along the walk.

"Oh, my God, what have I done? I beg your pardon!" I helped the dazed, hurt woman to her feet, brushing off her soiled skirt, and futilely, her pink blouse, split and torn on her lacerated arm and shoulder. I stopped dead when I felt myself experiencing erotic sensations.

Irina Filipovna held a handkerchief to her bloody nostril and wept a little. We sat on a stone bench, a girl of ten and her little brother watching us. Irina said something to them in Russian and they moved off.

"I was frightened of you also as you are of us," she said. "I trust you now because Levitansky does. But I will not urge you to take the manuscript. The responsibility is for you to decide."

"It's not a responsibility I want," I said unhappily.

She said as though to herself, "Maybe I will leave Levitansky. He is wretched so much it is no longer a marriage. He drinks. Also he does not earn a living. My brother Dmitri allows him to drive the taxi two, three hours of the day, to my brother's disadvantage. Except for a ruble or two from this, I support him. Levitansky does not longer receive translation commissions. Also a neighbor in the house—I am sure Kovalevsky—has denounced him to the police for delinquency and parasitism. There will be a hearing. Levitansky says, he will burn his manuscripts."

"Good God, I've just returned the package of stories!"

"He will not," she said. "But even if he burns them he will write more. If they take him away in prison he will write on toilet paper. When he comes out, he will write on newspaper margins. He sits this minute at his table. He is a magnificent writer. I cannot ask him not to write, but now I must decide if this is the condition I wish for myself for the rest of my life."

Irina sat in silence, an attractive woman with shapely legs and feet, in a soiled skirt and torn blouse. I left her on the stone bench, her handkerchief squeezed in her fist.

That night—July 2, I was leaving the Soviet Union on the fifth —I experienced massive self-doubt. If I'm a coward why has it taken so long to find out? Where does anxiety end and cowardice begin? Feelings get mixed, sure enough, but not all cowards are anxious men, and not all anxious men are cowards. Many "sensitive" (Rose's word), tense, even frightened human beings did in fear what had to be done, the fear calling up energy when it's time to fight or jump off a rooftop into a river. There comes a time in a man's life when to get where he has to go—if there are no doors or windows—he walks

through a wall.

On the other hand, suppose one is courageous in a foolish cause—you concentrate on courage and not enough on horse sense? To get to the point of the problem endlessly on my mind, how do I finally decide it's a sensible and worthwhile thing to smuggle out Levitansky's manuscript, given my reasonable doubts of the ultimate worth of the operation? Granted, as I now grant, he's a trustworthy guy and his wife is that and more; still, does it pay a man like me to run the risk?

If six thousand Soviet writers can't do very much to squeeze out another inch of freedom as artists, who am I to fight their battle—H. Harvitz, knight-of-the-free-lance from Manhattan? How far do you go, granted all men, including Communists, are created free and equal and justice is for all? How far do you go for art, if you're for Yeats, Matisse, and Ludwig van Beethoven? Not to mention Gogol, Tolstoy, and Dostoevsky. So far as to get yourself intentionally involved: the HH Ms. Smuggling Service? Will the President and State Department send up three loud cheers for my contribution to the cause of artistic social justice? And suppose it amounts to no more than a gaffe in the end—What will I prove if I sneak out Levitansky's manuscript and all it turns out to be is just another passable book of stories?

That's how I argued with my-self on more than one occasion, but in the end I argued myself into solid indecision.

What it boils down to, I'd say, is he expects me to help him be-cause I'm an American. That's quite a nerve.

Two nights later—odd not to have the Fourth of July on July 4 (I was listening for firecrackers) —a quiet light-lemon summer's evening in Moscow, after two mo-notonously uneasy days, though I was still writing museum notes, for relief I took myself off to the Bolshoi to hear *Tosca*. It was sung in Russian by a busty lady and handsome tenor, but the Italian plot was unchanged, and in the end, Scarpia, who had promised "death" by fake bullets, gave in sneaky exchange a fusillade of hot lead; another artist bit the dust and Floria Tosca learned the hard way that love wasn't what she had thought.

Next to me sat another full-breasted woman, this one a lovely Russian of maybe thirty in a white dress that fitted a well-formed mature figure, her blond hair piled in a birdlike mass on her splendid head. Lillian could look like that, though not Rose. This woman—alone, it turned out —spoke flawless English in a mezzo-soprano with a slight ac-cent.

During the first intermission she asked me in friendly fashion, managing to seem detached but interested: "Are you American? Or perhaps Swedish?"

"Not Swedish. American is cor-rect. How did you happen to guess?"

"I noticed, if it does not bother you that I say it," she remarked with a charming laugh, "a certain self-satisfaction."

"You got the wrong party," I said.

When she opened her purse a fragrance of springtime burst forth—fresh flowers; the warmth of her body rose to my nostrils. I was moved by memories of the hungers of youth—dreams, long-ing.

During intermission she touched my arm and said in a low voice, "May I ask you a favor? Do you depart from the Soviet Union?"

"In fact tomorrow."

"How fortunate for me. Would it offer too much difficulty to mail wherever you are going an air-mail letter addressed to my hus-band, who is presently in Paris? Our airmail service takes two weeks to arrive in the West. I shall be grateful."

I glanced at the envelope ad-dressed half in French, half in Cyrillic, and said I wouldn't mind. But during the next act sweat grew active on my flesh and at the end of the opera, after Tos-ca's shriek of suicide, I handed the letter back to the not wholly surprised lady, saying I was sorry. Nodding to her, I left the theater. I had the feeling I had heard her voice before. I hurried back to the hotel, determined not to leave my room for any reason other than breakfast, then out and into the wide blue sky.

I later fell asleep over a book and a bottle of sweetish warm beer a waiter had brought up, pretending to myself I was relaxed though I was as usual concerned beforehand with worried thoughts of the departure and flight home; and when I awoke, three minutes on my wristwatch later, it seemed to me I had made the acquaintance of a spate of new nightmares. I was momentarily panicked by the idea that someone had planted a letter on me, and I searched through the pockets of my two suits. Nyet. Then I recalled that in one of my dreams a drawer in a table I was sitting at had slowly come open and Feliks Levitansky, a dwarf who lived in it along with a few friendly mice, managed to scale the wooden wall on the comb he used as a ladder, and to hop from the drawer ledge to the top of the table. He leered into my face, shook his Lilliputian fist, and shouted in high-pitched but (to me) understandable Russian, "Atombombnik! You massacred innocent Japanese people! Amerikansky bastards!"

"That's unfair," I cried out. "I was no more than a kid in college."

That's a sad dream, I thought. Afterwards this occurred to me:

Suppose what happened to Levitansky happens to me. Suppose America gets caught up in a war with China in some semi-reluctant stupid way, and to make fast hash of it—despite my frantic loud protestations: mostly I wave my arms and shout obscenities till my face turns green—we spatter them, before they can get going, with a few dozen H-bombs, boiling up a thick atomic soup of about two hundred million Orientals—blood, gristle, marrow, and lots of floating Chinese eyeballs. We win the war because the Soviets hadn't been able to make up their minds who to shoot their missiles at first. And suppose after this unheard-of slaughter, about ten million Americans, in self-revulsion, head for the borders to flee the country. To stop the loss of wealth, the refugees are intercepted by the army in tanks and turned back. Harvitz hides in his room with shades drawn, writing in a fury of protest a long epic poem condemning the mass butchery by America. What nation, Asiatic or other, is next? Nobody in the States wants to publish the poem because it might start riots and another flight of refugees to Canada and Mexico; then one day there's a knock on the door, and it isn't the F.B.I. but a bearded Levitansky, in better times a Soviet tourist, a modern, not medieval Communist. He kindly offers to sneak the manuscript of the poem out for publication in the

Soviet Union.

Why? Harvitz suspiciously asks.

Why not? To give the book its liberty.

I awoke after a restless night. I had been instructed by Intourist to be in the lobby with my baggage two hours before flight time at 11 a.m. I was shaved and dressed by six, and at seven had breakfast—I was very hungry—of yogurt, sausage, and scrambled eggs in the twelfth-floor buffet. I then went out to hunt for a taxi. They were hard to come by at this hour but I finally located one near the American Embassy, not far from the hotel. Speaking my usual mixture of primitive German and French, I persuaded the driver by first suggesting, then slipping him an acceptable two rubles, to take me to Levitansky's house and wait a few minutes till I came out. Going hastily up the stairs, I knocked on his door, apologizing when he opened it, to the half-pajamaed, iron-faced writer, for awaking him this early in the day. Without peace of mind or certainty of purpose I asked him whether he still wanted me to smuggle out his manuscript of stories. I got for my trouble the door slammed in my face.

A half hour later I had everything packed and was locking the suitcase. A knock on the door—half a rap, you might call it. For the suitcase, I thought. I was momentarily frightened by the sight of a small man in a thick cap wearing a long trench coat. He winked, and against the will I winked back. I had recognized Levitansky's brother-in-law Dmitri, the taxi driver. He slid in, unbuttoned his coat, and brought forth the wrapped manuscript. Holding a finger to his lips, he handed it to me before I could say I was no longer interested.

"Levitansky changed his mind?"

"Not changed mind. Was afraid your voice to be heard by Kovalevsky."

"I'm sorry, I should have thought of that."

"Levitansky says not to write to him," the brother-in-law whispered. "When is published book please send to him copy of Das Kapital. He will understand message."

I reluctantly agreed.

The brother-in-law, a short shapeless figure with sad Jewish eyes, winked again, shook hands with a steamy palm, and slipped out of my room.

I unlocked my suitcase and laid the manuscript on top of my shirts. Then I unpacked half the contents and slipped the manuscript into a folder containing my notes on literary museums and a few letters from Lillian. I then and there decided that if I got back to the States, the next time I saw her I would ask her to marry me. The phone was ringing as I left the room.

On my way to the airport, alone in a taxi—no Intourist girl accompanied me—I felt, on and off, nauseated. If it's not the sausage and yogurt it must just be ordinary fear. Still, if Levitansky has the courage to send these stories out the least I can do is give him a hand. When one thinks of it it's little enough he does for human freedom in the course of his life. At the airport if I can dig up a bromo or its Russian equivalent I know I'll feel better.

The driver was observing me in the mirror, a stern man with the head of a scholar, impassively smoking.

"Le jour fait beau," he said.

He pointed with an upraised finger to a sign in English at one side of the road to the airport: "Long live peace in the world!"

Peace with freedom. I smiled at the thought of somebody, not Howard Harvitz, painting that in red on the Soviet sign.

We drove on, I foreseeing my exit from the Soviet Union. I had made discreet inquiries from time to time and an Intourist girl in Leningrad had told me I had first to show my papers at the passport-control desk, turn in my rubles—a serious offense to walk off with any—and then check luggage; no inspection, she swore. And that was that. Unless, of course, the official at the passport desk found my name on a list and said I had to go to the customs office for a package. In that case—if nobody said so I wouldn't remind him—I would go get the books. I figured

I wouldn't open the package, just tear off a bit of the wrapping, if they were wrapped, as though to make sure they were the books I expected, and then saunter away with the package under my arm. If they asked me to sign another five copies of a document in Russian I would write at the bottom: "It is understood that I can't speak or read Russian" and sign my name to that.

I had heard that a KGB man was stationed at the ramp as one boarded a plane. He asked for your passport, checked the picture, threw you a stare through dark lenses, and if there was no serious lack of resemblance, tore out your expired visa, pocketed it, and let you embark.

In ten minutes you were aloft, seat belts fastened in three languages, watching the plane banking west. Maybe if I looked hard I might see in the distance Feliks Levitansky on the roof waving his red-white-and-blue socks on a bamboo pole. Then the plane leveled off, and we were above the clouds, flying westward. And that's what I would be doing for five or six hours unless the pilot received radio instructions to turn back; or maybe land in Czechoslovakia or East Germany, where two big-hatted detectives boarded the plane. By an act of imagination and will I made it some other passenger they were arresting. I got the plane into the air again and we flew on without incident until we touched down in London.

As the taxi approached the Moscow airport, fingering my ticket and gripping my suitcase handle, I wished for courage equal to Levitansky's when they discovered he was the author of a book of stories I had managed to sneak out and get published, and his trial and suffering began.

Levitansky's first story of the four in English was about an old father, a pensioner, who was not feeling well and wanted his son, with whom he had had continuous strong disagreements, and whom he hadn't seen in eight months, to know. He decided to pay him a short visit. Since the son had moved from his flat to a larger one and had not forwarded his address, the father went to call on him at work. The son was an official of some sort with an office in a new State building. The father had never been there although he knew where it was because a neighbor on a walk with him had pointed it out.

The pensioner sat in a chair in his son's large outer office, waiting for him to be free for a few minutes. "Yuri," he thought he would say, "all I want to tell you is that I'm not up to my usual self. My breath is short and I have pains in my chest. In fact, I'm not well. After all, we're father and son and you ought to know the state of my health, see-ing it's not so good and your mother is dead."

The son's assistant secretary, a modern girl in a short tight skirt, said he was attending an important administrative conference.

"A conference is a conference," the father said. He wouldn't want to interfere with it and didn't mind waiting although he was still having nauseating twinges of pain.

The father waited patiently in the chair for several hours; and though he had a few times risen and urgently spoken to the assistant secretary, he was, by the end of the day, still unable to see his son. The girl, putting on her pink hat, advised the old man that the official had already left the building. He hadn't been able to see his father because he had unexpectedly been called away on an important State matter.

"Go home and he will telephone you in the morning."

"I have no telephone," said the old pensioner impatiently. "He knows that."

The assistant secretary; the private secretary, an older woman from the inside office; and later the caretaker of the building, all tried to persuade the father to go home, but he wouldn't leave.

The private secretary said her husband was expecting her and she could stay no longer. After a while the assistant secretary with the pink hat also left. The caretaker, a man with wet eyes and a ragged mustache, tried to persuade the old man to leave. "What sort of foolishness is it to visit all night in a pitch-dark building? You'll frighten yourself out of your wits, not to speak of other discomforts you're bound to suffer."

"No," said the sick father, "I will wait. When my son comes in tomorrow morning I'll tell him something he hasn't learned yet. I'll tell him what he does to me his children will do to him."

The caretaker departed. The old man was left alone waiting for his son to appear in the morning.

"I'll report him to the Party," he muttered.

The second story was about another old man, a widower of sixty-eight, who hoped to have matzos for Passover. Last year he had got his quota. They had been baked at the State bakery and sold in State stores; but this year the State bakeries were not permitted to bake them. The officials said the machines had broken down but who believed them.

The old man went to the rabbi, an older man with a tormented beard, and asked him where he could get matzos. He was frightened that he mightn't have them this year.

"So am I," confessed the old rabbi. He said he had been told to tell his congregation to buy flour and bake them at home. The State stores would sell them the flour.

"What good is that for me?" asked the widower. He reminded the rabbi that he had no home to speak of, a single small room with a one-burner electric stove. His wife had died two years ago. His only living child, a married daughter, was with her husband in Birobijan. His other relatives—the few who were left after the German invasion—two female cousins his age—lived in Odessa; and he himself, even if he could find an oven, did not know how to bake matzos. And if he couldn't what should he do?

The rabbi then promised he would try to get the widower a kilo or two of matzos, and the old man, rejoicing, blessed him.

He waited anxiously a month but the rabbi never mentioned the matzos. Maybe he had forgotten. After all he was an old man burdened with worries and the widower did not want to press him. However, Passover was coming on wings, so he must do something. A week before the Holy Days he hurried to the rabbi's flat and spoke to him there.

"Rabbi," he begged, "you promised me a kilo or two of matzos. What has happened to them?"

"I know I promised," said the rabbi, "but I'm no longer sure to whom. It's easy to promise." He dabbed at his face with a damp handkerchief. "I was warned one could be arrested on charges of profiteering in the production and sale of matzos. I was told it could happen even if I were to give them away for nothing. It's a new crime they've invented. Still, take them anyway. If they arrest me, I'm an old man, and how long can an old man live in Lubyanka? Not so long, thank God. Here, I'll give you a small pack but you must tell no one where you got the matzos."

"May the Lord eternally bless you, rabbi. As for dying in prison, rather let it happen to our enemies."

The rabbi went to his closet and got out a small pack of matzos, already wrapped and tied with knotted twine. When the widower offered in a whisper to pay him, at least the cost of the flour, the rabbi wouldn't hear of it. "God provides," he said, "although at times with difficulty." He said there was hardly enough for all who wanted matzos, so he must take what he got and be thankful.

"I will eat less," said the old man. "I will count mouthfuls. I will save the last matzos to look at and kiss if there isn't enough to last me. God will understand."

Overjoyed to have even a few matzos, he rode home on the trolley car and there met another Jew, a man with a withered hand. They conversed in Yiddish in low tones. The stranger had glanced at the almost square package, then at the widower, and had hoarsely whispered, "Matzos?"

The widower, tears starting in his eyes, nodded. "With God's grace." "Where did you get them?" "God provides." "So if He provides let Him provide me," the stranger brooded. "I'm not so lucky. I was hoping for a package from relatives in Cleveland, America. They wrote they would send me a large pack of the finest matzos but when I inquire of the authorities they say no matzos have arrived. You know when they will get here?" he muttered. "After Passover by a month or two, and what good will they be then?"

The widower nodded sadly. The stranger wiped his eyes with his good hand and after a short while left the trolley amid a number of people getting off. He had not bothered to say goodbye, and neither had the widower, not to remind him of his own good fortune. When the time came for the old man to leave the trolley he glanced down between his feet where he had placed the package of matzos but nothing was there. His feet were there. The old man felt harrowed, as though someone had ripped a nail down his spine. He searched frantically throughout that car, going a long way past his stop, querying every passenger, the woman conductor, the motorman, but no one had seen his matzos.

Then it occurred to him that the stranger with the withered hand had stolen them.

The widower in his misery

asked himself, would a Jew have robbed another of his precious matzos? It didn't seem possible. Still, who knows, he thought, what one will do to get matzos if he has none.

As for me I haven't even a matzo to look at now. If I could steal any, whether from Jew or Russian, I would steal them. He thought he would even steal them from the old rabbi.

The widower went home without his matzos and had none for Passover.

The third story, a tale called "Tallith," concerned a youth of seventeen, beardless but for some stray hairs on his chin, who had come from Kiev to the steps of the synagogue on Arkhipova Street in Moscow. He had brought with him a capacious prayer shawl, a white garment of luminous beauty which he offered for sale to a cluster of Jews of various sorts and sizes—curious, apprehensive, greedy at the sight of the shawl—for fifteen rubles. Most of them avoided the youth, particularly the older Jews, despite the fact that some of the more devout among them were worried about their prayer shawls, eroded on their shoulders after years of daily use, which they could not replace. "It's the informers among us who have put him up to this," they whispered among themselves, "so they will have someone to inform on."

Still, in spite of the warnings of their elders, several of the younger men examined the tallith and admired it. "Where did you get such a fine prayer shawl?" the youth was asked. "It was my father's who recently died," he said. "It was given to him by a rich Jew he had once befriended." "Then why don't you keep it yourself, you're a Jew, aren't you?" "Yes," said the youth, not the least embarrassed, "but I am going to Bratsk as a komsomol volunteer and I need a few rubles to get married. Besides I'm a confirmed atheist."

One young man with fat unshaven cheeks who admired the deeply white shawl, its white glowing in whiteness, with its long silk fringes, whispered to the youth he might consider buying it for five rubles. But he was overheard by the gabbai, the lay leader of the congregation, who raised his cane and shouted at the whisperer. "Hooligan, if you buy that shawl, beware it doesn't become your shroud." The Jew with the unshaven cheeks retreated.

"Don't strike him," cried the frightened rabbi, who had come out of the synagogue and saw the gabbai, with his cane upraised. He urged the congregants to begin prayer at once. To the youth he said, "Please go away from here, we are burdened with enough troubles as it is. It is forbidden for anyone to sell religious articles. Do you want us to be accused of criminal economic activity? Do you want the doors of the shul to be closed forever? So do us and yourself a mitzvah and go away."

The congregants moved inside. The youth was left standing alone on the steps, but then the gabbai came out of the door, a man with a deformed spine and a wad of cotton stuck in his leaking ear.

"Look here," he said. "I know you stole it. Still, after all is said and done, a tallith is a tallith and God asks no questions of His worshippers. I offer eight rubles for it, take it or leave it. Talk fast before the services end and the others come out."

"Make it ten and it's yours," said the youth.

The gabbai gazed at him shrewdly. "Eight is all I have but wait here and I'll borrow two rubles from my brother-in-law."

The youth waited patiently. Dusk was thickening. In a few minutes a black car drove up, stopped in front of the synagogue, and two policemen got out. The youth realized at once that the gabbai had informed on him. Not knowing what else to do he hastily draped the prayer shawl over his head and began loudly to pray. He prayed a passionate kaddish. The police hesitated to approach him while he was praying, and they stood at the bottom of the steps waiting for him to be done. The congregants came out and could not believe their ears.

No one imagined the youth could pray so fervently. What moved them was the tone, the wail and passion of a man truly praying. Perhaps his father had indeed recently died. All listened attentively, and many wished he would pray forever, for they knew that when he stopped he would be seized and thrown into prison.

It has grown dark. A moon hovers behind murky clouds over the synagogue steeple. The youth's voice is heard in prayer. The congregants are huddled in the dark street, listening. Both police agents are still there, although they cannot be seen. Neither can the youth. All that can be seen is the white shawl luminously praying.

The last of the four stories translated by Irina Filipovna was about a writer of mixed parentage, a Russian father and Jewish mother, who had secretly been writing stories for years. He had from a young age wanted to write but had at first not had the courage to—it seemed like such a merciless undertaking—so he had gone into translation instead; and then when he had, one day, started to write seriously and exultantly, after a while he found to his surprise that many of his stories, about half, were about Jews.

For a half-Jew that's a reasonable proportion, he thought. The others were about Russians who sometimes resembled members of his father's family. "It's good to have such different sources for ideas," he told his wife. "This way I can cover a varied range of experiences in life."

After several years of work he had submitted a selection of stories to a trusted friend of university days, Viktor Zverkov, an editor of the Progress Publishing House, and the writer appeared at his office one morning after receiving a hastily scribbled cryptic note from his friend, to discuss his work with him. Zverkov, a troubled man to begin with—he told everyone his wife did not respect him—jumped up from his chair and turned the key in the door, his ear pressed a minute at the crack. He then went quickly to his desk and withdrew the manuscript from a drawer he first had to unlock with a key he kept in his pocket. He was a heavy-set man with a flushed complexion, stained teeth, and a hoarse voice; and he handled the writer's manuscript with unease, as though it might leap up and wound him in the face.

"Please, Tolya," he whispered breathily, bringing his head close to the writer's, "you must take these dreadful stories away at once."

"What's the matter with you? Why are you shaking so?"

"Don't pretend to be so naïve. You know why I am disturbed. I am frankly amazed that you are submitting such unorthodox ma-terial for publication. My opinion as an editor is that they are of doubtful literary merit—I won't say devoid of it, Tolya, I want to be honest—but as stories they are a frightful affront to our society. I can't understand why you should take it on yourself to write about Jews. What do you know about them? Your culture is not the least Jewish, it's Soviet Russian. The whole business smacks of hypocrisy and you may be accused of anti-Semitism."

He got up to shut the window and peered into a closet before sitting down.

"Are you out of your mind, Viktor? My stories are in no sense anti-Semitic. One would have to read them standing on his head to make that judgment."

"There can be only one logical interpretation," the editor argued. "According to my most lenient analysis, which is favorable to you as a person of let's call it decent intent, the stories fly in the face of socialist realism and reveal a dangerous inclination—perhaps even a stronger word should be used—to anti-Soviet sentiment. Maybe you're not entirely aware of this—I know how a story can pull a writer by the nose. As an editor I have to be sensitive to such things. I know, Tolya, from our conversations that you are a sincere believer in our socialism; I won't accuse you of being defamatory to the Soviet system, but others may. In fact, I know they will. If one of the editors of *Oktyabr* were to read your stories, believe me, your career would explode in a mess. You seem not to have a normal awareness of what self-preservation is, and what's appallingly worse, you're not above entangling innocent bystanders in your fate. If these stories were mine, I assure you I would never have brought them to you. I urge you to destroy them at once, before they destroy you."

He drank thirstily from a glass of water on his desk.

"That's the last thing I would do," answered the writer in anger. "These stories, if not in the tone or subject matter, are written in the spirit of our early Soviet writers—the joyous spirits of the years after the Revolution."

"I think you know what happened to many of those 'joyous spirits.' "

The writer for a moment stared at him. "Well, then, what of the stories that are not about the experience of Jews? Some are pieces about homely aspects of Russian life; for instance the one about the pensioner father and his invisible son. What I hoped is that you might personally recommend one or two such stories to *Novy Mir* or *Yunost*. They are innocuous sketches and well written."

"Not the one of the two prostitutes," said the editor. "That contains hidden social criticism and is adversely naturalistic."

"A prostitute lives a social life."

"That may be but I can't recommend it for publication. I must advise you, Tolya, if you expect to receive further commissions for translations from us, you must immediately rid yourself of this whole manuscript so as to avoid the possibility of serious consequences both to yourself and family, and to this publishing house that has employed you so faithfully and generously in the past."

"Since you didn't write the stories yourself, you needn't be afraid, Viktor Alexandrovich," the writer said coldly.

"I am not a coward, if that's what you're hinting, Anatoly Borisovich, but if a wild locomotive is running loose on the rails, I know which way to jump."

The writer hastily gathered up his manuscript, stuffed the papers into his leather case, and returned home by bus. His wife was still away at work. He took out the stories, and after reading through one, burned it, page by page, in the kitchen sink.

His nine-year-old son, returning from school, said, "Papa, what are you burning in the sink? That's no place for a fire."

"I am burning my integrity," said the writer. Then he said, "My talent. My heritage."

Questions for Analysis and Discussion

1. Comment on the beginning of the story. How is the reader's interest aroused? How is the narrator characterized? What do you learn about the narrator in the first three paragraphs? We learn later that the narrator is a writer. What skills of a writer does he reveal in the first paragraphs? What skills of a writer does he reveal in his description of Levitansky?

2. In the first conversation between Harvitz, the narrator, and Levitansky, the taxi driver, they learn some basic facts about one another. What does each learn about the other? Why does Levitansky call himself a marginal Jew?

3. In his reverie about his recent past experiences Harvitz tells the reader much about himself. What do you learn from this exercise in recall? Why was Harvitz so fearful during his visit to Kiev? Is there any suggestion in Harvitz's account of his visit to Kiev that he was self-conscious because he was Jewish? What activity in Kiev impresses Harvitz the most? Why?

4. What motives did Harvitz have in bringing five copies of a poetry anthology to Russia? Is this an indication that he was a simple and naive man or a brave and foolhardy one? Why was he disturbed when the anthologies were confiscated? What problems did Harvitz face in his solitary walks in Kiev? How does the author wish you to interpret the actions of the Russians whom Harvitz encountered? This story presents three views of experience: the author's, the narrator's, and those of the Russian Jewish writer. See whether you can distinguish among the three.

5. Harvitz defends democracy and Levitansky defends communism. Evaluate each one's position. Are they the orthodox views or are there variations from accepted concepts? How does the author suggest that Levitansky has some doubt about his views of the communist state?

6. What kind of a writer does Harvitz say he is? Levitansky, too, is a writer. What does he mean when he says he writes for the drawer? Why does he compare himself to Isaac Babel? (Check on the life and work of Isaac Babel to understand the allusion.)

7. When Harvitz leaves the Chekhov Museum, Levitansky is waiting for him. What does Levitansky ask of Harvitz? Why does Harvitz

agree? What in Levitansky's stories surprises him? Harvitz is persuaded to read Levitansky's stories. Why cannot he be persuaded to
smuggle them out of the country? What is there about the stories that
strengthens his resolve?

8.   Why does Harvitz visit Levitansky at his home? How do you explain that Harvitz is able to move about Moscow so freely? (Check
to see whether this was possible at the time of the story. Would Harvitz for any reason be given special privileges?) Why is Levitansky's
wife worried about Harvitz's visit?

9.   As you review the story check the following: How does the
author build up the world of his story? How does he foreshadow
Levitansky's quarrel and disenchantment with his Communist world?
In your view, is the author being objective? Or is this story propaganda against the Communist system?

10.   The questions that Harvitz asks Levitansky indicate that he
believes some of Levitansky's stories to be autobiographical. What are
Levitansky's views concerning the writing of fiction? Why does Harvitz think that Levitansky was a brave man to submit for publication
stories about Jews? Read again the summaries of the four stories that
Harvitz smuggled out of Russia. Why would a Russian editor in a land
where all people are considered to be equal, regardless of religion,
object to these stories? If Dostoevski and Tolstoy, some of whose
stories have religious overtones, are acceptable, why not Levitansky?

11.   What criticisms did the editors make of Levitansky's work?
Check to determine what the Russian government means by socialist
realism. What faults does Levitansky find in the government's treatment of its artists?

12.   The story is called "Man in the Drawer." How is "the drawer"
used symbolically in the story? What is your view of "the drawer" as
the central image of the story? Is it effective? Would the image of
"prison" or "cell" or "cave" or "hell" have been better?

13.   An artist must have an audience, someone to read his work,
look at his painting or drawing, listen to his music. Else he suffocates
and is nothing. Do you agree with this view of Levitansky's? Isn't it
enough that an artist through his work purges his mind and soul of the
pain and unrest that trouble him or expresses his wonder and awe at
nature's miracles? Is an audience really necessary? Harvitz uses the
Kiev episode as an excuse to refuse to smuggle Levitansky's stories
out of the country. Is his reason a good one? What are the dangers?

Is Levitansky's anger justified? Against whom is Levitansky's anger really directed? What significance is there in Levitansky's throwing the picture of Pasternak against that of Mayakovsky?

14. Harvitz visits Leningrad. In recording his feeling during a walk, he comments, "It's the Soviet Union but it's still Russia." What does he mean by this statement? Why was Harvitz disturbed by the two encounters on Leningrad streets? In what ways does the author let the reader know that Harvitz is considering Levitansky's request?

15. When Harvitz returned from Leningrad, how did Levitansky know where to find him? What advice does Harvitz give Levitansky? Why does Levitansky find it impossible to accept this advice? How does Levitansky use the image of a drowning man to persuade Harvitz to help him? What new reasons does Harvitz give for again refusing?

16. How have Levitansky's views concerning his communist state changed? What faults does he find with the system and with revolution? Have you found fault with American democracy? What views of yours have changed as the result of the operations of American politics? The artist in America seems to have almost complete freedom to say or depict what he wishes. Do you think this is good?

17. Is it accident or design that Levitansky leaves his manuscript on the bed in Harvitz's room? Why does Harvitz feel the compulsion to return the manuscript immediately? Why does Harvitz apologize when he returns the manuscript?

18. On the way out of the house, Harvitz accidentally knocks down Irina who is on her way in. What information about Levitansky does she give him? What has led her to trust Harvitz? What purpose in the story does this scene serve? Is it necessary?

19. Back at the hotel, Harvitz mentally debates his situation vis-à-vis Levitansky. Why is this a problem for him? Is it because he is a writer? because he is an American? or because he is a Jew? What clues, if any, does the author give the reader to explain Harvitz's dilemma?

20. A Russian lady whom Harvitz meets at the opera asks him to mail a letter for her outside the country. Why does he first agree and later change his mind? Has the author prepared the reader sufficiently for this act of fear? What purpose does this scene serve? Does the story need this scene? Is the author overdoing Harvitz's fears? Or is

the author building up the state of secrecy and intrigue inspired by a repressive regime? What is your view?

21.   How do the nightmares define the nature of Harvitz's unrest and fears? Are the nightmares believable? In what ways do the nightmares persuade Harvitz to smuggle Levitansky's stories out of the Soviet Union? Has the author prepared the reader adequately for this act of heroism?

22.   On the way to the airport, Harvitz reviews in his mind what he will undergo before he boards the plane. Why does he imagine the possibility of his plane's being rerouted for his arrest but does not consider the possibility of his being caught when his luggage is checked at the airport? How effective a fictional device is it to describe Harvitz's departure as anticipatory while he is driving to the airport rather than retrospective after he has arrived home safely? What, in the narrator's view, will be Levitansky's fate if his stories are published in America?

23.   The author ends his narrative with a summary of four of Levitansky's stories. Are these summaries necessary to the story? Are they anticlimactic? What if anything do they add to the story? What is the theme of each of the stories? Which of the themes of the main story is repeated, strengthened, or awakened by a repetition in the summary stories?

Suggested Activities

1.   In the story Levitansky mentions the names of a number of Russian writers whom he admires: Vladimir Mayakovsky, Boris Pasternak, Anton Chekhov, Maxim Gorky, Isaac Babel, Osip Mandelstam. Get information concerning the life and work of each of these writers and report your findings to the class. A basic subject to investigate is the extent to which each of the writers was a defender of his world and the extent to which he was a critic of his world. Another subject to investigate is why Levitansky would link Isaac Babel with Checkhov and Gorky.

2.   Set up the classroom as a trial courtroom. Levitansky is on trial in the Soviet Union for undermining the ideals and integrity of the state. The witnesses in the action are Harvitz, Irina, Dmitri, and a

member of the Kovalesky family. The evidence against Levitansky is the four stories that he had submitted to Russian editors and that he had attempted to smuggle out of the country. There is a prosecuting attorney and a defense attorney. There is no jury, but a panel of three judges. Write a script of the trial and enact it.

3. In a moment of great self-doubt, Harvitz thinks: "There comes a time in a man's life when to get where he has to go—if there are no doors or windows—he walks through a wall." Write a series of biographies of well-known people or ordinary folk who showed the kind of heroism described in the statement. (John Kennedy wrote a book of a different kind of heroism called *Profiles in Courage*.)

4. The condition of the Jews in Russia is dramatically presented in a play by Elie Wiesel called *Zalmen and the Madness of God*. Read the play and report to the class how each of the characters depicts a different response to the authoritarian decrees of the state against religious involvement and observance. Discuss what you consider to be the theme of this play.

5. An increasing number of Soviet Jews have settled in this country. If you can contact a Soviet immigrant, invite him to visit your class or to be interviewed privately by a class delegation. Learn first-hand what prompted this Soviet citizen to leave his country. Write an account of the visit or the interview for the school newspaper.

Glossary

In the stories in this anthology and in the introductions to the stories, you may have found references to people, places, objects, rituals, customs, and so forth, that were strange to you. This glossary defines such allusions.

Aliyah
The word means "going up," an ascension. It describes the permanent return to Israel of any Jew living in the Diaspora (lands outside of Israel).

Auto-da-Fé
The word means "act of faith." It was a public ceremony at which the officers of the Inquisition pronounced judgment and sentenced those tried as heretics. It also refers to the execution of heretics, by burning at the stake.

Das Kapital
The major work of Karl Marx (1818–1883), German political philosopher and socialist. It is the source of socialist and communist theory.

Dizengoff
One of the main streets and squares in Tel Aviv, named after the first mayor of the city.

Galilee
A region in the northern part of Israel. According to the New Testament, Jesus spent the early years of his life there.

Haganah
The voluntary military organization in Israel during the British Mandate. Its primary purpose was to defend Jewish life and property against Arab attack. It was the immediate forerunner of the Israeli army.

Kabalah
A system of Jewish mysticism which sought to probe man's relationship to God and his universe. Study, prayer, fasting, and piety were elements of the life-style of the Kabalist.

Kaddish
A prayer recited during religious service. It is also recited by mourners, though it is not primarily a prayer for the dead. It sanctifies the name of God

and voices a plea for the realization of God's king-
dom on earth.

Marrano

A Spanish term for a Jew who converted to Chris-
tianity. It was an insulting term originally meaning
swine. Another term that was used was *converso*,
one who converted. Many of the *marranos* practiced Jewish rites and observances in private.

Matzos
(plural for
matzah)

Unleavened bread which Jewish tradition states
must be the only bread eaten during the week of
Passover. Leavened bread and utensils used during the rest of the year are called *hometz* and may
not be used during Passover.

Mizrah

The word means "East." When Jews pray, they face
the East, toward Jerusalem. To remind them which
direction is east, pious Jews place a decorative ornament containing the word *Mizrah* on the eastern
wall of their home. A similar plaque is found on
the eastern wall of many synagogues.

Mogen David

The star of David, a symbol of Judaism and now
of the State of Israel.

Passover

The spring holiday, which celebrated the exodus
(departure) of the Israelite slaves from Egypt ap-
proximately 3500 years ago. Its main observance is
the Seder, a family supper, during which many colorful rituals are observed.

Phylacteries

Jewish people who follow traditional practice wear
phylacteries during weekday morning prayers.
Within the containers worn on the arm and forehead are slips containing selected passages from
Exodus and Deuteronomy.

Rosh Hashonah

The Jewish New Year. A phase of the prayer service is the blowing of the shofar, the ram's horn.
The shofar was used by the ancient Hebrews in
sacred festivals.

Rosh Yeshiva

The head or principal of a religious school or
academy devoted largely to the study of Talmud.

Shalom The Hebrew word for peace. It is used for "hello" and "good-bye."

Siddur The Jewish prayerbook.

Tallit The prayer shawl worn at traditional religious services by Jewish men and by Jewish boys after Bar Mitzvah (confirmation). It has specially prepared fringes at its four corners.

Talmud The laws of the Bible were orally interpreted and, for many centuries, applied by rabbis and scholars to ever-changing social, economic, and religious situations. The discussions of these interpretations and applications, together with much folklore and historical and anecdotal information, were ultimately set down. They form the Talmud which defines the spiritual relationships between man and God, and the moral, ethical, and legal relationships of mankind.

Torah Originally, the term meant "teaching." It came later to describe the first five books (the Pentateuch) in the Bible. Still later, in a broader sense, it came to refer to the Pentateuch and its various interpretations by Jewish sages through the ages.

Yom Kippur The Day of Atonement. This is the holiest day in the Jewish calendar. It is a time for fasting and repentance.

Zionism The theory and desire to establish a Jewish national (or religious) community in Palestine (now the State of Israel).

Bibliography

Anthologies

Some of the anthologies contain works written by American Jewish authors only. Others contain works by European and Israeli Jewish authors as well as American. A third category is the multiethnic anthology in which appear works by American Jewish writers. Some of the anthologies contain examples of poetry, essay, and biography as well as fiction. The works below are listed because in each there are excellent examples of fiction written by American Jewish authors dealing with Jewish themes and characters.

Angoff, Charles and Levin, Meyer, eds. *The Rise of American Jewish Literature: An Anthology of Selections from the Major Novels.* New York: Simon and Schuster, 1970.

Bellow, Saul, ed. *Great Jewish Short Stories.* New York: Dell Publishing Co., 1963.

Chapman, Abraham, ed. *Jewish American Literature: An Anthology.* New York: New American Library, 1974.

Charles, Gerda, ed. *Modern Jewish Stories.* Englewood Cliffs, New Jersey: Prentice-Hall, 1966.

Dann, Jack, ed. *Wandering Stars: An Anthology of Jewish Fantasy and Science Fiction.* New York: Harper and Row, 1974.

Eisenberg, Azriel, ed. *The Golden Land: A Literary Portrait of American Jewry, 1954 to the Present.* New York: Thomas Yoseloff, 1964.

Faderman, Lillian and Bradshaw, Barbara, eds. *Speaking for Ourselves.* Chicago, Illinois: Scott, Foreman and Company, 1969.

Gross, Theodore L., ed. *The Literature of American Jews.* Glencoe, Illinois: The Free Press, 1973.

Leftwich, Joseph, ed. *Yisroel: The First Jewish Omnibus.* New York: The Beechhurst Press, 1952.

Lewis, Jerry D., ed. *Tales of Our People: Great Stories of the Jew in America.* New York: Bernard Geiss Associates, 1969.

Malin, Irving and Stark, Irwin, eds. *Breakthrough: A Treasury of Con-*

temporary American-Jewish Literature. Philadelphia: The Jewish
Publication Society, 1965.

Podhoretz, Norman, ed. *The Commentary Reader: Two Decades of
Articles and Stories.* New York: Atheneum, 1966.

Ribalow, Harold U., ed. *My Name Aloud: Jewish Stories by Jewish
Writers.* New York: Thomas Yoseloff, 1969.

———. *A Treasury of American Jewish Stories.* New York: Thomas
Yoseloff, 1958.

Schwarz, Leo W., ed. *Feast of the Leviathan: Tales of Adventure,
Faith and Love.* New York: Rinehart and Co., 1956.

———. *The Jewish Caravan: Great Stories of Thirty-Five Centuries.*
New York, 1935. Revised and enlarged in paperback. New York:
Schocken, 1976.

Simon, Myron, ed. *Ethnic Writers in America.* New York: Harcourt,
Brace, Jovanovich, Inc., 1972.

Sobel, Samuel, ed. *A Treasury of Jewish Sea Stories.* New York: Jona-
than David, 1965.

Walden, Daniel, ed. *On Being Jewish: American Writers from Cahan
to Bellow.* Greenwich, Connecticut: Fawcett Publications, 1974.

Collections of Short Stories
by Individual Jewish Writers

American Jewish authors wrote short stories on many subjects, not
solely on Jewish ones. Some, in fact, never used their Jewish experiences in their work at all. However, many did write about Jewish
characters and subjects, about the problems of being Jewish in an
American world, ghetto and suburban life, the effects of poverty and
affluence, the conflict of generations, the hold of the past, the impact
of history upon Jewish thought and action, and so forth. The collec-
tions listed below contain stories that deal with Jewish themes, people,
and conduct.

Ansell, Jack. *Summer.* New York: Arbor House, 1973.

Calisher, Hortense. *In the Absence of Angels.* Boston: Little, Brown
and Co., 1948.

Charyn, Jerome. *The Man Who Grew Younger.* New York: Harper &
Row, Publishers, 1966.

Elkin, Stanley. *Searches and Seizures.* New York: Random House, Inc., 1973.

Elman, Richard. *Crossing Over and Other Tales.* New York: Charles Scribner's Sons, 1973.

Epstein, Seymour. *A Penny for Charity.* Boston: Little, Brown and Company, 1965.

Fast, Howard. *Departure and Other Stories.* Boston: Little, Brown and Company, 1949.

Fiedler, Leslie A. *A Nude Croquet.* New York: Stein & Day Publishers, 1969.

Gerber, Merrill Joan. *Stop Here, My Friend.* Boston: Houghton Mifflin Company, 1965.

Gold, Herbert. *Love and Like.* New York: The Dial Press, 1960.

Greenberg, Joanne. *Summering.* New York: Holt, Rinehart and Winston, Inc., 1966.

Halper, Albert. *On the Shore.* New York: The Viking Press, Inc., 1973.

Hurst, Fannie. *Humoresque.* New York: Harper & Row, Publishers, 1920.

Jacobs, Harvey. *The Egg of the Glak and Other Stories.* New York: Harper & Row, Publishers, 1969.

Kaplan, Bernard. *Prisoners of this World.* Grossman Publishers, 1970.

Kessler, Jascha. *An Egyptian Bondage and Other Stories.* New York: Harper & Row, Publishers, 1967.

Lewisohn, Ludwig. *The People.* New York: Harper & Row, Publishers, 1933.

Malamud, Bernard. *Idiots First.* New York: Dell Publishing Co., Inc., 1950.

———. *The Magic Barrel.* New York: Random House, Inc., 1950–58.

———. *Rembrandt's Hat.* New York: Farrar, Straus & Giroux, Inc., 1968.

Miller, Arthur. *I Don't Neet You Any More.* New York: The Viking Press, Inc., 1967.

Nissenson, Hugh. *A Pile of Stones.* New York: Charles Scribner's Sons, 1964.

———. *In the Reign of Peace.* New York: Farrar, Straus, & Giroux, Inc., 1968.

Ozick, Cynthia. *The Pagan Rabbi.* New York: Alfred A. Knopf, Inc., 1971.

Paley, Grace. *Enormous Changes at the Last Minute.* New York: Farrar, Straus & Giroux, Inc., 1974.

———. *The Little Disturbances of Man.* New York: Doubleday & Company, Inc., 1959.

Roth, Philip. *Goodbye, Columbus*. New York: Bantam Books, Inc., 1963.

Schwartz, Delmore. *The World Is a Wedding*. New York: New Directions Publishing Corporation, 1948.

Shaw, Irwin. *Selected Short Stories*. New York: Random House, Inc., 1955.

Weidman, Jerome. *The Horse that Could Whistle "Dixie."* New York: Simon & Schuster, Inc., 1939.

Wilner, Herbert. *Dovisch in the Wilderness and Other Stories*. New York: The Bobbs-Merrill Co., Inc., 1968.

Yezierska, Anzia. *Children of Loneliness*. Boston: Houghton Mifflin Company, 1923.